CW01313091

The Life and Death of Paul McCartney 1942-66

A very English Mystery

NICHOLAS KOLLERSTROM

The Life and Death of Paul McCartney 1942-66

A very English Mystery

Produced by Ole Dammegård

MOON ROCK BOOKS

Moon Rock Books has earlier published: '
And I suppose we didn't go to the moon either? The Beatles, the Holocaust and other mass illusions' 330 pp,
edited by Jim Fetzer and Mike Palacek, 2015.

Copyright, 2015 by Moon Rock Books

All rights exclusively reserved. No part of this book may be reproduced or translated into any language or utilized in any form or by any means, electronic or mechanical, including photocopying, recording or by any information storage and retrieval system, without permission in writing from the publisher.

The Life and Death of Paul McCartney 1942-66
ISBN 9781517283131 Hard Copy Soft Cover Book

Cover design and layout by Ole Dammegård

Disclaimer and Reader Agreement

Under no circumstances will the publisher, Moon Rock Books, or author be liable to any person or business entity for any direct, indirect, special, incidental, consequential, or other damages based on any use of this book or any other source to which it refers, including, without limitation, any lost profits, business interruption, or loss of programs or information. Regarding Beatle lyrics' copyright issues, see Appendix D, "Copyright Issues".

*The princess and the prince discuss
Whats real and what is not ...
There are no truths outside the Gates of Eden*

Bob Dylan, Gates of Eden, 1965

Thanks to:

*Frank McGillian, Jonathan Reese,
Toby Malamute and Clare Kuehn*

CONTENTS

1. The Duality	*11*
2. The Summer of Love and Peace	*25*
3. A Fractured Identity	*31*
4. Secret of the Songs	*39*
5. The Newcomer steps into History	*57*
6. Magical Mystery Tour	*67*
7. Birth and Death of the PID Story	*73*
8. The Mirror Reveals	*89*
9. Through a Glass Darkly	*97*
10. From Jane to Linda	*107*
11. Glimpses of Paul	*123*
12. Clue-Bearing Albums	*137*
13. Doom of Lennon	*147*
14. The Disclosure Process	*157*
15. A Magic Touch	*167*
16. Nine Nine O Nine	*179*
17. Endgame	*191*
Chronology	*203*
Appendix A: Tara Browne - A Mystery Death	*209*
Appendix B: The Endeavour of Forensic Analysis	*215*
Appendix C: Two Alleged Disclosures	*225*
Appendix D: Copyright Issues	*229*
Bibliography	*231*
Index	*233*

The Duality

Terri managed a smile. "I was sort of hoping you were going to play a Beatles record backwards. The one where it says 'Paul is dead.'
"Abbey Road", Monk answered. "Never liked it."
                                                    Eyes of a Child by R.N.Patterson 1996.

Is Paul McCartney the world's most successful musician, or has he been dead for 50 years? We are here talking about the primal, the ultimate, urban legend of rock 'n' roll. The literary genre on this topic has fallen into two categories: either sceptical of the story –i.e reviewing the 'clues' as having all been a monster hoax, to sell Beatles' records – or, trying to tell 'the truth' of what happened, while proclaiming itself to be fictional. For legal reasons, attempts to narrate the incredible tale have all had to be formulated as being fiction.

But this book is no work of fiction. It endeavours to be a study of history. It is a tale of death, transfiguration and the Swinging Sixties. I was there, I used to stroll past Abbey Road on my way to school and then later, fate took me to San Francisco in the summer of '67, listening to *Sgt Pepper* – or rather experiencing *Sgt Pepper* if you know what I mean - and now as an old man with a few grey hairs left I pen the startling tale, of the death and replacement of the multifaceted Paul McCartney.

Whether I am competent to do so, you can decide for yourself: as a philosopher, I discern the difference between what is real and what is illusory. I enjoy telling that difference, in the same way that a dog enjoys gnawing a bone or a cook enjoys making a meal.

Were we deceived? Yes we were, but in the nicest possible way and for some quite acceptable reasons. I don't think there are any bad guys in this story, or only quite peripherally. The show had to go on, it could not stop just because of one death, and what a show it was!

It's high time we had an English book on the topic, as the several books on the subject are all American. A flood of disclosures has been emerging in recent years making these texts quite dated.

It would be nice if this could have been written by an avid Beatles' fan, who would know the music better than me, or even by someone who understood music theory. I was never part of the screaming crowd – but then, maybe it needs more of a detached onlooker to evaluate this stranger-than-fiction tale. I can hardly tell the difference between a sharp and a flat, between major and minor keys. But, I've consulted a friend who can! And, when I've given talks on the subject or posted blogs, people keep strangely saying, you should write a book on the subject! At least four different people have said that to me. So here it is ....

This is a tale of a replacement, who was far better than he had any right to be, the tale of a man who stepped through an opaque glass screen onto the stage of history, to 'mend the broken band'. If you are expecting to be told who he was or where he came from – well, please mull over this book's title! This is a deeply Shakespearean mystery, indeed some feel that 'Billy Shears' kind of meant William Shakespeare, catch my drift? Billy Shears is, you may recall, introduced in first song on the *Sgt Pepper* album, as being the new member of the band. Here we have the most interesting kind of mystery, that of real identity... who is the mystery man? Or, more answerable perhaps, what did John Lennon think of him? Rather bossy maybe .. but, we're jumping ahead.

Because we can't answer that key question, can't solve it, we cannot fold up the subject and file it away, it's still here to haunt us. Those still alive who know the answer or know something are unlikely to speak. I'm not here to solve it for you.

I am here to praise. I praise the genus of a young 24-year old lad, an English Orpheus, the Beautiful Boy. We here ask: *who ever achieved so much for his country in a life of a mere four-and-twenty years?* I wish to praise the magnificence of that achievement.

For three years Beatlemania echoed around planet Earth, our world was in its grip, the intensity of which may be hard to imagine, if you only saw it on TV. And it happened *because of* one young man. Girls screamed, cried, fainted, hardly knowing what had hit them. They were taken out of themselves, it was ecstasy in the literal sense of 'standing-outside' oneself, i.e. they were pulled out of their usual world. Then once he departed it vanished, quite suddenly. No-one could do it without him. Paul was England's troubador singer of gentle love-ballads, but also he could hit that wild, Dionysian frenzy, I mean just listen to him singing Little Richard's *Long Tall Sally*.

The Duality

Come September 1966, it was suddenly gone: from then on Beatlemania was just a memory. Empty excuses had to be made, why the Band could never again perform in public. The adoring fans had all been abandoned – and nobody could even tell them why. Then the great miracle happened, and *Sgt Pepper* was produced, in a studio. This was the mystery, which had quite a lot to do with that wonderful Summer of Love and Peace. They all sang separately on that album - the blissful concordance of Lennon and McCartney singing together into a microphone, or of George and Paul singing together, has gone forever. From now on, it was only history. The amazing concordance the band used to have, with their unique vocal harmonies, that produced Beatlemania had gone, replaced by solo pieces.

This book aims to remind you what the real, actual Paul McCartney looked like, because your memory at present will be very largely conditioned by the fellow (or fellows, according to certain conspiracy theorists...) who has been claiming to be him for the past fifty years. This replacement, who is called Faul ('false Paul') on websites all around the world, is truly skilled at singing old Beatles songs: he was after all the 'man with a thousand voices' of the *Magical Mystery Tour* (MMT, late 1967) i.e a versatile session musician. He had a higher voice than the original, more musically trained and not much of a Liverpudlian accent; the first Paul had a velvety, deep mellifluous tone of voice, more rough and throaty.[1]

And yes the new man was taller, several inches taller. That is the simplest reason why he and Lennon could never be allowed to sing into the same mike - it would be too obvious. No surgery could ever change that. He was a bigger guy.

The real Faul, so to speak, is heard once he appears solo with Linda McCartney and in *Wings,* when he is no longer so bothered about sounding like Paul. He has a mid-Atlantic accent that is somewhat Scottish. Whose was the lovely voice we hear singing in the various Beatles albums then? It's in the nature of a studio recording that we do not ultimately know who is singing, or what the great maestro producer George Martin did with the voices. At this point I probably should confess, that I'm not keen on the voice of Beatles Bill, or Faul, or Bill Shepherd, or whatever we want to call him, and having to listen to albums liken *Ram* or *Give my regards to Broad Street*

---

[1] 'McCartney's voice *was* different in the later recordings! In the pre-1967 selection, it was raw, nasal, resonant. In the post-1967 selection, it was smooth, dulcet almost flute-like in places.' from the novel by John Perkins, 'A Day in the Life' (2005, p.82). His hero had selected *'I saw her Standing There, Drive my Car* and *Got to Get you into my Life'* from pre-'67 and then *Mother Nature's son, Let it Be* and *Get Back'* from later; and decided not to use any *Sgt Pepper* songs because 'he couldn't be sure anymore when the songs involving McCartney had been recorded.'

is no fun for me, in fact I find it quite dire. He does good videos and he has in recent years assembled a very talented band. When a hundred thousand people gather for a McCartney concert, I can't avoid the feeling that they are enjoying it because of who they believe he is. Feel free to disagree with me here.

All I'm saying is, please do not ever compare him with the real, the one and only James Paul McCartney, Genius of Beatlemania. Faul is a more intellectual character, more complex. Generally of a larger size, he had a bigger head. Lennon's words here come irresistibly to mind, while a-plonking on his grand piano in a field in *Magical Mystery Tour:*

'Man you've been a naughty boy, you let your face grow long'

The one thing Faul did not have and could never have, was adorability. Paul was, quite simply, totally adorable, he could, as his early girlfriend Dot said, 'charm the birds out of the trees'. Whereas, in a clown-like manner, Faul sung, 'Silly love songs.' (*Wings,* 1976)[2] The baffled fans were manipulated.

Every Beatle song is up on the web thrice, as lyrics, then as Youtube and as Wiki for information. So, we can readily listen to all the old classics. For example, just type in 'Silly love songs McCartney' and it's all there. Starting in 2014, a whole new newspaper archive has opened at the British Library enabling access to all the period music mags such as *Melody Maker* and *New Musical Express, Disc and Music Echo,* the monthly *Beatles Book* as well as *International Times,* plus all the newspapers: making this the first account you have come across whereby the author has been able to check out conspiracy stories against papers and journals of the time.

Did a transfer of identity take place? Let's hear the mystery voice of 'Billy Shears':

Those silly love songs led him right down that road of life (that he crashed on) to me. Paul followed his life's music to his own dead end, passing through the door to eternity, leaving me standing in for him on this other side of the road. (p.526)

Moving words, but who on Earth spoke them? Let's hear a bit more from the same source:

**Herein is an epic of our hero
Paul McCartney,
who entered the underworld,**

---

2 See Ch. 12 for this song being in Dave Berry's *Book of Worst Love-Songs.*

and then returned,
by taking possession of me,
an unknown session musician.

These words are so beautiful, but are they true? They were published in 2009, in a book which claims to be fictional but in its content assures us that it is disclosing the real, biographical truth. It claims that Sir Paul met its author and reached a deal, to 'tell the story' except that any info about where he had originally come from had to be concealed. The book's author a Mr Thomas E. Uharriet wrote *The Memoirs of Billy Shears* in 666 pages.[3]

Those *Memoirs* were published in the US by 'Peppers Press' a subsidiary of MACCA Corp, on Wednesday 9th September of 2009, i.e. 9.9.09. On that same date the entire Beatle corpus of songs was republished in digitally-remastered form, by Apple Corps, produced at Abbey Road studio – it was a final statement, following on from what was earlier published as 'The Anthology,' and totalled 14 CDs; it also synchronized with production of 'The Beatles: Rock Band' video game. Three things were published on the same day on different sides of the Atlantic: the music, a game, and a biography!

So, was the switchover fated? For example, the last words sung on '*Revolver*' the last album Paul ever sung on were 'This is the end of the beginning.' One of the last things the young Paul got to hear about (on 9.9.66) was that *Revolver* had gone Platinum with its sales i.e. sold a million copies, and so was the 20th platinum disc the band had made. I won't be answering that big question, I mean who can?

But it is an option so to speak. If we could summon up Will Shakespeare maybe he would speak some cryptic words on the matter. *So let me introduce to you, the one and only Billy Shears...* Yes, this is a deep subject, it goes deep. Who said 'Lend me your ears'? Why Mark Anthony of course, standing over the corpse of Julius Caesar. It's the wonderful speech in the Shakespeare play where Mark Anthony laments the death of the person he loved more than anyone else in the world. And *therefore* the phrase comes in, at the start of *Sgt Pepper*. Like everything they would do thereafter, it was stuffed with clues about the unsayable truth.

Not a single one of the Beatles ever wrote an autobiography.[4] Ah, how they would have sold! What millions 'Paul McCartney' has been offered, if

---

[3] The name may sound unlikely but Uharriet seems to be a real person: see his Facebook page, plus www.billyshears.com/
[4] George Harrisson's *I, Me, Mine* featured some songs and documents he wanted preserved, plus a few conversations of his, but I doubt if anyone would call that an autobiography.

only he would do that! Or, what about Neil Aspinall, who knew more about the Fab Four than he did? In his orbituary, Beatle biographer Hunter Davies recalls how he used to beg Neil to spill some of the secrets[5,6]. Or for that matter Jane Asher, she was at the centre of things, she saw it all, how her memoirs would sell! Why on Earth will she not breathe a single word about her memories? I can answer that, and don't worry I will. In the meantime, let me suggest that *The Memoirs of Billy Shears* is the nearest thing to an autobiography of Sir Paul McCartney you will ever come across.

The replacement, was he a fraud or an impostor? Some have called him that, but I'm certainly not going to - as *Billy Shears* tells us, 'I would probably pass a lie-detector test while saying that I am him – even though my body is not like his.' (*Memoirs*, p.572) The firm Apple Corps was set up after Paul's death, and try to experience that that name really means, 'A Paul corpse.' Up till now our response to Beatles songs has been *subjective*, 'I like that' or 'I never liked that,' because that is what the Beatles' legacy is built on - whereas now, after all the years, we are here going on a journey together to discover an *objective* approach, whereby we experience the soul-drama that went on within that astonishing group, its creative ferment.

And, one could add, of various other groups, who were gobsmacked by the new stranger turning up: the Stones (while Brian Jones was still alive), the Who, the young Elton John, Donovan. You will now be able to listen to *Ruby Tuesday* and for the first time get a sense of what it was really about. We all heard the haunting *Come Together* sung by Lennon in the British Olympic Games in 2012, but what did it mean? I don't want to comment just yet, but am respectfully disagreeing with the expert view of Ian MacDonald, that it was 'a stream of self-confessed 'gobbledygook.''[7]

John was a poet and that song is his most direct expression of the nightmare of his dead aka 'undead' dearest companion haunting him; coming back as it were after his death, allegedly in a car-crash. Let's admit here and now, that nobody can prove that any such car-crash happened, but it has long been a rather central part of the urban legend.

Lines of old songs will acquire a new meaning for you, for example

Take these broken wings and learn to fly

---

[5] Hunter Davies "When I pressed him for inside stories, he used to say he couldn't remember" *Guardian* orbituary, 25.3.08.
[6] Some people believe that Neil Aspinall penned *The True Story of the Beatles* by 'William Shepherd' back in 1964, but if so he kept very quiet about it.
[7] Macdonald, *Revolution*, 359.

– the operating instructions given to Faul. He had impossibly difficult requirements, in stepping forward to rescue the Band: not only a ton of plastic surgery and having to mug up on Paul's life-history, but he had to learn to play Paul's bass-guitar left-handed. These words express a resurrection motif, of recovering from death. The line continues 'All your life / You were only waiting for this moment to arise.' The new stranger had mysteriously stepped forward, as if from nowhere. Reassuringly for him, Jane Asher did like him, she appreciated the way he was trying to continue the being-ness of her beloved Paul. She may not have slept with him but they were an item. Having the approval of that ginger-haired beauty was quite important for his arrival, and credibility.

My pal Jim Fetzer, a former professor of logic, summarised in ten points what he saw as the main points of evidence on this topic. The replacement he here calls 'Sir Paul'[8]:

'As I see it, the situation is more or less as follows:

(1) Sir Paul is both taller and larger than Paul with a bigger chest and upper body;
(2) Sir Paul learned to play left-handed, while Paul was born left-handed;
(3) Paul had terrible teeth, but Sir Paul has teeth in very good condition;
(4) Sir Paul concealed the difference in their ears by wearing false ears;
(5) Sir Paul appears to be more intellectual and cerebral than Paul;
(6) Paul had a decidedly cheerier disposition and was rather adorable;
(7) Sir Paul is less cheery and does not have that same personal appeal;
(8) They stopped doing concerts after the date of the apparent accident;
(9) John›s sketch is inexplicable unless Paul actually died (it is nothing like a doodle);
(10) there are many clues in «Sgt. Pepper» and elsewhere that support this conclusion.'[9]

Not a bad summary, though I'd put at number one the green eyes of Faul compared to the big chocolate-brown eyes of Paul – a flutter of whose eyes used to drive the girls wild. On *Magical Mystery Tour* at 7-8 minutes you get to gaze into the big green eyes of the new Faul, while Lennon is singing 'nothing is real.' We also get to view his tall silhouette, looking nothing whatever like Paul. Watching the video *Hey Jude* we are again startled to look into the newcomer's big, green eyes. The Sir Paul who is around now tends to have bright blue eyes, I don't know where he came from.... To look into the brown eyes of the real one-and-only Paul McCartney, I suggest watching

---

8 He follows Clare Kuehn's convention, of using 'Sir Paul' even before his knighthood was awarded in 1997. I have alluded throughout to 'Faul' and Paul.
9 See the 'comments' section of a debate between me and Clare Kuehn on Jim Fetzer's Real Deal 19 February 2014.

the colour film *Help!* (1965). That's the one with with Eleanor Bron and a story about various 'rings of power' plus a sacrificial victim (NB, don't worry about Fetzer's item 9, we'll come to that later).

Complications arise because of different editions of songs and videos being edited. In for example video releases of *Strawberry Fields,* debates go on as to whether the green eye colour has been adjusted at any stage. If that sounds unduly conspiratorial, then try listening to the original *Strawberry Fields* single, the 'e.p.' record release, or modern equivalent (released Xmas '66, the first song with Faul's voice). After the song seems to be over it strangely starts up again, in a somewhat eerie manner, with sounds that could resemble an ambulance siren and maybe blood pumping out somewhere, and then Lennon distinctly says 'I buried Paul.'

Readers are urged to go onto Youtube and listen to this, turning up the volume at the end of the song, and be satisfied that he really did speak these words and not any other. When asked about this – after the whole 'Paul is dead' story exploded in October 1969 – Lennon claimed he had said 'Cranberry sauce.' Let the reader ascertain that those were *not* the words there spoken, this is important.[10]

After he had put in all the amazing clues, Lennon, when confronted with them was obliged to deny that he had done any such thing, and he would give irritating and mundane interpretations. The Blue Album *'the Beatles 1967-70'* has the same song, but *no trace of any such words* can be heard, they have been deleted! That was done in 1969. That is re-mastering, i.e. George Martin just removed it.[11]

Isn't that proof? If the whole thing had been just a stunt to re-sell the records, why delete those scary words from the truth-teller Mr Lennon? "Strawberry Fields cemetery also lies within the city" (of Liverpool) according to www.merseyside.com, and they should know. But also (on Beatle tours of the city), Strawberry Fields is an orphanage children's home. Incidentally, it is quite hard to confirm that Lennon could have been around at Paul's burial, as he was out of the country acting in a film over that period.

You can impress your friends by opening up that Blue double album, to see the two pictures of the Fab Four on the same staircase, on the back and front covers. They clearly feature the two different Pauls, its so obvious once you see it.

---

10 Neil Aspinall gave an honest answer, that it sounded to him as if John were indeed saying 'I buried Paul': see The Rotten Apple 1 (November 2006) at 1:30 minutes.
11 Later on, in the "take 7 and edit piece" version of the song that appeared on *Anthology II* (1996), the words do sound like "cranberry sauce."

Can we add to those ten points of Jim Fetzer? Paul loved wearing elegant clothes, stylish suits and white shirts, and he drew up the sketches for the design of their velvet-collared mohair suits[12] that Brian Epstein ordered; whereas his replacement Faul would hardly bother to appear in a suit and would lounge around in any old T-shirt. Paul wore the trendy Cuban boots which made him look taller, as he was quite short, whereas Faul wore casual trainers. While Paul was alive the Beatles would usually appear in the *same* attire, usually suits. That was part of their charm, whereas once the replacement had blended in they all wore different attire, expressing the way they no longer enjoyed their old unity.

Paul never got into drugs like John or Faul. Faul encouraged youngsters to take LSD which would have been unthinkable for Paul. At the Cavern the lads took amphetamine-type drugs, giving them the stamina to keep playing for eight hours at a time, and Paul may have smoked dope a bit – but, he was never a serious advocate of the weed, or any other drug. His creative power *did not come from* or through drugs: as the magic of *Sgt Pepper* very obviously did.

George Martin tells how once when John was having a bad trip on some acid, and his companions were worried he might try to 'fly' off the roof of the Abbey Road studio: then Paul took a tablet of LSD for the first time 'so I could get with John' as he said: causing George Martin to wonder, 'What about that for friendship?'[13]

While Paul was alive, the interviews given were nearly all with the four Beatles together. That's what everybody wanted to hear, it was just *so* cute to hear the four of them bantering together. But, once Paul had departed from this limited space-time world, the interviews were almost all of separate individuals – for obvious reasons. Why the Fab Three would have wanted to carry on at all is a difficult question, with which we will have to grapple, but they were far from keen on appearing in public with the newcomer as a foursome.[14]

---

12 The Bio, C.S. p142.
13 Making, GM, 110.
14 The listed Beatle interviews www.beatlesinterviews.org/ shows that, up to August/ September 1966 they were mostly of the Fab Four together, after which such group interviews became rare. I counted yearly totals of interviews with the group together, such that each yearly period started in September and ended in August:
Yearly total Fab Four Interviews
1962-3: 5, 1963-4: 33, 1964-5: 24, 1965-6: 15
1966-7: 1, 1967-8: 1, 1968-9: 0
Thus, eighty percent of all the interviews given were of the group together, until August 1966, after which only 5% of them were.

9/11 and Real Identity

Moving on, deeper into the core of the mystery, we come to the strange notion that the death of Paul McCartney happened either on November 9th or on September 11th. The former was initially favoured, because of the way the story broke in America… If we write 9/11/2001 that means September 11th, 2001, because Americans put the month first. This may be sounding rather obscure, but hang on. An English person writing that date would put 11/9/2001. So what is that mystery date about?

In the year 1998 the film *The Matrix* was released. Seventeen minutes into the film, the lead character Neo is being grilled over his dual identity by Agent Smith. He is Anderson, the office worker, but also Neo, a subversive computer-hacker. Smith flicks open Neo's passport. Hold it right there! We see, clearly, his birthdate: September 11th, 2001. Thus the world's greatest sci-fi movie gives us a date linking that century to this one. Who really is he? And what has that date got to do with it?

The mystery of his identity has got something to do with that date. We know how upon that date a monstrous fiction, a phoney fabricated falsehood, was perpetrated upon mankind, imposing a momentum of ruin upon humanity, from which it can break free only by seeing through that illusion. Heavy stuff, but what's the connection? Why did the Empire want to give us that date in advance in a movie?

The 9/11 date is so important to us today but back then nobody knew about it of course, it did not have 'meaning.' And yet, in the story we have here to tell, that date keeps echoing and reverberating through the years:

September 11th, 1962 First studio recording by Beatles at Abbey Road, of two singles written by Paul *Love Me Do* and PS *I Love You*; George with black eye[15].

September 11th, 1966 Paul McCartney dies on that Sunday evening. (Whether you accept this may depend on whether you believe he was present at the *Melody Maker Awards* two days later on the 13th, see Chapter 8)

September 11th, 1967 The Magical Mystery Tour begins, at 10.30 that morning.

September 11th, 1968[16] Lennon recorded his *Glass Onion* song at

---
15 George's black eye came from livid fans at the Cavern in Liverpool, angry at Pete Best's replacement by Ringo.
16 These dates are Claire Kuehn's findings.

Abbey Road. Two songs where Lennon is haunted by Paul's presence are *Come Togethr* and *Glass Onion*. The former has all the nightmare of his violent death, while the latter is Lennon yearning for the spirit of Paul his great companion ('You know we're as close as can be, man').

September 11th, 1969 The PID story broke in America: 'Is Beatle Paul McCartney Dead?' appeared in the student newspaper The Drake-Times Delphic at Drake University, Ohio on 17th September.

September 12th, 2005 McCartney's album *Chaos and Creation* is released, appearing as a kind of dialogue between Paul out in the beyond and Faul. It couldn't have been released the day before on the 11th which was a Sunday. (*Ordo ab Chaos* being the motto of 3rd degree masonry)

September 11th, 2010 The one-hour video online *The Winged Beetle* was published, by 'Iamaphoney.' This was a massive stage of the disclosure-process clearly made by insiders, with access to Beatle archive material: who evidently believe in magic, as we'll consider later.

911 is the emergency number to dial in America. In *retrospect* now in the 21st century that date September 11th becomes deeply meaningful. And that in turn *undermines* the narrative I hope to try and describe here, of a tragic accident, and pushes us into a more deeply 'conspiratorial' tale whereby the death had to have been planned, with that date intended.

'Those whom the gods love, die young.'[17] The fascination of the urban legend came from the feeling that Paul was somehow *too* happy, too successful and too good-looking, to stay alive in this world of grief and sorrow... The above death-date was a couple of days before the New Moon nearest to the Autumn Equinox. Was Paul was so good, so true, so beautiful, that he just had to be ... the perfect sacrifice?

From that date September 11th 1966 an illusion was imposed upon us. Yes, catastrophe was covered up - or how many girls around the world would have committed suicide? But a fictional narrative starts from that date. Questions will now be a-buzzing around in your mind, I will be able to answer some of them, not all, but you'll have to be patient.

On the next page are two early JPM pics, and the following page another one of him with Brian Epstein a couple of years later: In contrast, below on page 22 are a couple of Faul images from later on, 1968/69.

---

17 'Quem di diligunt, adulescens moritur' Plautus, *Bacchides*, IV, 7, 18.

Nicholas Kollerstrom

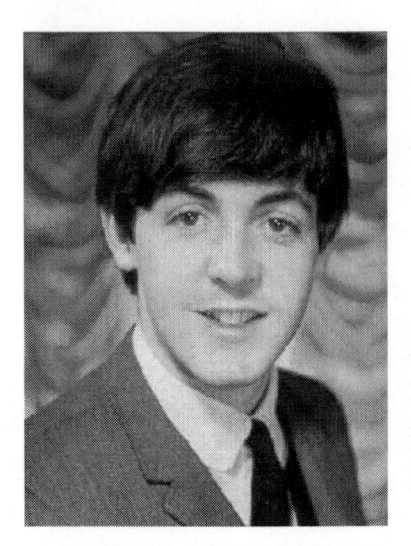

Try putting 'Paul McCartney' into Google Images and you'll mainly get the replacement, a mere one-third or so will be the real JPM. Others are the Faul we've just been looking at – plus various other weird replacements! But, try putting in

>Billy Shears (of *Sgt Pepper*),
>or Billy Pepper (of the *Pepperpots*),
>or William Campbell (of the band *Marmalade*),
>or Phil Akrill (of the *Diplomats*),
>or Viv Stanshall (of *Bonzo Dog Band*)
>or Denny Lane (of the *Diplomats*, then *Wings*)
>or Dino Danelli (of the *Rascals*)

The Duality

- and each time you'll be flooded with mystery images of *duality*, as the characters endlessly blend and morph into the ever-mutable figure of Faul: indicating how PID-ers have quested over years, seeking the inscrutable identity of the newcomer, but could they find it?

Where after all does this story begin, where does it end? Would you rather have it told in terms of what might have happened in the sixties, or would you prefer an account of the sequence of disclosure? Given the uncertain, fragmentary nature of what we know, the latter approach could be more sensible. I've put the songs fairly early, near the beginning, and that way you are able to refer back to them as new issues arise.

This book has a purpose: to enable you to enjoy more interesting conversations with your mates in the pub. A gleam will come into the eye of old codgers as memories of their youth come flooding back: 'No!' and 'But that's impossible!' These old memories should lead to some lively discussion, but without the sense of dark malevolence and hopelessness that tends to arise with other conspiracy theories. Then everyone drives back to the home of whoever has a vinyl record deck: does the *White Album's* 'Revolution' 'Number Nine, Number nine…' really play backwards as 'Turn me on, Dead Man? (Or, backwards recordings of such tracks are nowadays online). When checking out 'clues' on the *Sgt Pepper* cover, then indeed are we 'far from the twisted reach of crazy sorrow.'

The Summer of Love and Peace

Ken Tynan in *The Times* said *Sgt Pepper* was 'a decisive moment in the history of Western civilization'[1] – no, don't laugh, it really was. It was after all the Summer of Love and Peace and the 'Youthquake miracle' was happening in *Swinging London*. Skirts were short, hair was long, the good times were rolling, the beautiful people were strolling around, British bands dominated the charts, and *Sgt Pepper* set the optimistic tone.

Nowadays people may not understand the mystery, that which created a philosophy of optimism, and suppose it was 'just drugs.' Well hullo, if you take drugs now you are unlikely to get an inspiration like *Lucy in the Sky with Diamonds*. Don't expect cellophane flowers and newspaper taxis to come and take you away, or to meet the Girl with the Sun in her Eyes.

More likely you'll just get wasted, as happened to Lennon not long after the period we are looking at. Two substances aided the sixties *Zeitgiest*: the birth-control pill and LSD, but only a shallow materialism would suppose that they produced it.

Harold Wilson said 'No' to war, and he was the last-ever British Prime-minister to be capable of denying an American request for war-support: British troops *did not go* to Vietnam. That had a lot to do with the tenor of optimism of that period. We had a government that could govern, in the sense that it was capable of not going to war. That was the 'peace', in The Summer of Love and Peace.

> most critics and fans agree that the Beatles reached their creative apogee at some point between the spring of 1966 and the spring of 1967 and that the band's innovative impact, the overall quality of their work, and the Beatles' influence on contemporary and later generations of rock

---

[1] Quoted in *Revolution in the Head*, Ian MacDonald, p.249

musicians began to decline thereafter – that is, with the summer and fall singles of 1967 and with *Magical Mystery Tour.*[2]

If such a thing as a cultural 'contact high' is possible, it happened here. *Sgt Pepper's lonely Hearts club Band* may not have created the psychic atmosphere of the time but, as a near-perfect reflection of it, this famous record magnified and radiated it around the world.'[3]

Possibly no other album in history brought about as much change in musical direction as this work. It ushered in a new era, filled with psychedelic sounds that drenched our imaginations in shades of fluorescent colours and pulsating rhythms.'[4]

Of the war, David Crosby of the Byrds and later of Crosby, Stills, Nash and Young fame said: 'Somehow *Sgt Pepper's* did not stop the Vietnam War. Somehow it didn't work. Somebody isn't listening… I would've thought *Sgt Pepper's* could have stopped the war just by putting too many good vibes in the air for anybody to have a war around.'[5] Ah well, a rainbow only appears against a stormy background. The album was voted the greatest rock album of all time by critics and broadcasters in Paul Gambaccini's *The Top 100 Rock and Roll Albums of All Time,'* in both the 1977 and 1987 editions.

We peer through the numinous awe to see how the 'five magicians' as they called themselves (on MMT) had woven it. They *were not the Beatles* any more, the famous Band was buried -on the front cover! They were four separate guys, just a 'Lonely Hearts Club Band' who had acquired a new member. The new guy had been introduced the previous December on the cover of Golden Oldies, the long, tall dude who did not resemble any of the Fab Four. But, that was rather low-key.

The music came about through Paul and John interacting with George Martin, their producer. He was a realizer of dreams! George Martin had produced comedy records with the Goons and they liked his humorous approach. Let's quote him:

> [John] would have an image in his mind, but he would not necessarily have a very good idea of how to get there, in practical terms. Paul was much more articulate about what he wanted, much more focussed. John would tell me what kind of mood he wanted on the song, whereas Paul

---

[2] *The Beatles* Ed Womack, CUP 2009, p.97
[3] Ibid 250.
[4] Patterson, *The Walrus Was Paul*, p.49
[5] Patterson, *Walrus Was Paul* 14, quoting William Dowlding, *Beatlesongs*, NY 1983, p.163.

would ask for a cello, say, or a trumpet at a certain point. Then at the end of everything, John would be unhappy that he had not quite got the final result he wanted. (p.87)

The *psychedelic* message concerns how to make manifest the soul, from Greek *psyche* the soul and *delos* to make manifest. George Martin realized their dreams, in that unique summer, he had a happy job.

There were four musicians who could not read music, an orchestra, and George Martin! Fortunately Mr Martin had been taught at the Guildhall School of Music and Drama by Mrs Asher, mother of Jane Asher, so he was up to the challenge. Concerning *A Day in the Life* George Martin wrote of Lennon's voice: 'I was always enormously captivated by his voice, and on this track it is at its best. I miss hearing that voice terribly.' (Ibid p.60)

During the rehearsals, George Martin asked, 'What do you want this symphony orchestra to do, exactly?'[6] We may doubt whether Paul would have had an answer to that question, or indeed whether he would have wanted a symphony orchestra in the studio in the first place! But Faul could answer, after all he had been listening to avant-garde music by the likes of John Cage, Stockhausen and Luciano Berio.

The album *begins* with a song about how, we don't really want to stop the show – as if a show was about to end:

> You're such a lovely audience
> We'd like to take you home with us
> We'd love to take you home
> I don't really want to stop the show
> But I thought that you might like to know
> That the singer's going to sing a song
> And he wants you all to sing along
> So let me introduce to you
> The one and only Billy Shears
> And Sgt. Pepper's Lonely Hearts Club Band

These are the opening words, when the show is just beginning, but do they not sound more like an ending? They don't want to stop the show, and *therefore* the mystery newcomer is introduced. Then in the next song, his insecurity and uncertainties are disclosed:

> What would you think if I sang out of tune,
> Would you stand up and walk out on me.

---

6 *Making*, p56.

> Lend me your ears and I'll sing you a song,
> And I'll try not to sing out of key.
> I get by with a little help from my friends,

How could the world's most famous band be having such worries?[7] Ringo the least accomplished singer in the band does this number. The song continues as if journalists are quizzing Faul over how he is going to manage:

> I get by with a little help from my friends,
> I get high with a little help from my friends,
> Going to try with a little help from my friends.
> What do I do when my love is away.
> (Does it worry you to be alone)
> How do I feel by the end of the day
> (Are you sad because you're on your own)
> No I get by with a little help from my friends,
> Do you need anybody,
> I need somebody to love.
> Could it be anybody
> I want somebody to love.
> Would you believe in a love at first sight,
> Yes I'm certain that it happens all the time.

The goddess Lakshmi is shown bottom centre of the *Sgt Pepper* cover, signifying abundance and prosperity. Yes the good times were rolling - but behind all this, was John in torment? His biographer noted:

The photos of John Lennon taken during the *Sgt Pepper* sessions are disquieting... Here is a man who has suddenly aged about forty years. The eyes behind his granny glasses look like those of dead fish. His dry, droopy moustache belongs on the face of an old geezer. His slumped posture is that of an ancient door keeper.'

Of the latter half of that year, he recalled: 'I was still in a real big depression after Pepper. I was going through murder.'[8] I suggest that even his somewhat jaundiced biographer Albert Goldman[9] is unable to account for this. Lennon had the best possible studio, the best possible band to work

---

7 This may remind us of the laconic comment by George in his *Only a Northern Song* (1967): 'When you're listening late at night/ You may think the band are not quite right If you think the harmony/ Is a little dark and out of key ...'
8 Alan Clayson, *John Lennon*, 2006, p.162.
9 Albert Goldman had an $850,000 deal to write this, and there seems a consensus that his 'Lives of John Lennon' is unduly destructive. Admittedly, all biographies and histories I've seen of the latter part of Lennon's life, living with Ms Ono, express varying degree of pity and nausea.

with, the best possible producer in the form of George Martin, a symphony orchestra hired to help realise the sounds that he heard in his head, a fine home in Surrey plus a lovely wife and child, and had just co-produced the biggest smash-hit rock'n'roll album of all time, whereby he had a key role in giving form to a real period of human optimism. Only (I suggest) the ghastly bereavement he has just suffered can account for this change, well-noted but not understood by Goldman.

Depressed? He had just produced and sung what would soon become the *world's favourite song,* 'A Day in the Life.' He had co-sung it with his new buddy, who had stepped out of nowhere. As the beautiful finale to *Sgt Pepper* his song reached its grand orchestral climax on an E-major, which had to be the most dramatic musical finale since Sibelius' Seventh Symphony. And then he was *depressed*?

Faul, embracing his new identity, was welcomed by the Band:

How does it feel to be one of the beautiful people?
Baby you're a rich man now![10]

From the other side of this single he received some helpful Lennonesque advice: 'Nothing you can do but you can learn how to be you in time. It's easy…'

July '67, *All You Need is Love*

---

10 'Billy Shears' tells the story, whereby on meeting up in Paris after the crash (See Chapter 5), Neil Aspinall said those very words to the new guy: 'How does it feel to be one of the beautiful people? You're a rich man now!': *Memoirs* p.211

Nicholas Kollerstrom

A Fractured Identity

Reflecting on the different aliases under which Faul has performed and published – Apollo C. Vermouth, Viv Stanshall, Percy Thrillington, The Fireman, Billy Martin, the Liverpool Sound Collage – O and yes I nearly forgot, Paul McCartney - one can easily despair of finding out the real identity of this mercurial character. But, let's have a go.

Mother Nature's Son (August 1968, released on the White album)
>Born a poor young country boy
>Mother Nature's son
>All day long I'm sitting, singing songs for everyone
>
>Sit beside a mountain stream
>See her waters rise
>Listen to the pretty sound of music as she flies
>
>Find me in my field of grass
>Mother Nature's son
>Swaying daisies, sing a lazy song beneath the sun

Paul who grew up in urban Liverpool could never have sung this, telling as it does of a non-urban childhood. There again, it's not easy to imagine a complex character like Faul sitting around all day contemplating a mountain stream. It reminds us of Faul singing about a home in Scotland, where the 'Holy people' live:

Heart of the Country (Ram, 1971)
>I look high, I look low,
>I'm lookin' everywhere I go,
>Lookin' for a home in the heart of the country.
>
>I'm gonna move, I'm gonna go,
>I'm gonna tell everyone I know,

> Lookin' for a home in the heart of the country.
> Heart of the country where the holy people grow,
> Heart of the country, smell the grass in the meadow,
> Wo, wo, wo.
>
> Want a horse, I want a sheep,
> I wanna get me a good night's sleep,
> Livin' in a home in the heart of the country

From the *Ram* context we feel he must be alluding to Scotland, though it doesn't actually say so. Scotland was traditionally the 'land of second sight' and so, 'where the holy people grow' which I doubt if anyone would say about the English countryside. Later on he expressed a deep sense of belonging, that he *felt most at home* in Scotland, in the lovely 'Mull of Kintyre.'[1]

The farm seems to have been purchased by Paul in June '66 mere months before his death, far out in the windy wilds off Scotland's West coast, while Paul's luxury Cavendish Avenue home was still being done up (in his last-ever interview in the first week of September '66 he said it was more or less ready except that it did not yet have a piano, so he couldn't practice). These two big property investments synchronized well with Faul's arrival!

That farm off the west coast of Scotland meant a lot more to him than it ever did to Paul. A Semi-derelict house consisting of two rooms plus a kitchen, grey skies and rain, sheep on the hills, rough manual labour - Faul went and lived there, together with Linda and their two kids. It had a a strategic role in Faul's crushing the PID story when it erupted, in late '69 (Chapter 7). When *Wings* band members were expected to stay there they found it hard to appreciate the rough living. Some have surmised that Faul was indeed Scottish, and maybe involved with Scottish masonry: the centre of Scottish-rite masonry, the Kilwhynnin Lodge, some forty miles away, is older than any English lodge.

His haunting song *Blackbird* (1968) remembers the strange change he was put through:

> Blackbird singing in the dead of night
> Take these broken wings and learn to fly
> All your life
> You were only waiting for this moment to arise.

---

1 : 'My ancestors are Scottish and Irish...My heritage and ancestors feel closest to me when I am out on my farm in Scotland.' *Memoirs of Billy Shears* 2009, p.420.

> Blackbird singing in the dead of nigh
> Take these sunken eyes and learn to see
> All your life
> You were only waiting for this moment to be free.
>
> Blackbird fly Blackbird fly
> Into the light of the dark black night.
> Blackbird fly Blackbird fly
> Into the light of the dark black night

It starts with a death-image 'Blackbird singing in the dead of night.' Then someone is given instructions to 'take these broken wings... take these sunken eyes' as if there is a corpse of someone who has crashed out, maybe Icarus flying too close to the Sun. It has to be picked up, he has to *learn to see, and learn to fly.*

This is the big moment his whole life has been leading up to, he was 'only waiting for this moment to be free.' To do that, he has the frightening experience of flying into 'the dark black night' i.e forgetting his previous life, blotting out memories, and then mysteriously he emerged *into the light.*[2]

Or again, to change the metaphor, there was a 'mighty crash' whereby the two of them 'fell into the Sun' (on his *Band on the Run* album):

> Well, the rain exploded with a mighty crash
> As we fell into the sun
> And the first one said to the second one there,
> "I hope you're having fun."

- suggesting that Faul has not got a great deal of his own life-memories, or that they are quite distant for him. He can recall Paul's life with uncanny detail (Barry Miles' biography of McCartney *Many Years From Now* is little more than Faul 'remembering'), but what of his own?

His song 'Jet' (*Wings,* 1974) may recall his Father having been a fighter-pilot. There is an interview where he says he had worked in one or two factories before joining the band. Faul said "I had a couple of jobs in factories" before becoming a Beatle, which Paul never did.[3] In a 1963

---

[2] The song can be interpreted in different ways. Faul in America explained that by the 'blackbird' he had meant a black woman, and 'arise' alluded to the civil rights struggle (Wiki).
[3] Quote from the discerning Tina Foster, who found this: 'I have yet to come across a biography of Paul that says he had one factory job, much less "a couple!"' http://plastic-macca.blogspot.co.uk/2010/01/oops-things-faul-says-sometimes.html

interview, Paul was asked about working and his reply excluded his having any such factory job:

> Q:But you›ve been working since '58, haven›t you?
> Paul: Well, yeah... not working, you know. I mean, strictly speaking we've been out of work since '58 and we've been doing this as a hobby. 'Cuz we've only been doing it as semi-pros. I left school and went right into it. And we were only sort of picking up a few quid a week, you know. It really wasn't work. I think the main thing is now that, as we've got ourselves a bit of security... we don't really have to worry, at the moment anyway, what we're gonna do after it. So we don't.[4]

Paul learnt to play the piano at his family's home, his musical father Jim McCartney taught him. Both his father and grandfather played in bands.

Strangely, Sir George Martin has averred: "When I first met him [Paul] *he could not play the piano at all*. It was a very short time indeed from then to *Lady Madonna*, which is a very complicated and extremely good piano track played entirely by Paul, and a measure of his great musicianship.'[5] It is just not possible to believe that either Paul or Faul were unable to play the piano at any point when Sir George met them, so his comment must remain enigmatic.

We are bewildered by the different faces of Faul, but what does he feel about them? In the year 1989, when he no longer had Linda around to reassure him, he sung this on his 'My Brave Face'[6] (the *Wings* album, 'Flowers in the Dirt'): *Now I'm alone again / Can't stop stop breaking down again / ...Take me to that place, Where I can't find my brave face / I've been living a lie.'* Faul has thoroughly put his life-experience into his songs, which helped him to cope emotionally with all he went through.

Faul's Xmas video release for 1979 'Wonderful Christmas time' shows him bustling around, happy with Linda the love of his live. He confronts his *doppelganger* at 1 minute 50 seconds: the alter-ego he meets is not a mirror-image, because their chins are different, so are the ears: the first, long-faced Paul says "so lift the glass ..." and the other round-faced Paul stares back and sings "And don't look down!"

---

4 www.beatlesinterviews.org/db63.html
5 Martin, *Making*, p.86. Some conspiracy-theorists believe that the *Lady Madonna* piano is just too good, and someone else eg Elton John must have done it, with Faul singing.
6 The 'Paul McCartney Tribute: My Brave Face' online video made for his 66th birthday is continually ricocheting from Paul to Faul and back again, comparing their faces - quite effective for this song.

A Fractured Identity

Faul frequently comments on his identity problem. The replacement *feels the old being* of Paul in him, as if he is two people.[7]

'I joined the Beatles, an already set-up affair' - Paul joined the Quarrymen in 1957 then co-founded the Beatles in 1960, no way did he join a 'set-up affair.'

'In a way, I think of Paul McCartney as 'Him'... I do wake up some mornings and think, Jesus Christ, am I really that guy, is this the same body I'm inhabiting? It is quite strange.' (RA 60 2)

'I'm very good at forgetting who I am, because as far as I'm concerned, Paul McCartney is a name I was given ... I didn't really do all that. It's like a dream really, It's going to stop soon.'[8]

'I've learnt to compartmentalise' ... 'There's me and there's famous Him. I don't want to sound schizophrenic, but probably I'm two people.' (Sir Paul confronts the ghosts of his past, *Sunday Times* – no longer online)

'I Look in the mirror and just think, I in this shell, am the guy I've read so much about .. I dunno whether it's a schitzo thing, ….. Paul McCartney is like the successful bit of it all, that I'm very proud of, but you know, I don't imagine I am him, 'cause otherwise it would just blow my head off.'[9]

'They shouldn't be paying me this money, I'm y'know I'm not him, I'm some kid masquerading as this guy, who'se like the famous guy - and Oh no, I'm a clone, y'know.'[10]

'So I thought, being Paul McCartney the whole bit is really, you know, too much to live up to: the advantages, I like to think they outweigh the disadvantages.'

About 'Yesterday, Paul McCartney's most famous' song:
'I dreamed it, didn't believe it was mine really, *I didn't even write it really in a way….*'

---

7 Most of these quotes were assembled by Tina Foster for her excellent *Plastic Macca* site. They don't all have source references: mostly Google will find them.
8 'live fo rehtaf' video (2008).
9 Three sources for this: 'Faul McCartney?' video by 911archive, 2009; 'Paul is Dead - The Shocking Clues Collection' by SgtPepperChannel, 2013, 5:20-30; and *Rotten Apple* 78, at the start.
10 'Paul is Dead - The Shocking Clues Collection', by SgtPepperChannell, 2013, 5:20 mins.

See Faul give a big wink, when the band is asked about 'all the time you've been Beatles.'[11]

'In America, I was asked a thousand times *if I was Paul or his clone*. I prepared a ready-made answer: "I am neither Paul nor his clone, but I went out last night with your wife."'

Of Beatle songs composed long ago: "In a way, someone else did write them - it was a 24 year old me. And I look back *on him* and think, I'm looking at his writing as if he's, like, another person, some of the lyrics thinking 'that wasn't bad - it was good the way he did that." *Daily Mirror* 21/12/2011

As regards stepping into Paul's shoes, «You work it up from there, y›know, and you gradually find this new identity for yourself, that›s what I was trying to do...› (*Rotten Apple* 78, 2:20)

On being endlessly asked the same question (about Paul's death) his replies were sometimes humorous – e.g., 'I'm not actually dead at this minute anyway' (RA 78, 0:30-0:35) – and sometimes quite startling:

Faul: 'There was a theory a few years ago that I was dead ...
Question: I was going to ask you about that. Are you, erm...
Faul: No I'm not actually dead, not actually ... just a good, er, replica.[12]

In 1972 while touring in Sweden with Linda his sardonic comment was:
Faul: My name actually is Yan Shoderbuk, and I am actually a Swedish chap who's standing in for Paul McCartney tonight to make a lot of money and just run off with it.'
Question: Why do you think that the rumours come?
Faul: Why do they come about? Because Paul McCartney's dead of course.[13]
That seems clear enough! One more time - and here we note the amused expressions shared by other members of his *Wings* group as it is put to him (on RA 76, 4:25-4:40):
Question: And what about the rumours going around that you had died and that there is a double standing in for you?
Faul: It's not true. I'm almost alive.

---

11 Video: 'Conspiracy theory #1968: Paul is dead!'
12 RA 72 'Just a good replica', 5:25.
13 'Paul McCartney funny interview,' 1972 interview by Claes Elfberg, uploaded 12.9.09..

In the pub

Faul is in a Liverpool pub, jostling around with a crowd that seems excited to have a Beatle in their midst. We are probably in the late '60s and Faul is trying to look as if he's got some kind of family around. See the *Rotten Apple* 36 (1:0 - 1:45)[14].

By way of introducing this scene he says 'Liverpool, a city of .. pubs, relatives' *as if* we are seeing him in a pub with his relatives. Are we? 'Hullo Billy,' an old lady calls out to him, with an affectionate smile upon her face: 'Hullo Billy, you going to sit here?' There is unmistakeable warmth and recognition in her voice, without malice. Faul calls out to someone called Joe, then he says 'Hullo Dad' and we see Jim McCartney smiling broadly.

Does he just happen to bump into his own father in the pub? It's clearly an act, and he is being filmed, and Jim evidently enjoys the theatre of being called 'Dad' by a famous Beatle. Jim McCartney has endorsed and surely rescued the identity of the famous Faul, by accepting the 'Dad' role.

A discerning blogger commented of Faul, 'He is between a rock and a hard place, but he's got a helluva lot of cash to ease the pain. We don't really know what Faul goes through. "Trapped inside these four walls...". ...*forced* to move into a nice London Georgian mansion and forced to drive an Austin Martin DB6 and forced to live with nice antique furniture and Oriental rugs and forced to grab another's man big fat bank account..'[15]

A Machine behind him?

Heather Mills after her divorce from Sir Paul in 2008, walked off with a cool twenty million, plus she retained at least technically her title, Lady McCartney, as having been married to a knight of the realm. She wasn't popular: the British people reacted quite strongly against a former high-class hooker with one leg moaning about being married to a Beatle. When she was asked in 2007: "Knowing what you know now about Paul, would you have married him in the first place?" she firmly replied "Never."

There was, she added, 'A lot of fear of the truth coming out from a certain party.' Her ex-husband 'had betrayed me immensely, I mean, beyond belief

---

14 As usual with the *Rotten Apple* series, we could do with a bit more context but are not given it. This video series tends to flicker and flitter quickly over bewilderingly different topics, for which reason I'm here suggesting a limited time in seconds over which to watch it.

15 Comments from 60if page 2005, mainly 'Bishop.' 'Trapped inside these four walls' is a quote from McCartney's *Band on the Run* album, see next chapter.

– and I don't mean infidelity, or anything like that ... If you pop me off, the truth will come out ... *People don't want to know what the truth is, 'cause they could never, ever handle it*; they would be too devastated. And that's why I have stayed quiet. *I married a legend and there's a machine behind.* I can't really go into it, but, you know, you have to read between the lines.... I still love him and he's the father of my child. And, you know, there's things go on. Things are not what you see...[16] I have a box of evidence, and should anything happen to me it will come out... I found out that someone I had loved for a long time had betrayed me immensely, and I don't mean infidelity or anything like that, like, beyond belief'.[17]

Whatever it was, she has accepted a big sum to keep quiet. No wonder the press were mystified.

---

16 CNN Larry King Live: Interview With Heather Mills, March 20, 2007.
17 Quotes from *Plastic Macca* site, plus *The Winged Beetle* 2012 1hr 24 mins.

Secret of the Songs

I'll Follow the Sun

One day, you'll look
To see I've gone.
But tomorrow may rain, so I'll follow the sun.
Someday, you'll know
I was the one.
But tomorrow may rain, so I'll follow the sun.

And now the time has come,
And so, my love, I must go.
And though I lose a friend,
In the end you will know.

One day, you'll find
That I have gone.
But tomorrow may rain, so I'll follow the sun.

Yes Paul, you were the one; and yes, you had to go. You left this old world behind (I'll follow the Sun...). Farewell, Orpheus![1]

That was a very early McCartney song 'written almost before the Beatles' as Lennon remarked, but recorded in 1964.

As regards what Beatlemania was then like, Sir George Martin recalled: 'In 1964, in the USA, you could tune right across the frequency spectrum of a transistor radio, station after station, and hear nothing at all over the airwaves but that one sound – the Beatles.'[2]

---

1 In the Greek myth, Orpheus the musician descends with his lyre into the Underworld, and comes back again. The poet Pindar called him 'the father of songs.'
2 The Making, p.12.

Stones tribute in Ruby Tuesday: (composed in November-December '66, released in January 1967 –Brian Jones presented an early version of this haunting melody to the rest of the Rolling Stones according to Marianne Faithfull.

> She would never say where she came from
> Yesterday don't matter if it's gone
> While the sun is bright
> Or in the darkest night
> No one knows
> She comes and goes
>
> Goodbye, Ruby Tuesday
> Who could hang a name on you?
> When you change with every new day
> Still I'm gonna miss you...
>
> Don't question why she needs to be so free
> She'll tell you it's the only way to be
> She just can't be chained
> To a life where nothing's gained
> And nothing's lost
> At such a cost
>
> There's no time to lose, I heard her say
> Catch your dreams before they slip away
> Dying all the time
> Lose your dreams
> And you will lose your mind.
> Ain't life unkind?

This beautiful song regrets the passing of Paul 'Still I'm gonna miss you…Ain't life unkind?', but also expresses some awe of the newcomer 'She would never say where she came from', whose identity cannot be pinned down 'who could hang a name on you?' Wake up people, this haunting lyric is *not* a love song!

Tuesday is a key day in the story, said in the *Billy Shears Memoirs* to signify the day Lennon got to hear of his comrade's death, two days earlier. The story is that Lennon was briefly told by Epstein the news in a telegram, who however was greatly delayed in getting to Hamburg, so Lennon was tortured by the long wait, making that afternoon 'never-ending:' 'Tuesday afternoon is never-ending' ('Lady Madonna', 1968)

It was that Tuesday which impacted most terribly upon his soul, so when he came to tell the story later on to the Stones it became 'Ruby Tuesday.'

Donovan sees the change

In December 1966 Donovan at the EMI Abbey Road studio must have seen the newcomer arrive. He composed 'Epistle to Dippy' recounting how a good friend of his had been going through some startling changes: "Through all levels you've been changing/ Getting a little bit better, no doubt," adding "The doctor bit was so far out" (i.e., the plastic surgery). His song alluded to the terrible accident: "Through all levels you've been changing/Elevator in the brain hotel/ Broken down but just as well."

As to the mystery identity of this "broken down" person we are only told, "Doing us paperback reader" - alluding to a transform, which followed on from the earlier Paul's song *Paperback Writer*. "Looking through crystal spectacles/I can see you had your fun" is a theme of this song, i.e. the singer needs special spectacles to perceive the very strange thing that has happened to his pal.

The song enquires about the identity of the newcomer, after all these changes: 'Over dusty years, I ask you/ What it's been like being you?' One had to focus from different points of view to try and get a grip on what had happened: 'Looking through all kinds of windows/ I can see you had your fun.'

This song was only released in the USA, being too close to the bone to be permitted in the UK. The *Billy Shears Memoirs* recall how Donovan called Faul DOP, Duplicate of Paul, however Faul wasn't happy about that, it sounded like dope or dopey, and instead he suggested 'DIP', Duplicate *in* Paul. So Donovan called him 'Dippy,' and his song was entitled, 'Epistle to Dippy.'[3]

The song opens with a monk meditating in the Himalayan mountains, indicating that there is some transcendent meaning to the topic, beyond ordinary ken.

Sgt Pepper: Lennon, **A Day in the Life,** spring '67

> I read the news today, oh boy
> About a lucky man who made the grade
> And though the news was rather sad
> Well I just had to laugh

---

[3] *Memoirs of Billy Shears,* pp273-274.

> I saw the photograph.
> He blew his mind out in a car
> He didn't notice that the lights had changed
> A crowd of people stood and stared
> They'd seen his face before

A poll by Q magazine said this was the best British song of all time! Composed in January 1967, it alludes to the car-crash of Tara Browne on 18 December 1966. The heir to a fortune, he was associated with the *Indica Gallery* scene, and his Father was in the House of Lords ('Nobody was sure if he was from the House of Lords'). In view of its great significance as the last song, and with a whole symphony orchestra at the end sounding like a car-crash, it is also I suggest alluding to a tragic event of a more immediate importance to the Beatles.

There are different levels on which death-motifs appear in Sgt Pepper: the grave on its cover, 'lend me your ears' as part of a funeral speech, the song *Good morning, good morning* which has the words 'Nothing to do to save his life;' and finally 'A Day in the Life.' And inside Paul has what looks like 'OPD,' 'Officially Pronounced Dead' on his sleeve. There is a whole debate about that which we needn't here go into.

Ex-band member Stuart Sutcliffe features on the front cover, but Pete Best doesn't. And why is that? It's because the former was dead, the latter alive. The colourful crowd on the *Sgt Pepper* cover are mainly persons who have died, gathered together to welcome Paul into the Great Beyond. Bob Dylan went through what the papers called a near-death experience, vanishing from public view for quite a while, over the period of Paul's disappearance, so it was decided to include him.

At the end of the MMT (November 1967), the *Bonzo Dog Band* comes on, in a strip club, and its lead singer Viv Stanshall gives an Elvis parody. This is the best account of the urban legend, in which Paul may be alluded to as 'cutie'(i.e, the good-looking Beatle) calling a cab, which we have to interpret as driving in his smart new Aston-Martin. He picks up a hitch-hiker then starts driving too fast while being distracted by her pretty curves, and in fact is she the 'cutie'?

Death Cab for Cutie

> That night Cutie called a cab, uh huh huh
> (baby don't do it)
> She left her East Side room so drab uh huh huh
> (baby don't do it)

Secret of the Songs

> She went out on the town
> Knowin' it would make her lover frown
> (Death-cab for Cutie)
> (Death-cab for Cutie)
> Someone's gonna make you pay your fare
>
> The cab was racin' through the night, mm mm mm
> (baby don't do it)
> His eyes in the mirror, keepin' Cutie in sight, uh huh huh
> (baby don't do it)
> When he saw Cutie, it gave him a thrill
> Don't you know, baby curves can kill
> (Death-cab for Cutie)
> (Death-cab for Cutie)
> Someone's gonna make you pay your fare
> Cutie, don't you play with fate
> Don't leave your lover alone
> If you go out on this date
> His heart will turn to stone
>
> Bad girl, Cutie, what have you done, uh huh huh
> (baby don't do it)
> Slippin' slidin' down-a Highway 31, mm mm mm
> (baby don't do it)
> The traffic lights changed from green to red
> They tried to stop but they both wound up dead

This is *the* song about the car-crash - if you want to believe it. This gripping song has two people killed - a vital part of the urban myth: the hitch-hiker Paul picked up also met her fate. If the whole of MMT was about the replacement of Paul and his new identity, then does this tell us something about how close the Bonzo Dog Band (presumably also with the Ruttles, a comic pastiche version of the Beatles, with whom they were quite close) were to the Fab Four, to be invited to sing this last song?

The whereabouts of 'Highway 31' remains a mystery. But why they would entrust this awful secret story to a bunch of clowns like the Bonzo Dog Doo Dah band and even allow a comic parody? Our next chapter will comment upon this!

Also in MMT (released a couple of months earlier as a single) *The Fool on the Hill* enigmatically juxtaposes two very different people, or maybe archetypes:

Day after day, alone on the hill
The man with the foolish grin
Is keeping perfectly still

But nobody wants to know him
They can see that he's just a fool
And he never gives an answer

But the fool on the hill
Sees the sun going down
And the eyes in his head
See the world spinning around

Well on the way, his head in a cloud
The man of a thousand voices
Talking perfectly loud

But nobody ever hears him
Or the sound he appears to make

Somebody is immobile on a hill, with a vacant grin and whose expression does not change. He never gives an answer, and all he sees is the world revolving and the sun rising: that is Paul, now out of this world. We are shown a picture of what has to be him in the brochure for MMT, looking clearly Paul-like and wearing stylish clothes as he liked to – but, there is a huge crack in his head! His left hand, deftly drawn by John Lennon, expresses his death: it's ghostly and limp, with only four fingers.

In contrast the 'Man with a thousand voices' is walking by with 'his head in a cloud.' He is tall and he has a different kind of problem, that he talks 'perfectly loud / But nobody ever hears him.' The camera here pans to the tall figure of Faul, appearing in colour for the first time (8-9 minutes of MMT).

Nobody really hears what he is saying; and there is 'the sound he appears to make,' which might mean for example that he is not really making the Beatles-recorded music. He's very versatile, can sing in different voices, but may not be what he appears to be. This song needs to be seen visually in the film.

Hey Jude

In August of '68 *Hey Jude* appeared, which became the Beatles' biggest hit, but what was it really about? It was composed while Faul was driving down to visit Cynthia Lennon and her son Julian.

Secret of the Songs

She was feeling very much abandoned by her husband, who hardly ever came to see his son, and in her memoirs said that her son Julian saw more of Paul McCartney than he did his father. That June day when he came to visit her he gave her a rose.

People think it's a drug song because of the words 'let her under your skin,' after which, 'you'll feel better.' But that is far from adequate to account for the amazing mood which this song generates, causing it to be regularly voted as one of the best songs of all time. People who decline to believe that Paul McCartney could have been replaced, will tend to point to this song as evidence: how could a replacement ever compose a song as good as this? That is assuredly *the* question.

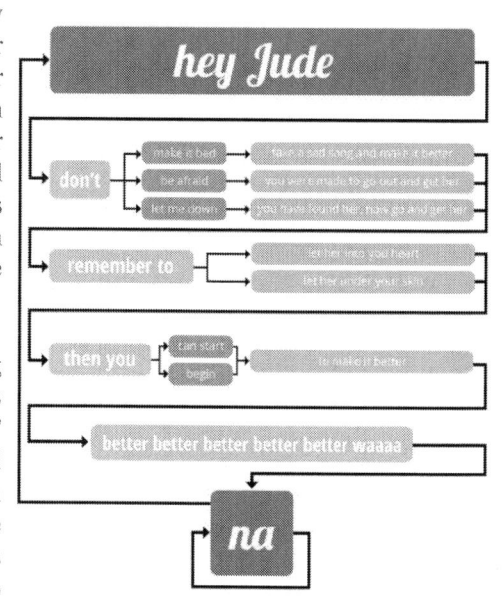

No-one knew what its opaque lyrics were about: 'It's me!' exclaimed Lennon on hearing the song, to which McCartney replied 'No-it's me!'[4] A common view would be that this song isn't really about anything, a bit like e.g. 'A Whiter Shade of Pale' (see diagram).

We understand this song from the explanation give in the *Billy Shears Memoirs*, whereby it is Paul addressing Faul, encouraging him and explaining to him how to become a proper Beatle and fulfil his Beatle-potential: 'Hey Jude is about me, the brother[5] of James Paul, fully letting him into my heart. It is about me forsaking my reluctance to be totally one with him.'(*Memoirs* p.319)

Faul is told, 'Take a sad song, and make it better' by way of overcoming the tragedy of the death. Empathising too much with the Departed One could make him liable to get hit by the enormous pain that Paul is still suffering: 'And anytime you feel the pain, hey Jude, refrain / Don't carry the world upon your shoulders.'

---

4 Ian Macdonald, *Revolution in the Head*, p.303.
5 Billy Shears has just made the slightly far-fetched claim that 'Jude' alludes to Judas who is the brother of James in the New Testament.

45

But conversely, he is also advised against becoming too detached: 'It's a fool who plays it cool, making the world a colder place.' There follows the cryptic comment 'The movement you need is on your shoulder:' On several occasions the *Billy Shears Memoirs* allude to the way, when Faul felt Paul was with him, he would feel via his left shoulder.

The cryptic words of this song are interpreted by each hearer in their own way, which is why the song has such a universal appeal. On Thursday 1st August 1968 a huge orchestra was hired, to play four chords over and over again: 'The monumentality of the orchestral contribution to *Hey Jude* – so simple, so surprising – was typical of the Beatles… the huge chords suggesting both Jude's personal revelation and, along with the accompanying chorale, a vast commonality in which artists and audience joined in swaying to a single rhythm, all around the world.'[6]

The *White Album* of 1968 showed the Band as fully atomised, their old unity gone. Many of Lennon's songs for that album had been composed in Rishikesh, India at the Maharishi's ashram earlier that year. They worked on the album in George Harrison's wonderful Kinfauns home in Surrey, its walls all psychedelically painted (have a look at some web-pictures of it). Donovan was around and commented: 'We'd play for hours on end and so much of ths became part of the White album.' Lennon sang -

Glass Onion

> I told you 'bout strawberry fields
> You know the place where nothing is real
> Well, here's another place you can go
> Where everything flows
>
> Looking through the bent backed tulips
> To see how the other half live
> Looking through a glass onion
> I told you 'bout the walrus and me, man
> You know that we're as close as can be, man
> Well, here's another clue for you all
> The walrus was Paul
> Standing on the cast iron shore, yeah
> Lady Madonna trying to make ends meet, yeah
> Looking through a glass onion
>
> Oh yeah, oh yeah, oh yeah
> Looking through a glass onion

---

6 Ian MacDonald *Revolution in the Head* p.303.

> I told you 'bout the fool on the hill
> I tell you man he living there still
> Well, here's another place you can be
> Listen to me
>
> Fixing a hole in the ocean
> Trying to make a dovetail joint, yeah
> Looking through a glass onion

Like a seer Lennon here peers through into the misty Beyond, as if the 'glass onion' is some crystal ball or scrying-stone.[7] He is looking out at the never-never land of Strawberry Fields, 'where nothing is real' and 'everything flows' – while he, in contrast, stands on the firm 'cast-iron shore' of this world. His lines 'Looking through the bent backed tulips / To see how the other half live' recall the tulips around the Beatles' grave on the *Sgt Pepper* cover.

Lennon had had too many people close to him pass away strangely, starting with his Mother in 1958 in a violent car-crash when he was only 17, then Stuart Sutcliffe his best friend at art college, then Paul, then just recently Brian Epstein his manager; it was all too much, no wonder he as a poet felt that there was a 'hole in the ocean' he was attempting to fix. How come a down-to-Earth rocker is singing about 'fixing a hole in the ocean?' People think these are just druggie visions but they're not.

In MMT the Fool on the Hill does nothing all day, except watch the world going round: that image of the dead Paul, removed from them, John here alludes to, assuring us that that figure *is really there*: 'I tell you man...'.

Another White Album song by Ringo, Don't Pass me by:

Don't Pass Me By

> I listen for your footsteps
> Coming up the drive
> Listen for your footsteps
> But they don't arrive
> Waiting for your knock dear
> On my old front door

---

7 'Psychic vision to me is reality. Even as a child. When I looked at myself in the mirror or when I was 12, 13, I used to literally trance out into alpha. I didn't know what it was called then. I found out years later there is a name for those conditions. But I would find myself seeing hallucinatory images of my face changing and becoming cosmic and complete.'- John Lennon, 1980 *Playboy* interview

> I don't hear it
> Does it mean you don't love me any more?
>
> I hear the clock a'ticking
> On the mantel shelf
> See the hands a'moving
> But I'm by myself
> I wonder where you are tonight
> And why I'm by myself
> I don't see you
> Does it mean you don't love me any more?
>
> Don't pass me by don't make me cry don't make me blue
> 'Cause you know darling I love only you
> You'll never know it hurt me so
> How I hate to see you go
> Don't pass me by don't make me cry
>
> I'm sorry that I doubted you
> I was so unfair
> **You were in a car crash**
> **And you lost your hair**
> You said you would be late
> About an hour or two
> I said that's alright I'm waiting here
> Just waiting to hear from you.

Ringo has here – in the first Beatles song he wrote by himself - lost someone whom he used to see more or less daily. He even compares himself to a wife who would hear her husband's footsteps a-crunching up the gravel drive every day. How could Ringo have been so abandoned, such that the person who has forsaken him 'will never know it hurt me so'?

There is *no-one else Ringo loves as much* as this person: 'you know darling I love only you.' In the last lines we are astonished to receive the explanation, 'You were in a car-crash / And you lost your hair,' which gives form to the traditional urban myth, of McCartney being suddenly decapitated by a dreadful car-crash - no wonder he isn't coming back any more!

In that story Ringo, seeing Paul storm out – maybe from Abbey Road Studio in the evening of Sunday, September 11th - had expected him back in an hour or two, but had been left waiting. There is also a suggestion that Paul had sensed it was coming and had tried to tell people about it[8]: 'I'm sorry that

---

[8] *Memoirs of Billy Shears*, Ch.3

I doubted you.' Equally intense is a *White Album* song by Faul, expressing a mystical communion, if you want to believe that:

I Will

Who knows how long I've loved you?
You know I love you still
Will I wait a lonely lifetime?
If you want me to, I will

For if I ever saw you
I didn't catch your name
But it never really mattered
I will always feel the same

Love you forever and forever
Love you with all my heart
Love you whenever we're together
Love you when we're apart

And when at last I find you,
Your song will fill the air..

Here again we have the love of a lifetime, which is *still going on* ('you know I love you still'), such that one of these two will 'love you forever and forever.' But, hang on a minute, the person speaking didn't even catch the other's name! I mean, did they ever meet ('if ever I saw you')?? It is not impossible that Paul did at some stage meet the person who was to become Faul, to which that second verse alludes.

Now that is impossible, you may say! In that case, please tell me what this song is about? 'When' they do meet up, in the Great Beyond – and we appreciate a certain amount of confidence here that this is indeed going to happen – he will recognise the other by the song: which 'will fill the air'. I dare not comment upon this!

The song title here, 'I, Will' alludes to the identity of the young man who bravely stepped into Paul's shoes, whether we want to call him Bill Shepherd or William Campbell.

George on the *White Album* sings 'While My guitar Gently Weeps', voted 10th in the *Rolling Stone* list of 100 greatest Beatle songs, plus number 7 on their list of a hundred greatest guitar songs of all time. We clearly hear George murmuring 'Paul, Paul, Paul' towards the end[9] which gives us some idea what the song is about: 'I look at you all see the love there that's sleeping / While my guitar gently weeps' – where 'love' here signifies the vitality and joy that the band used to have, that is now gone. Then suddenly he – most unfairly - blames Faul, accusing him of being an unnatural and 'controlled' character:

> I don't know how someone controlled you
> They bought and sold you
>
> I don't know how you were diverted
> You were perverted too
> I don't know how you were inverted
> No one alerted you

The gentle George had taken quite a dislike to the new fellow.

In January 1969 as the Beatles approached their break-up, the exquisite melody 'The long and Winding Road' on their last album *Let it Be* was composed and sung by McCartney.

> The long and winding road that leads to your door
> Will never disappear
> I've seen that road before it always leads me here
> Leads me to your door
>
> The wild and windy night that the rain washed away
> Has left a pool of tears crying for the day
> Why leave me standing here, let me know the way
> Many times I've been alone and many times I've cried
> Anyway you'll never know the many ways I've tried
> And still they lead me back to the long and winding road
> You left me standing here a long, long time ago
> Don't leave me waiting here, lead me to your door

What happened 'a long, long time ago' on a windy, rainy night, on a 'long and winding road'? The singer cannot escape from the situation, and he keeps crying about it when alone, because 'you left me standing here'? Long ago the rain has washed away the sad remains, yet the singer keeps begging 'lead me to your door' - as if it could still be found. This has to be alluding to the crash, with Faul's identity tied up with another, who is dead. The door resembles some door of Heaven, and the winding road is his life's path.

---

9 At 3.40-4.20 minutes of the song.

The compelling but nightmarish *Come Together* was sung by Lennon as the first song on Abbey Road (nowadays their best-selling album), recorded in September 1969:

Come Together

Here come old flattop he come grooving up slowly
He got joo-joo eyeball he one holy roller
He got hair down to his knee
Got to be a joker he just do what he please

He wear no shoeshine he got toe-jam football
He got monkey finger he shoot coca-cola
He say "I know you, you know me"
One thing I can tell you is you got to be free
Come together right now over me

He bag production he got walrus gumboot
He got Ono sideboard he one spinal cracker
He got feet down below his knee
Hold you in his armchair you can feel his disease
Come together right now over me

He roller-coaster he got early warning
He got muddy water he one mojo filter
He say "One and one and one is three"
Got to be good-looking 'cause he's so hard to see
Come together right now over me

The horror haunts Lennon, as a vision of the crumpled-up once-beautiful Paul, his dearest friend now come back like one of the Undead to haunt him.

'Old flat-top' has to allude to the top of Paul's head shorn off in the crash. 'He one spinal cracker' i.e his spine was smashed up by the accident. He's one 'holy roller' who is 'so hard to see', *because* he's not in this space-time world any more.

'He shoot coca-cola' could (I suggest) mean, that while other members of the band were on hard liquor or drugs, cheerful Paul was just knocking back the Coca-cola. 'He got early warning' could suggest Paul had sensed in some way his approaching demise. 'He wear no shoeshine' could allude to the front cover of Abbey Road, with Faul as the barefoot Beatle allegedly signifying that he is dead.

The three ('one and one and one is three') remaining Beatles here get the instruction to 'Come together right now over me' – over his terrible dead body, they must come together.

A drawing by Lennon on an album in a private collection[10], shows a grizly decapitation, seemingly a visual equivalent to this song.

The Sun is going down on a youngster who is lovable as shown by a dog licking him. He is digging his own grave, the fashionable groovy boots he liked to wear are all undone. The entire top of his skull has been broken and something's flowing out from it, the side of his head has been impacted, so that he's left with an awful "joo-joo eyeball." Despite being decapitated the lad appears as still alive, he's *undead*, like the character in Lennon's nightmare *Come Together*.

A couple of *Abbey Road* songs by Faul are very simple, and set up paradoxes like cries for help indicating his strange condition.

Carry that Weight

> Boy, you gotta carry that weight
> Carry that weight a long time
> …And in the middle of the celebrations
> I break down

A 'boy' carries a burden, for a long time. The hardest part of this turns out to be, not on some long, ardous journey as one might suppose, but rather 'in the middle of the celebrations.' Then 'I,' the singer, i.e. Faul, is liable to break down. The singer has to be that 'boy' and the song alludes to a false identity, that is most liable to be exposed during celebrations, after a bit of alcohol.

That song was recorded in August, 1969, on the same day as *Golden Slumbers*, the two being adjacent on Abbey Road. They flow together as one piece in the album's well-crafted ending. *Golden Slumbers* tells us:

---

10 The image is shown by Clare Kuehn, 70% of way down her www.youcanknowsometimes.com blog on the PID topic. It's in someone's private collection and I guess Clare is not at liberty to say more. But the image is not signed by Lennon so we do really need some kind of validation. This is 'John's sketch' alluded to by Jim Fetzer in Chapter One.

Once there was a way to get back homeward
Once there was a way to get back home
Sleep pretty darling do not cry
And I will sing a lullaby

Golden slumbers fill your eyes
Smiles awake you when you rise

A fast-asleep 'darling' is being consoled - while Faul is also lamenting that there is no way for him to get back home. He once used to be able to do that: but, whatever could that have to do with 'golden slumbers'? Faul is here suffering from the loss of his identity, of his folks and the old friends of yore, plus *nobody* is allowed to call him 'William' or Bill. He can't find the way back to where he came from, and that is deeply connected with the 'darling' who is in a 'golden slumber:' the dead Paul.

In 1971 Lennon is heard griping against Faul, disliking his albums:

How do you sleep?

The sound you make is muzak to my ears
You must have learned something in all those years
caustically adding, "You better see right through that Mother's eyes" as if there was something deceptive about Faul. Never, ever would he have said such a thing about his beloved soul-mate Paul. Let's not quote further from this unpleasant rant (on the *Imagine* album); even though one may feel a certain sympathy with this characterization of Faul's post-Beatle *oeuvre*.

This attack was followed a year later by Ringo (with George's help) scoffing at Faul[11] in the single *Back off, Boogaloo*. Boogaloo here refers to a genre of popular Latin/American dance music, in other words this insult is not so different from Lennons' 'sounds like Muzak to my ears' jibe.

Back off Boogaloo

Wake up, meat head
Don't pretend that you are dead
Get yourself right off the cart
Get yourself together now
And give me something tasty
Everything you try to do
You know it sure sounds wasted

---

11 There is a degree of consensus here, that 'Boogaloo' alludes to McCartney, see *Wiki* on this song.

"Back off, boogaloo", I said
Back off, boogaloo, you think you're a groove

- with a picture of Frankenstein on the cover! The remaining Beatles are now uneasy about the success of Faul, who was, after all, 'invented' to rescue the broken band - but he has now broken off and gone away on his own career.

Frankenstein was an artificial creation which, once unleashed, could not be recalled, because it had its own awful life: here depicted as having broken his chain and smoking a huge joint!

This attack continued the next year (1973) with Lennon composing the satirical 'I'm the Greatest' for Ringo to sing, again alluding to 'boogaloo' and scoffing at Faul. They are irked at the way he is now more successful than the 'real' Beatles, and hurl at him this jibe:

I'm the Greatest
I was in the greatest show on earth
For what it was worth
Now I'm only thirty-two
And all I wanna do is boogaloo, hey
Yes my name is Billy Shears
You know it has been for so many years

Boogaloo is now a verb and the person is Billy Shears. Ringo had sung the *Billy Shears* song on *Sgt Pepper*, alluding to the newcomer Faul. Now scoffing at this character 'Billy Shears', they imply that he is a real person and was not just dreamed up for that album, and also that he did not always have that name ('it has been for so many years').[12]

Band on the Run

Faul to his credit never replies to these taunts. After all his position was rather delicate.[13] Doing so would not have been hard, with Lennon's once-

---
12 In MMT Faul gives his age as thirty, filmed on September 1967, when Paul would have been 25.
13 'You can knock me down with a feather, but you know it's not allowed' 3 Legs,

lovely voice having been reduced to a mere hoarse croak in these days, from all his years of smoking, drugs and booze. Instead, we hear more intense introspection from Faul. His *Wings* song (December 1973) 'Band on the Run' starts with him feeling imprisoned, and locked in:

> Stuck inside these four walls, sent inside forever
> Never seeing no one nice again like you
> Ah, if only he could 'get out':
>
> All I need is a pint a day
> If I ever get out of here

He then recalls –as we've alluded to in Chapter Three - the stupendous moment of transformation, when his life changed forever:

Well, the rain exploded with a mighty crash as we fell into the sun
And the first one said to the second one there I hope you're having fun

That's his memory! His feeling of being imprisoned derives from that moment, when 'we fell into the sun.' Who are the 'we,' who together 'fell into the Sun'? That's the duality present in his memory, where 'the first one says to the second one there I hope you're having fun' – as if the dead Paul were wishing his successor well. Water and fire are here juxtaposed, with the crash of rain (that rainy night of Paul's crash) followed by, the Sun.

This strangely-bestowed identity makes him feel like he is forever 'on the run' -
> Band On The Run, Band On The Run
> And the jailer man and Sailor Sam were searching everyone

The song ends with a flashback to Paul's funeral, where hardly anyone turned up (aka *The long and Winding Road'*):

Well the undertaker drew a heavy sigh seeing no-one else had come.
It was hardly a public event.

2005 *Chaos and Creation*

This garrulous album has Faul playing most of the instruments, and listening to it may not be much fun. One song 'Friends to Go' reads as secret dialogue with his soulmate Paul on the Other Side;

> I've been waitin' on the other side, for your friends to leave

---
Ram 1971.

So I don't have to hide, I prefer they didn't know
So I've been waiting on the other side, for your friends to go

I've been sliding down a slippery slope, I've been climbing
Up a slowly burning rope, but the flame is getting low
I've been waitin' on the other side, for your friends to go

You never need to worry about me, I'll be fine on my own
Someone else can worry about me
I've spent a lot of time on my own
I've spent a lot of time on my own

I've been waitin' till the danger's passed, I don't know
How long the storm is gonna last, if we're gonna carry on
I'll been waiting on the other side, till your friends are gone

The 'I' here is not him, can it belong to his companion out in the Beyond?[14]

---

14 Faul averred that George Harrison had inspired him from the Beyond to write this song. He composed it three years after the latter's death: "… I felt as if I was almost George Harrison during the writing of that song, I just got this feeling, this is George…. it just wrote itself very easily 'cause it wasn't even me writing it." (Wiki)

The Newcomer Steps into History

In 1964 the UK entertainment industry was pulling revenues into the country over and above any other industry, because of the Beatles, with every country buying up their albums faster than they could be run off the presses. Most countries around the world were pre-ordering millions of records even before they had been composed, the Beatles were 'outselling all other groups combined worldwide'.[1] The huge baby-boom teen population in Britain in the 1960s were thrilled by the Beatles / Rolling Stones polarity. The Wilson government was able to avoid devaluing the pound because of the Beatles' contribution to revenue and exports (NB Lennon's complaint 'One for you nineteen for me' in Mr Taxman, on *Revolver*). Harold Wilson came from Huddersfield, not so far from Liverpool.

So, when and if something catastrophic happened to the Band, there was an overriding priority that the show had to go on. If there was a high-level government imperative for a replacement to be put swiftly into place, persons concerned would bear in mind that violating the Official Secrets Act was a *capital* offense.[2]

The last-ever interview with the original Fab Four Beatles took place on 28th August towards the end of their American tour. Enjoy watching it on Youtube, seeing Paul being his usual relaxed and charming self. They are all recovering from the trauma caused by John Lennon's comments about Jesus Christ, earlier in the year, with Beatles records being burnt all over the States (at least the covers were, but the vinyl was too toxic to burn and just had to be stomped upon). Paul's own last interview came a week later, in

---

1 This data comes from Schultz, Beatles the Untold Story, p.12.
2 The Official Secrets Act 'is a law, not a contract, and individuals are bound by it whether or not they have signed it.' (Wiki) The original law of 1911 Section 2 had the 'unauthorized disclosure of any information on any subject an offence,' whereas the 1989 Act replaced this with a more limited statement.

the days before 10th September, by Penny Valentine of *Disc & Music Echo*. Then on September 13th the *Melody Maker* Awards were given out, where the Beatles and Paul McCartney in particular received various top awards. Does that not prove they were still around? Or, does it rather show the contrary, by the rather strange nature of the reporting of that event? You will have to wait until later, for my in-depth analysis of this event, for it is a crucial step of the argument, if I'm claiming that he was by then dead.

Neil Aspinall the Beatles' roadie recalled how:

On the night of Thursday September 15th we travelled by train from Hamburg to Paris, met up with Paul there for a couple of, days, and then flew from France to Spain the following Sunday, while Paul and Brian Epstein returned to London. (in 'Neil's Column' in *The Beatles Book* monthly)

What was the point of this meeting? John Lennon was busy filming in Germany, and its action scene was then due to move down to Spain. Would the busy Brian Epstein have wanted to fly out with Paul to Paris and spend two whole days there Friday and Saturday, just so that John and Paul could have a chat? Those two had known each other for so many years, and, had they wanted to meet, they would hardly have wanted their managers to be present!

The answer has to be that it was the brand-new Faul who had been speedily recruited by Mr Epstein, who had truly risen to the crisis. We come back later to the big question of how Eppie could have known this fellow and selected him at such short notice. The story has him working with the aid of British intelligence, because *the show had to go on* to prevent anything appearing in the newspapers after the crash. Lennon then had to decide, did he want the band, his band, to go on? No-one could force him, could they??

The story here is that John had a lot of recordings of Paul, and of the two of them together, to use, so he agreed to keep the band going until they were recorded[3]. Or, the story is that he told Faul, OK we'll try and use you but you won't be any good for public appearances, you can never look like Paul - this being before Faul had had *any* plastic surgery.

Or, the story is that Faul told Lennon that if he was moving in, there would be 'no more silly love songs.' Replied Lennon, huh, that's all we do, love songs, what else do you have in mind? Epstein had heard Billy doing some songs, covering some Beatles numbers, and Lennon would have needed to hear his opinion concerning the credibility of the operation. The newcomer

---

[3] Urban legend has 'She's leaving Home' on *Sgt Pepper* a being the last song sung by Paul to have been recorded - you'll have to make up your own mind on this one.

realised that he was holding strong cards if he was indeed going to step in to 'mend the broken band.' The sage judgement of both Aspinall and Epstein was needed, for this huge destiny-decision. Ah to have been a fly on the wall, in the Paris café where they mulled over things!

Throughout the month of October, 1966, there are no reports or engagements of Paul McCartney, it's just a blank, he's absent from the scene. One hears it claimed that on 3rd October Epstein put out a statement that the Beatles would never perform again (*The Winged Beatle,* 2012, 8 mins) but that is not so: what *Melody Maker* reported on October 7th was that Epstein had replied to their questions by saying there were 'no plans at present' either for the Beatles to make their usual Christmas album or for them to undertake any UK concerts 'before the end of the year.'

That was a very strange statement. Every year the fans had some Xmas album from the Fab Four, and why would Epstein be doubting that this would happen again? Surely, if they were not touring they would have more time to make such an album, would they not? In the event they did produce one – *Golden Oldies,* and an entirely new phase of their lives began, with subtle 'clues' being added, to both back and front covers.

Life goes on, except that poor Brian Epstein has to spend ten days in a mental hospital, in the latter half of October.[4] What's he doing there? Recovering from a tiff with his boyfriend, *not.*

In November, Brian Epstein's house was besieged by indignant fans.[5] Fifty of them rattled his windows, but he refused to emerge. Why had there been no Beatles tour this year they asked, and what about the awful rumours that they might never perform again? Epstein refused to accept their petitions, each one signed by a thousand fans, demanding a British tour. 'Nothing has been decided' he said. Poor fellow, what could he say?

As Clare Kuehn[6] explained to me, the biographies and histories become quite vague over the key period of late summer and autumn of '66. *The Beatles Book* (monthly) kept using pics of Paul. My impression is, that through that year it used slightly stretched-out pics of his face, as if it were concerned that the images should blend together when the newcomer arrives. Generally

---

4 Epstein's ten days in hospital in Priory hospital Putney from 27 September: Ray Coleman, *Brian Epstein, the Man who made the Beatles,* 1989, p.329.
5 Daily Mail, 14 Nov.
6 See her site, 'you can know sometimes.' I did a PID debate with Clare on Jim Fetzers *Real Deal,* February 2014. She's Canadian, lives in Vancouver, and somehow has tuned in deeply to the story. She gave an excellent talk at Jim Fetzer's 9/11 conference in Toronto, about what made the Towers collapse; at which I also contributed, as the only British citizen ever to be invited to speak at a US 9/11 truth conference.

I recommend re-activating your memory of what Paul looked like by using film rather than photos because the later have been so much processed and manipulated.[7]

A grand meetup took place on 20th of November, the day after Mal Evans and Faul had returned from Kenya. John had returned from filming in Spain and George had returned from India. Faul and Mal Evans the roadie had been to Kenya, and John had not seen him for six weeks. Then at Paul's Cavendish Avenue home in St John's Wood, London, the gang assemble. We get to hear of this epic event from a page of manuscript by the trustworthy Big Mal,[8] which has turned up in an extraordinary manner. Two treasures emerge after Mal Evans' death in 1976: his film of Faul in Africa, and this one-page manuscript – less so his diary which has only been made public in a very incomplete manner.

This single page 146 of his manuscript *Living the Beatles Legend* may be all that is left of his book, the intention to publish which may have brought about his demise..It tells how Epstein assigned to Mal Evans the unsavoury task of summarily dismissing Paul's butler / housekeeper George Kelly, so the latter never gets to see the new Faul, who arrived soon after. Mal then moved in with Faul for the next four months.

> George Kelly was not very happy about it. He didn't understand it, but I had no choice. Brian could have sent somebody else to tell him the bad news, but the easy way was letting me tell him, even though I was closer to George Kelly and his wife than the others. I felt so bad and was actually crying in front of Brian, begging him to not letting me do this. Brian thought that it was a splendid idea to tell George that because of the article, we could no longer trust him and he was fired. Poor George, he didn't understand a thing. Why, he cried bitterly, why? He kept asking this question again and again.

> I was standing there as a butcher with his knife. My body was shaking and I was fighting to hold the tears back but big boys don't cry. It was a pretty ** moment, not having a chance to tell him the truth. George and his wife left Cavendish the same evening.

---

7 E.g., *The FAUL Guy* video at 11.30 minutes: 'In Remembrance of Paul'
8 Clare Kuehn has more or less discovered this page, as having been released in 2010 by insider(s) 'Iamaphoney' right at the end of *The Winged Beetle* film. Scroll down about 75% on Clare's page www.youcanknowsometimes.blogspot.co.uk. The film was released in 2010 (See http://vimeo.com/16353230 at 1 hour), then the 2012 extended version https://www.youtube.com/watch?v=8W9_qN64S4s at 1½ hrs. She showed how there were several images of this page on different videos, some with words deleted others not, enabling it to be largely reconstituted as you read here.

The Newcomer Steps into History

Brian Epstein, Mal Evans, Neil Aspinall, the three Beatles and the newcomer, plus 'Anita' and 'Robert' are gathered[9] (we're not sure who they are, but would these be included if this were a forgery?), and they are appreciative of the plastic surgery, during the African visit: "Everybody was excited and stunned. It was amazing. They did a good job in Narobi ...Paul came up with an idea we already had talked a lot about when at the clinic in Kenya,[10] the Sargeant Peppers Lonely Hearts Club Band." In the context, a plastic surgery operation is indicated. Mr Lennon was shocked but soon recovers:

The next day Paul arrived. We were all there, Neil, Robert, John, Brian, Ringo, Anita, George and Tony. Everybody was excited and stunned. It was amazing. They did a good job in Narobi * was really happening, it was like we had known him forever.

A strange attunement of the new band is experienced, '*like we had known him forever.*'

Brian was afraid ** Neil assured him that he could trust Pete but Brian needed a commitment from him. John was paralysed. Just don't go there he said, we don't need friggin' Pete involved. I don't need to see him again, just don't let him near us. I felt bad again, starting .. I tried to tell that I had to see my family sometimes, but Brian and John insisted that I should stay with Paul for a while. In those days we were so out of it, and I see now that I left my beloved **ces alone and unsafe. When I was thinking too much about it, I felt real low and I had to get high. We all had to get high. It was so unreal and that is why John invented Strawberry Fields. Nothing is real, he said again and again. We didn't really understand it until he showed us what wasn't real in the lyrics. John is a genius a real one. It blew my mind when he played it backwards. What a way to tell a story.. Paul really gave him a new direction, a new way of art. Good and bad. Black and white. In November they started to record the album or what we thought was the new album.

It sounded right the song and we were all very pleased. The idea of making a new sound on the album. Paul came up with an idea we already had talked a lot about when at the clinic in Kenya, the sargeant peppers lonely hearts club band. We were playing around with the moustache *** he needed to have the kind of thing that could take...

[* indicates text that I could not read] This page has an authentic sense of a Beatle meetup, where Faul for the first time ever meets the gang. Lennon

---

9 Jane Asher is absent: she had helped Paul furnish the new home in the spring.
10 For cryptic allusions about Mal and Faul at the Kenya clinic, see RA 78, 2:25-3:25.

is in deep shock as it begins to dawn upon him, that this new fellow might after all be presentable in public. They all apprehend that the Home Office has procured a new-identity passport for Faul, which enabled him to visit France and Kenya, implying high-level (Masonic-governmental) endorsement of what was going on.

John expresses concern about 'Pete' i.e. Pete Best the old drummer, they do not want him to be in the know. Mal Evans is impressed by Lennon's art, as he brews up his 'nothing is real' philosophy expressed in 'Strawberry Fields Forever.' And they all get high. Big Mal is awestruck when Lennon played the tape backwards and a message comes out! They would wear fake moustaches, because Faul was some years older than Paul had been and if they all wore them it might not look too evident. They decide to use this theme in the *Sgt Pepper* album – which worked very well.

Intense emotion is expressed in this very personal page: Mal's anguish at being told by Epstein to dismiss the butler pronto, then the tension builds up as the band all meet up and is resolved as they view the new band member. This all sounds quite believable and it gives us the very first historical mention of the *Sgt Pepper* title.

The First Photographs

Four and only four pictures of the newcomer were published in the year 1966, I ascertained.[11]

Here is my favourite picture of the newcomer, appropriately against a dark background because he is stepping out of nowhere (though actually, he's just in front of the door of his posh new Cavendish Avenue residence). This was 26th November, 1966, in *The New Musical Express* (NME)[12] with the caption -

---

11 I posted these on the Invanddis Proboards site, and invited anyone to cite any others published in that year, and no-one did so.
12 This image first appeared in the US *16 Magazine* article by Gloria Stavers, with the suggestive title: 'What are the Beatles Hiding from you?' November '66 (online). That featured a higher-resolution picture, dated 23 November. So *Melody Maker* obtained their pic from the US photographer, of Faul standing by the door of his Cavendish Avenue home.

The Newcomer Steps into History

'PAUL McCARTNEY returned to London this week from a nine-day holiday in Kenya. He is pictured above with the moustache and slightly shorter hair he used towards his disguise.'

Are they telling us it was a fake moustache? There are pictures of that Kenya 'holiday', together with Mal Evans their big roadie (on the web), but they only emerged many years later, so this is historically the first to appear.

The young man shyly steps forward and says 'I will,' yes he will forsake his own identity, his past and his folks, to rescue the Beatles.

One month later, 24th of December, the weekly *Disc & Music Echo* had this even more unlikely image of 'Paul McCartney,' cheeks stuffed with botox. Before we have heard him play a thing, we are told that he is composing a piece of music - which JPM never did.

GUESS WHO?

HAIRY BEATLE! PAUL McCARTNEY pictured composing the soundtrack for the new Hayley Mills film, "The Family Way." Looks quite serious about it, too. For a

On the same day, the *New Musical Express* showed the new Faul deep in study composing with the aid of George Martin: "at work in EMI's Paul's film music."

Neither Paul nor Faul could write music, the dapper George Martin did that. Mr Martin was trained in light classical music, Gershwin and Cole Porter, that sort of thing. In these pictures the newcomer has not yet trained his hair into the moptop Beatle style; and we might want to believe the stories that the moustache covers up plastic surgery.

Earlier in that year, Paul had categorically dismissed the idea that any of the Beatles

talk about th(

BEATLES

would write a musical: 'No I don't think any of us will write a play or a musical, not for a long time. People are always asking us that, but the thing is, we put all our imagination and ideas into our songs.' (NME 24 June) In contrast, when the new fellow arrives, the first thing he appears to be doing, is writing a musical! He's a more cerebral character.

On December 31st, NME featured the Fab Three without moustaches, plus in a quite separate image a different-looking fellow with a long, thin face: we can hardly avoid the impression that the journalist knew what was going on. Some cheerful dialogue was quoted, about how well they got on together, weren't breaking up but didn't want to perform.

Those are all the '66 pictures that I found. There was a press interview of the Fab Four on 20th December, however I saw no published photos from that (They may be on the web today, but let's here stick to what was then published).

A Faul image from early '67 appeared on the front cover of *International Times,* new the 'underground' paper, with its editor Barry Miles conducting a major interview with the newcomer. He *knew both Pauls quite well,* via his connection with the Indica Gallery just off Piccadilly which had opened in'65.

We'll cover this important interview to show the bright, cheerful optimism of this complicated intellectual character, his original mind, his belief in Crowleyite magic, and his love of avant-garde trends like Albert Ayler the jazz saxophonist and John Cage the US musician etc. Its so important to appreciate how creativity can come from a soul which has not gone through the mill of a university education. Also in this interview, there is the shared sixties presupposition that drugs are opening the 'doors of perception.'

These images give us a decent, coherent picture of the new Faul, who we then get to view in colour late in '67 in the MMT film. If you want more raw, less dolled-up images of him, go straight to covers of the post-Beatles albums, for example *Ram*, where he is no longer concerned to simulate the long-dead Paul.

Do you agree that the pictures here shown are of the same person?[13] Take your time, its an important decision. We've now looked at the four published in '66, one in early '67 and one unpublished for November. If so, then you

---

13 For the best sequence of Paul/Faul images, see http://60if.proboards.com/thread/3367 (NB, we'll come to 60if later on). There is an image of Faul turning up to record *Strawberry Fields Forever,* with a moustache, of which it says: 'November 24th, 1966. Here is the very first appearance of The Beatles with Faul, outside EMI. The other three members arrive clean shaven.'

The Newcomer Steps into History

The International Times No. 6 Jan 16-29, 1967 / 1s.
★ **Paul McCARTNEY**
★ **Norman MAILER**
★ **William BURROUGHS**
★ **Allen GINSBERG**
★ **Cerebral CORTEX**

might here want to check out the 'Golden Oldies' album front cover, released in December 1966.

A long, rather thin stranger here reclines, who is however looking quite groovy and surrounded by musical images. Is he not the newcomer? He's certainly not a traditional Beatle. If you agree, then this is historically the first 'clue.'

You may object that these images do not greatly resemble the fellow who we earlier saw running around on the Scottish farm in 1968? Maybe not, but I may not be able to resolve that for you, I'm no oracle.

Mal became Faul's very first friend after he emerged though that opaque-glass plate into the world, and years later was the *only* Beatle-related person to attend the marriage of Faul and Linda in 1969.

If there was one person who could have told the full story of what happened to Faul, it would have been him - no doubt why he was shot in LA just as he was completing his book *Living the Beatles Legend*, of which this would appear to be one page.[14]

---

14 Do not confuse this book manuscript with Mal Evans' diary. According to the *Sunday Times* (Mark Edmonds March 20, 2005) a cleaner found a trunk with Evans' diaries among other things in the basement of a New York city publisher in 1986, and contacted

65

Yoko Ono who arranged to have it shipped back to his family in London. Evans› widow kept the diaries in her attic for years and finally let *The Sunday Times* see and comment on them. The summary it published had totally deleted the year 1966!

The Magical Mystery Tour

On MMT indeed Faul is looking quite beautiful, a triumph of British plastic surgery. We can hardly believe this is the same awkward, shy-looking fellow who turned up a year ago. But then, he has just been through the radiant vibrations of the Summer of Love and Peace - and has a good woman who loves him.[1] There is indeed a *mystery* in this film, namely how could *anyone* believe the character here being showcased was Paul McCartney? View his big green eyes, at 7.30 minutes and 8.30 minutes into this film.

First shown on Boxing Day TV 1967 and seen in 3,930,000 homes, the film was slated as "Witless", "A colossal conceit," "Rubbish" etc – or, as the *Mirror* headlined it, "Beatles mystery tour baffles viewers." It was shown in black and white, color being essential to this film.

It was inspired by the American novelist Ken Kesey, who hired a bus with his group the Merry Pranksters, painted it psychedelically, and toured the US while serving drinks laced with LSD. Faul wanted to emulate this, and gathered some midgets, bizarre actors and assorted 'pranksters' and filmed what happened on a bus journey. 'I enjoyed the fish and chip quality of Magical Mystery,' recalled Lennon,[2] and yet it was widely regarded as the first failure the Beatles had come out with.

The bus started off at 10.45 on 11th September, 1967, a date and time which bears a heavy significance today: was that a year after Paul's death?

The film irks us by having everyone grinning the whole time, and we are grateful to George for not doing so. The old concordance has vanished and the lads hang about awkwardly, mostly performing solo. After '66 Lennon and McCartney would never again write a song together, sing together or spend time together. The band are now like angels cast out of heaven who cannot ever regain their old bliss, cannot ever return to experience the ecstasy

---

[1] Whether that lady was Jane or Linda, may hopefully be clarified in the next chapter.
[2] Miles, *Many years from Now*, 1998.

of concordance, that unique rock'n' roll sound they used to make, before enraptured fans. Instead, each one of them is doomed to wander off forging his own solitary path.

As the bus is driving along Faul tells an old lady, 'I myself am thirty, but I look a little younger due to the fair isle sweater which allows...' He thereby tells viewers that he is not JPM, but another who is five years older.[3]

At 27 minutes into the film, we see the Band merrily a-playing, but Faul has no shoes on, whereas some shoes have been placed adjacent to him, and there is a gap between the band members as if someone should be standing there. The shoes looks as if they have some red blood on them.[4] This symbolism links to the Abbey Road cover two years later, where he again is the only one not wearing shoes.

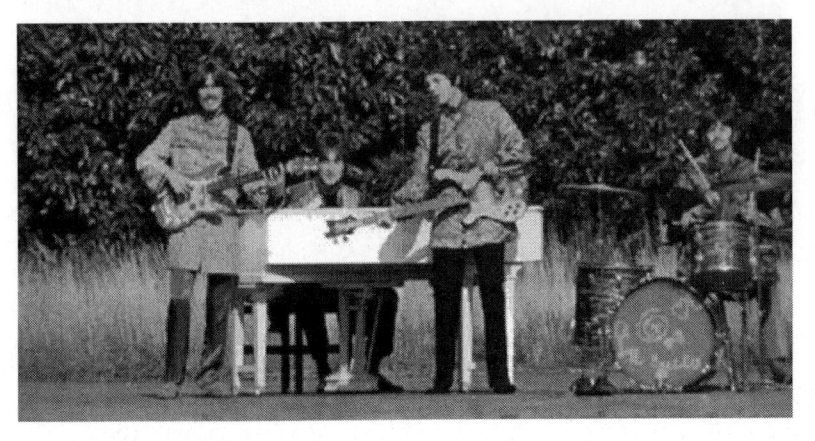

Figure: the shoes tell a story

Lennon sings 'No-one I think is in my tree' in his serene *Strawberry fields Forever*. He was feeling concerned that, if Paul could die and be replaced with apparently no-one noticing, could he be the next in line? That line could indicate, that no-one he hopes is tampering with his destiny.

At thirty minutes into the film, a hole in the sky opens up and voices are heard murmuring, 'Bury my body' and 'O untimely death,'[5] then at 39

---

3 As Clare Kuehn phrased it, that was 'his moment of getting real historical truth into the record.' (web comment)
4 'If you look to the right of Ringo's drumhead (which reads "LOVE THE 3 BEATLES) you can see an empty pair of shoes that appear to be covered in blood'- Gary Patterson, *The Walrus Was Paul*, p.97. For the trace of blood-red colour, see *The Winged Beatle* 22mins: image in MMT brochure as well as the film.
5 They are quoting from a King Lear passage, blended onto the end of 'I am a Walrus' on MMT, eg: Gloucester: What, is he dead? Edgar: Sit you down, father, rest you...

The Magical Mystery Tour

minutes while George is singing *Blue Jay Way* a blue, gruesomely decapitated corpse fills the screen.[6] Across its torso is written 'Magical mystery boy.'[7] That image *explains* the melancholy song or rather dirge which George is singing. He is waiting for his friend(s) to return, 'Please don't be long'(which he keeps repeating over a dozen times), and it's even getting past his bedtime.

George's distress at being left and having to wait and wait is overlaid by that dreadful image: song and image combine to remember that legendary evening when Paul drove off never to return, leaving him and Ringo waiting (the song transfers the location, as if it had happened in LA). A car with headlights on drives past him, with him apparently sitting in a road, then the film ends abruptly as a car with headlights on drives right up behind him, as if about to run him over: This song keeps highlighting the theme of some grizly road-accident.

George was into Eastern religion, and in Hindu mythology gods tend to be coloured blue to show they are not mortal. He may have been indicating something divine about his departed friend.

The bus journey ends up in the Raymond's Revue strip club in Soho (the Band used to perform in Hamburg strip clubs). 'Viv Stanshall' with his *Bonzo Dog Band* do an Elvis impersonation, singing *Death Cab for Cutie.*

Was that Faul?

Perusing the Stanshall biography *Ginger Geezer*[8], the big, round chin appears as a characteristic feature in its images, which (I suggest) he really doesn't have in MMT. Vivian Stanshall was a distinctive and unique British eccentric.

In the video 'Death cab for Cutie,' does the singer have that round chin, or can it be Faul in disguise? The MMT Elvis-impersonating singer had bright green-blue eyes, whereas Viv Stanshall's eyes

Lennon said that inclusion of that Shakespeare passage in *Walrus* was a random, chance affair: whereas it features in MMT just as a hole in the sky opens up, where those words spoken give a context for that to happen.
6 In the video it appears twice at 0.30 sec and 3.30 minutes.
7 This is hard to see in some videos. Reeve *Turn Me On, Dead Man* p.43: 'Handwritten across this body's chest is the phrase "MAGICAL MYSTICAL BOY"'.
8 Chris Welch, *Ginger Geezer The Life of Vivian Stanshall,* 2010. Mr Stanshall died as his Muswell Hill bed-sit went up in flames: 'Viking Funeral Pyre' was *The Telegraph's* front-page report, on 5 March 1995. Sir Henry Rawlinson had died a hundred years earlier on 5 March 1895, he being an alter-ego 'act' that Stanshall used to get into.

were unmistakably brown.[9] The book *Memoirs of Billy Shears* affirms that Faul here 'was' Viv Stanshall.

Mr Stanshall sometimes had to be treated for depression, and then he could not perform: it seems quite feasible

Figure: The 'Viv Stanshall' act (MMT, 47 mins) compared to early Faul pic.

that Faul could then fill in for him. Both of these characters enjoyed dressing up, as we readily see from Google images of 'Viv Stanshall.'

Here are a couple of old web-comments by 'SunKing' made in 2004:

'Vivian Stanshall on *Magical Mystery Tour*? No, Billy Shears performing his "previous" artistic job, the imitator!'[10]

And again,

Vivian and Bill were two well different persons. Only, in *Magical Mystery Tour* Bill performed Vivian to show us his "previous" job: singers' imitator.

In 1968 Faul helped produce the *Bonzo Dog Band*'s main hit single 'I'm the Urban Spaceman' under the alias Apollo C. Vermouth, so there was an interaction between them. Here is a quote from *Memoirs of Billy Shears* (2009):
... a song I wrote in collaboration with Neil Innes that we called 'Death Cab for Cutie.' I wrote and performed it as Vivian Stanshall. That is me, wearing the disguise, singing it in an unnatural voice at the end of our *Magical Mystery Tour* film. (p154)[11]

Fake teeth are unpleasantly flashed by 'Viv' in MMT towards the end of the song, obliging us to acknowledge that somebody is in disguise:

---

9 His brown eyes can be seen in the five-part colour video 'Vivian Stanshall-Crank'
10 Another clued-up blogger 'Abbey' agreed: 'Right, as always, SK (SunKing). When you see the two men side by side, the fact they are the same is SO obvious.' (from www.invanddis.proboards.com site where I post). 'SunKing' has been a major and respected source for PID material. He put together the two images here shown.
11 Faul sings 'Rocky Racoon' on the *White Album* in his American accent, does this resemble 'Viv's 'Death Cab for Cutie' voice? Compare his 'Elvis' voice on the 'Beatles Reunion '94' session singing 'blue moon of Kentucky.'

The Magical Mystery Tour

Notice how different my eyebrows look when I sing as Paul from when I sing as Vivian Stanshall. I only sing with my eyebrows pushed up for Paul, and only sing with them pushed firmly down for Vivian.

That distinction gives each their own look. More than Viv's fake teeth and latex, eyebrows changed the appearances, making each distinct.... An eyebrow pencil made Vivian's brows look thicker also, making them seem heavier on his face – the exact opposite of Paul's. (p.300)

Dare one say it, this Faul 'Viv Stanshall' was a deal better-looking than the original. Stanshall was a man of quite striking appearance.

The film's finale has the Four descending a splendid staircase (at 48 minutes) singing, 'Your Mother should Know,' wearing white suits with red carnations. But, Faul is wearing a black one.

He is then given a bouquet of the same red flowers, in order to emphasise the paradox, i.e. he is not just wearing a black one because 'they ran out of red carnations' – the fatuous excuse Faul came up with when asked about this.[12] Black carnations don't exist in nature, they are artificial. The Beatles would always give such trivial comments when asked about the 'clues' – they had no choice. Here we are reminded of the Fab Four in the *Sgt Pepper* cover, where only Faul holds a black musical instrument.

We see Lennon disguised as a waiter giving Ringo's aunt an important lesson concerning obesity, one which she may have needed but not wanted. Thus in a Shakespearean manner the two main characters appear in disguise, playing different roles.

You are now I suggest finally in a position to watch MMT, knowing its 'deep structure.' The film starts with a mystery song about 'The man with a thousand voices' and ends with us hearing one of them: the chamelion-like session musician who could 'do' Paul McCartney, also did Viv Stanshall! At last we can answer the anguished question, as to why the lads would allow an outsider to sing a humorous song about the death of their beloved Paul. We see John and George laughing while watching.

Yes death is funny – there is nothing funnier than Death, the Grim Reaper. But, they could only have allowed their very own Paul-replacement to do this death-humour piece. The joke is on us the audience, who do not realise that their mutable Faul is here telling in an Elvis accent the terrible fate:
'..,. but nobody ever hears him.'

---

12 'I was wearing a black flower because they ran out of red ones': *Life* magazine article 'Paul is still with Us, 7.11.69, Reeve p93.

What did Lennon say?

Living is easy with eyes closed
Misunderstanding everything you see.
(*Strawberry Fields Forever,* MMT 12 mins)

99% of viewers never realised *either* what the song *Death Cab for Cutie* is about *or* who was singing it. MMT was an open secret: the film fully presented its 'magical mystery' – 'Nothin' you can see that isn't shown', to quote their previous single – and yet the world was baffled, as indeed it had to be. The album's music was far more successful than the video. Lennon remarked, 'There are only about a hundred people in the world who understand our music.'[13] After reading this chapter, you are on the road to joining that elite group!

---

13 *Rolling Stone* review of MMT consisted only of this one sentence: Jan 20, 1968.

Birth and Death of the PID story

'I managed to stay alive through it all'
Faul to *Rolling Stone* magazine 31.1.74

It began in Detroit, which does seem a strange place for a story to begin. The centre of US motor-car manufacture, much of it is now a derelict ghost-city. On 12th October 1969 DJ's were being besieged with phone calls about the 'clues'. The year-old *White Album* had a cacophonous track *Revolution 9,* - its infernal racket being Yoko Ono's contribution together with Lennon of 'avant-garde music' – through which the words 'Number nine, number nine, number nine…' kept repeating. When these words were played backwards, one could distinctly hear the eerie words *Turn me on, Dead Man.*

Beatlemania surged back with a macabre twist as distraught fans sought for evidence that their hero was dead. Massive sales of the 'clue-bearing' albums began: *Sgt Pepper, Magical Mystery Tour, Abbey road,* and *The White Album.* 'It's the most well-planed publicity stunt ever' WAKR disc jockey Tony Jay told the *Akron Beacon Journal*. 'Only the Beatles could do it…so subtly with the planting of symbols of death.'

Abbey Road had been out only four weeks and wasn't

selling well because it cost two dollars more than earlier Beatles albums, but suddenly it got lift-off and started to sell by the million.

The heavy-going *White Album* surged up into the top 200 LP chart and by the end of 1970 it had sold over 6.5 million copies – the best-selling double album ever! Shops were giving away self-published clue-guides along with Beatle albums.

But, what was the motive? The Beatles were the most popular and financially successful music act in history, so they would hardly have done it for the money. Capitol records denied they had inaugurated any sort of death hoax to sell products, saying that they had no agents so creative! Where could it all have begun?

John Lennon kept denying that any of the clues meant anything; but remember that he had also denied that Lucy in the Sky with Diamonds had anything to do with LSD - there was a feeling that he had denied a bit too much.

The PID story blossomed only briefly, soon killed partly by Faul's sheer verve and nerve in the way he affirmed himself to be Paul, but also by a sense that the Brits *knew better*: raging primarily in America, it was doused by supercilious comments that Brits knew perfectly well that Paul was alive and so they weren't buying the story. It ended with the various American DJs going very quiet and feeling rather silly.

I guess the moral issue here is, that the 'clues' alone were a good start but insufficient to establish the story. The witty Faul did not fail to quote Mark Twain to the *Life* journo, 'Rumours of my death have been greatly exaggerated,' and added 'However if I was dead, I'm sure I'd be the last to know.' His false-identity claim was just done so well.

The word 'sly' may here occur to one. To plant all those clues surreptitiously and then deny them, for whatever reason, would assuredly require that attribute. Do you wish to attribute that to any of the Fab Four?

It's unthinkable! Nothing could be more inappropriate. On the contrary, we love the Fab Four because the lads put their life and experiences right into their songs, with emotional honesty.

'Saint Paul' by Terry Knight

In April 1969 *Saint Paul* by Terry Knight appeared, a song whose meaning was quite diffuse. It is credited with having catalysed the birth of the Paul-is-Dead movement, in Detroit. As an up-and-coming folk singer, Knight had received an invitation from 'Paul McCartney' to come to Apple Studios in London for an audition.

He went over there in August 1968[1], hoping to secure a contract with the newly-formed Apple company. Faul paid for his trip and arranged for him to be put up at Ringo's flat, but alas had no time to see him because the Beatles were right then experiencing severe problems:

Apple Corps had just been established but the Band was falling apart! Knight recalled, "I got to England just as The Beatles broke up. I was actually present at the studio the night the whole shit fell apart." Ringo had walked out on the others, just before Knight arrived.

In February back in Detroit he recorded his song, which transgressed the publishing rights of several Beatles songs ('Lucy', 'She Loves You' etc) perhaps intentionally.[2]

Saint Paul

I looked into the sky
Everything was high
Higher than it seemed to be to me

Standing by the sea
Thinking I was free
Did I hear you call or was I dreaming then, St. Paul?
You knew it all along
Something had gone wrong
They couldn't hear your song of sadness in the air
While they were crying out, "beware"
Your flowers & long hair

While you & Sgt. Pepper saw the writing on the wall

There is a lot more to this numinous song, which he wrote on the aeroplane flying back home after meeting the Beatles. 'Paul seems to be described as some sort of angel to which the singer prays for succour.'[3] It has a mood as if Paul is in the next world, without actually saying so. Knight

---

1 For Knight with the Beatles at the end of August 1968, see video *Who Buried Paul McCartney*, Netherlands Film and TV Academy.
2 He received a cease-and-desist order from the Beatles' record company MacLen. The startling upshot was its re-release in a 2nd edition by Maclen in May.
3 Reeve, *Turn me on Dead Man*, 179.

would never talk about it, then he was alas murdered in 2004 so took its secret to the grave.

We may surmise that Knight heard rumours of Paul's death and started to murmur it around Michigan once he knew that the first issue of 'Saint Paul' had been pulled for publishing violation and that it was coming back out with a revised 'MacLen' publishing credit: Lennon and McCartney's very own publishing company.

Why would they want to publish a virtually unknown musician's original song? It has a retrospective, otherwordly air as if Paul were something in the past. It was mainly played in the Detroit area. If it was about Paul having died, did this mean that the Beatles were promoting the idea?

As to what his song was about, with its airy symbolism: the line 'Isaac Newton knew that it would fall' alludes to newly-formed Apple (get it?) company and how it was imminently liable to fall, i.e. fall apart. But also, it alludes to the weight of this old world, in contrast with Paul who is now in the sky, as the song looks up to the sky to find him. I suggest it is a PID song, maybe the first, but not to a degree that would have gotten him in trouble or which he could not deny.

Some conjecture that it was written from his 'annoyance' at not getting to see McCartney. We may agree that his not seeing Faul was vitally important in his imagining of this song-dialogue with Paul. Had they met, Faul's charisma and his forceful I-am-Paul-McCartney manner would surely have extinguished any such reverie. This album appears as a *reason why* PID-mania blossomed on the other side of the world in Detroit later in the year.

Knight is remembered for his *Grand Funk Railroad* band, which sold more albums than any other American band in 1970, then the year after packed even more people into the Shea Stadium than had the Beatles.

September 11th

At a party on Friday the 12th September, given by a student named Dartanyan Brown, various long-haired musicians and girlfriends were jamming late into the night, and Brown there picked up a remarkable story[4].

Returning to campus the next Monday he wandered into the office of the student newspaper *The Drake-Times Delphic,* (of Iowa) and told it to the sports editor Tim Harper: 'I was rapping with the guitarist's old lady and she was laying this whole trip upon me about Paul McCartney being dead.'

---

4 Reeve, Ibid, p.20.

Harper printed the story in the college newspaper on September 17, 1969 and that is the earliest, printed, US account.

The *Billy Shears Memoirs* here avers that it had been the death of Brian Jones of the *Rolling Stones* earlier in the year that motivated the Beatles to start revealing to fans what had happened. Both bands, the Stones and Beatles, had lost central figures. So it was that on or around the 3rd anniversary of Paul's death September 11th the Beatles 'leaked the news to a Los Angeles musician,' resulting in the above news story.

A month later, on Sunday 12th October, Russ Gibb was DJ at the FM radio station WKNR in Detroit, Michigan and a 'Tom' phoned in, requesting him to play *Revolution No 9* backwards. That was done, then, another caller requested that the end of *Strawberry Fields Forever* be played. These are the two very clearest 'hidden massages.'

Soon the phone lines were all jammed up. A young Michigan student by the name of Fred Labour heard this program and swiftly assembled an article for the *Michigan Daily,* which appeared on the 14th October:

McCartney Dead; New Evidence Brought to Light

He became the Homer of the PID story! His article gave a comprehensive run-down of the 'clues'. For example, listening to 'Lady Madonna' from the *White Album* one hears Faul singing in his real voice, not trying to impersonate Paul, and was that not shockingly different? There is *no Liverpool accent*.[5] Many fans had supposed it must be Ringo's voice. Fred Labour placed the death in 'early November' of '66 without explanation.

The paper sold out by mid-morning and was twice reprinted that day. 'You could walk down and hear Beatles albums from one end of the street to the other, I mean every property, every house,' Labour recalled, for that day. He had creatively envisaged Faul as being a Scottish orphan called William Campbell - a name which stuck! There had been a talent contest (in Scotland, he reckoned), seeking for a McCartney lookalike, and 'William Campbell' won.[6]

---

[5] 'He was allowed to use his natural voice on 'Lady Madonna' which many listeners thought was Ringo at first' (Labour). The song was released in March 1968, and Faul's commented: 'It took my other voice to a very odd place' (Wiki). Others have said that the brilliant 1968 song 'Back in the USSR' sung by Faul (*White Album*) had little resembling a Scouse accent, likewise 'O Darling' of '69.
[6] There really was such a Paul McCartney lookalike contest (so Reeve informs us p.97) in the US in 1966, sponsored by *Tiger Beat* magazine, and James Barry Reefer won, and thereby got himself signed up by a music company.

Excited conversations went on in parties amongst stoned hippies, such as –

"Did you know Paul McCartney is dead?"
Summer grinned and took a swig of his ale. "Yeah. Him and Dylan, right? Jamming in rock'n'roll heaven."
"No really, the stranger continued, it's a big deal in my school right now."

We have this account of what it felt like then[7]:

> I was twelve years old when the events I am about to describe to you took place.
> In a few minutes, you'll see and hear everything you need to become a minor expert on this strange little episode in the history of mass communication.
>
> But there is something else I want to communicate as well.
> Something you can only learn from an eyewitness.
> I want you to know what it felt like to be almost a teenager in late October of 1969.
>
> I want you to know how it felt to be talking about this on the school bus, and in the cafeteria of my junior high.
> Huddling with friends at night around our record players, poring over our album covers, wondering.
> Staying up late with our parents to see what they would say on the 11 o'clock news.
>
> One of our heroes was missing.
> Some people were saying he was dead.
> The world's most beloved band, ambassadors of truth and love in an age of endless war and assassinations, had been caught in a monstrous lie.
>
> And their records, so full of joy and playfulness, had become the ever-present messengers of a creepy conspiracy.
> It was Halloween, and we were really scared.
> You may be wondering why anyone would make such a fuss over a bass player in a rock band.
>
> Those of you who did not raise your hands a minute ago probably know the reason already.

---

7 Oct '69 *USA Teen Life*, 'Who Buried Paul?' Presented at the San José Convention Centre on St. Patrick's Day 1999 by Brian Moriarty .

For the rest of you, it isn't easy to explain.
You see, this wasn't just any bass player.
And this was no ordinary band.

Paul-is-dead novelty songs were rushed into production: "Brother Paul," "The Ballad of Paul," "We're All Paul-Bearers" and "So Long, Paul," by Jose Feliciano.[8] OK, they were a bit silly:

Brother Paul, I'm crying
Are you really lying
Every night and day
Beneath the cold and lonely stone?

Are you getting older
Or just getting colder
Brother Paul, where did you fall
And are you still alone?
Can you hear me singing, Brother Paul?
Can you stand and sing your song?
Did you hear the trumpet when its called?
Can you tell me, is it true?
Are you gone?

(Billy Shears and the All-Americans)

The Ballad of Paul by the Mystery Tour:
Has Paul McCartney left this world?
Has he taken his last breath?
Have john and George and Ringo
told us of his death?
……

From Sgt Pepper to Abbey road
They led us on a chase
And if you know just where to look
It all falls into place
……

Of one fact I am certain
On one point crystal-clear
Alive or dead or just a hoax
The truth we'll never hear

---

8 Pseudonym 'Werbley Finster'

On the US radio station WKBW, host Jefferson Kaye reviewed the 'clues'. At the end of George Harrison's sad number *While my Guitar Gently Weeps*, he heard George calling repeatedly 'Paul, O Paul.'

There was a height difference, and Kaye cited page ten of the *Magical Mystery Tour* booklet to show that Faul was taller than anyone else in the group except Ringo: 'But here a taller McCartney is grouped with his mates.' Plus, that image from the MMT brochure showing Paul with no shoes:

> The empty shoes are the Greek equivalent of the American funeral wreath. It started in early Grecian days, when empty sandals would be placed outside the door of a Greek household and would say to the neighbours roundabout, 'Our son has died in battle.'

This 'clue' on the Abbey Road cover was scornfully dismissed by Faul a couple of weeks after that radio interview: 'I was walking barefoot because it was a hot day.'[9] On a hot day road tarmac becomes hot, soaking up the Sun's heat, and would one really want to walk across barefoot?

He was walking across the zebra with his eyes closed, a strange thing to do, was out of step with the other three, was barefoot and he was holding a cigarette in his right hand, whereas Paul was very left-handed.

A Scottish Farm

The story was denied and scoffed at but refused to die so long as no 'Paul McCartney' could be found in London or at any Beatle office. On 22nd of October, both *the New York Times* and *Washington Post* featured articles about the rumour and clearly something had to be done.

Any McCartney biography will tell the story, that he and his family were living out on their farm in Scotland during the month of October, just wanting a quiet life, until at the end of the month they became besieged by reporters, as a result of the preposterous rumours flying around. *Life* Magazine published that account in its November 2nd article, and that

---

[9] *Life* Magazine article 7.11.69; Reeve p.93; David Letterman interview 17 July 2009, shown at start of *The Winged Beetle* video.

would have been the only story - were it not for the fortunate act of a *Glasgow Herald* journalist.

On the evening of Wednesday 22 October, Mr McCartney with his wife Linda and her child were spotted at Glasgow airport, by a *Glasgow Herald* journalist acting on a tip-off, *on their way* to his Scottish farm. A drama was due to take place there, way out on the West coast miles from anywhere at High Park near Campbeltown. The photo published by the *Glasgow Herald* (here shown, from 23rd October)[10] is thus spontaneous and unprepared. Faul tells the reporter, that they were 'just going to the farm at Campeltown where we intend to have a holiday for a couple of weeks' but he declined to talk about the death-rumours. Only on the 24th, right after reaching his farm, did he give an interview with the BBC, his first since the rumours began: affirming that he wanted a more private life, etc.

We might wonder who was looking after that farm, for example feeding the large sheepdog Martha, prior to the McCartney family arriving on the 23rd? Faul's journey on 22nd was a shrewd move in response to the PID hysteria. He had wisely not been seen in the Apple studio over this period, or shrewd visitors from America such as Russ Gibbs would soon have commented, had he grown taller, had his eyes changed colour, how was his Liverpool accent coming on, etc?

Instead he went to a remote hill-farm, where distraught Beatle-fans could not reach him, and enacted the clever psycho-drama. Those who reported it were merely journalists: he did *not* want to be interviewed by DJs who had been fielding tricky questions and playing 'clues' over the airwaves.

Life magazine sent its London correspondent up to the wild and desolate Scottish moors, accompanied by a couple of photographers. The home had no road, no shops, no trees as far as the eye could see and as they approached their car got stuck in the mud. Martha, Paul's huge sheepdog, came bounding towards them and her barking brought McCartney, who angrily yelled at them to get off his property. They started filming him so he grabbed a bucket of water and doused them. They decided to leave. As they were getting into their car, and trying to start it up, a land-rover appeared with McCartney in it, who apologised to them for his uncouth behaviour and invited them in for a cuppa. That little drama took place on Wednesday 29th of October.

BBC Radio 4 sent their Chris Drake up to get a story, and he arrived on Friday, 31st October (Reeve p.93) and filmed a *bearded* fellow.[11] Faul had

---
10 A slightly different version of this picture is shown by Reeve, *Turn me on Dead Man* p.89
11 See Video, 'Paul McCartney Harassed by reporters at High Hill Farm.' For how this

no beard or facial hair in Glasgow station in 22nd, nor had he got any on 29th when *Life* interviewed him, yet suddenly on 31st he has a beard all over his face. These are clearly two different people and I suggest the bearded fellow had the air of living there, of looking after the farm.

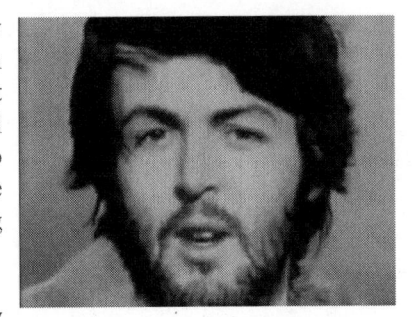

He *might* be the same as the heavy black-bearded fellow on the cover of *Let It Be* (1970), their last album[12] and could be the same black-bearded guy who performs in the 'rooftop concert' in January '69, the last-ever Beatles performance – far enough away from fans for the replacement to get away with it.[13]

Articles had been appearing in every leading newspaper, including *The New York Times*, the *Times* of London, the *Chicago Sun-Times*, the *Los Angeles Times, Billboard, Variety* and the *Washington Post. Time* magazine devoted a feature essay to the subject.

Special Paul-is-dead magazines appeared on newsstands, and were snapped up by the hundreds of thousands. Sales of the Beatles own records and licensed merchandise, especially their new *Abbey Road* album, went through the roof.

On November 2nd, the *New York Times* published an article intended to crush the rumour, entitled 'No, no, no, Paul McCartney is not dead.' This featured an image that had allegedly been sent by 'Newswire' on 22nd of October and had the subtext: 'NY Oct 22 NOT DEAD HE SAYS –Paul McCartney of the Beatles protested in London Wednesday that reports of his death were exaggerated. Al Wire photo 1969' Again a fake photo is used.

---

second or extra Faul appeared for Chris Drake's visit (for the BBC) to High Hill farm, on 31 Oct. , see RA 34.
12 Youtube video of Faul 'Harassed by Reporters at his Farm in high Park, Campbeltown' (from 'The Life of the Beatles' online)_
13 The 'Paul is dead' drama of October '69 involved various pictures of Faul appearing to 'prove' he was still alive, notably in the *Life* magazine article of early November, in none of which he had a beard (Chapter 7).

Its important to appreciate that Faul gave no press reports anywhere over this period leading up to his arrival on the farm on the 23rd, and thereby the tension built up, because he wasn't there, only the other three Beatles were visible in London. The *Newswire* picture of 22nd is not him, because his hair had never been that long during Beatle years (although in the future it would be, see eg the *Mull of Kintyre* video) and is incompatible with the other photos around this time.

The world was given a fictional story, a fictional image, and a quote from him that he only said in public one week later - to the *Life* reporters, quoting Mark Twain, about how reports of his death were exaggerated. This is all looking very planned.

Life Magazine's Nov. 7, 1969 issue with its cover story 'Paul is Still with Us' was one of the biggest-selling issues in its history[14]. Faul told them, 'I would rather be a little less famous' plus he gave them some shock news: 'The Beatle thing is over, it has been exploded, partly by what we have done and partly by other people.' Discussing various 'clues,' the article quoted Beatles' agent Derek Taylor as explaining that, at the end of *Strawberry Fields Forever*, Lennon had really said 'I'm very bored,' not 'I buried Paul.'

A couple of months later Lennon was to give a different version, whereby what he had really said was 'Cranberry sauce.'[15] It made no sense whatever to tack on those two words in a secretive manner at the end of this song, but that did not seem to matter.

Life magazine readers were assured that, if 'Revolution No 9' on the *White Album* were played backwards, then 'the terrifying sounds of a traffic accident' could be heard! A collision, crackling flames, plus the scary words 'He hit a pole, we better get him to see a surgeon [scream] ...Find the night watchman. A fine natural imbalance. Must have got it between the shoulder blades.' It could be heard on one stereo track, with the other turned down.

The whole issue had been brilliantly defused whereby, instead of answering the question, "Is the guy around now Paul McCartney?" a mere affirmation was made, that a person was still alive - which had never been in doubt. *Life* magazine showed a touching family portrait, of the newly married-couple with their child plus another from Linda's past. That settled it, didn't it?

---

14 I've only seen the International Edition of *Life* of 24 November, which has the same 'Paul is Still with Us' article, but its front cover image lacks the amazing see-through effect!
15 Lennon, *Rolling Stone* interview, 7 Feb 1970.

At Hofsra University, the *Is Paul McCartney Dead?* Society called its final meeting: in the light of recent developments, with Paul manifesting himself on the cover of *Life* magazine, there did not seem to be any point in its continuing. The fever gradually subsided on other campuses around America.

But you can't kill a good conspiracy theory that easily: it was soon noticed that, holding that *Life* magazine page up to the light, the car-advert on the previous page showed through, as if a car were driving right through Faul, and a heavy line along the top of the ad chopped off the top of his head!

The Starry Message

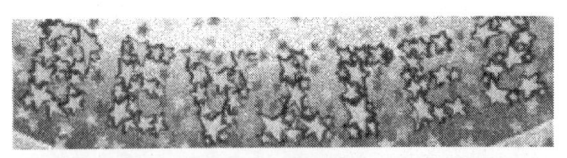

Meanwhile, stoned hippies had been decoding a secret phone number on the MMT cover. Some could see it in a pattern of stars which you had to hold upside down in a mirror... and if you managed to get through you could be quizzed on Beatles trivia. A correct answer would earn you a ticket to Pepperland!

This was maybe on the Greek island of Leso (remember the Sgt Pepper clue, 'BE AT LES$_O$'? If not, you may need to re-scrutinise the *Sgt Pepper* cover.) where Paul was said to be buried. The island Leso was part of a

Birth and Death of the PID story

private archipelago in the Aegean sea near Greece, almost purchased by the Beatles.[16] A yellow submarine is liable to turn up in this story.

There were various phone numbers thus 'seen' in the starry pattern, and a journo from the *Iowa State Daily* tried one of them. He naturally tried to phone at 'Wednesday morning at five O'clock'[17] but could not get through as all the switchboards were overloaded. Then he tried on Thursday instead, and the operator told him there was no such number, and "She also said there was no Billy, Bill or William Shears in London. She added that she had received so many calls to the number it was pathetic.' (Ah, remember the operators? I don't want to sound sexist but they were mainly female)[18] "You could have a date in Pepperland" sung *The Mystery Tour* in their 'Ballad Of Paul,' released on 29th October.

I never quite saw this clue, maybe because I didn't smoke enough dope. A *Guardian* journalist had one of the phone numbers thus 'seen.'[19] Stoned American hippies were not unduly aware of the time-zone difference US-UK so he kept being phoned in the middle of the night. He would be asked, "Hallo, can I speak to Sergeant J. Pepper?" with call charges reversed! He was receiving hundreds of phone calls each day. His article was published on 23rd October:

> For months I bravely lost nervous energy in an attempt to discover the secret of why all America wanted to ring me. Late at night I would awake as if in the midst of a nightmare and reach shakingly for the telephone to hear: "I have a collect call for Mr Billy Shears from Chicago, Illinois. Will you accept?"

They would ask him questions like, "Is it true Paul died Wednesday morning at five o'clock?" He found that, if he denied that Paul had died, then callers would refuse to believe they had phoned a wrong number. His months-long ordeal indicates how long the story had been gestating long before it was aired on Detroit radio. A couple of months after the whole story had died down, in February 1970, a TV show featured two angels in heaven[20]:

---

16 Lennon tried to buy a Greek island in the Aegean sea in 1967, with the help of their Greek technical wizard Alexis Mardus, but alas there were problems in getting sound equipment onto the island so the scheme fell through. Lennon did buy an island off Ireland: Alistair Taylor, (general manager of Apple Corps) *A Secret History*, 2003, p.159.
17 A line from 'She's Leaving Home' to which George Harrison points, on the back cover of *Sgt Pepper*.
18 Reeve, p113.
19 *The Guardian* Industrial correspondent Victor Keegan, 'Reverse Charge Dialogues' 23.10.69
20 *Rowan and Martin's Laugh-In* 23.2.70.

Angel One: Is there any truth in the rumour that Paul is still alive?
Angel Two: I doubt it. Where do you think we get those groovy harp arrangements?

Batman and Robin Solve the Mystery

Robin: 'Sure looks like him, and sounds like him.'
Batman: 'Dunno Dick, plastic surgery and voice training can do wonders.'

A June, 1970 *Batman* comic focussed on the rumour: Eden records (get it?) are benefiting from the story of a dead band member Saul Cartwright, from a top British rock 'n' roll group the 'Oliver Twists,' who is said to have died a year ago in a motorcycle accident. There was a *Gotham News* headline 'Alive ... or dead?' Robin (aka 'Dick Grayson') hangs around with his college buddies, listening to a radio broadcast of "Summer Knights", the latest record by the Oliver Twists.

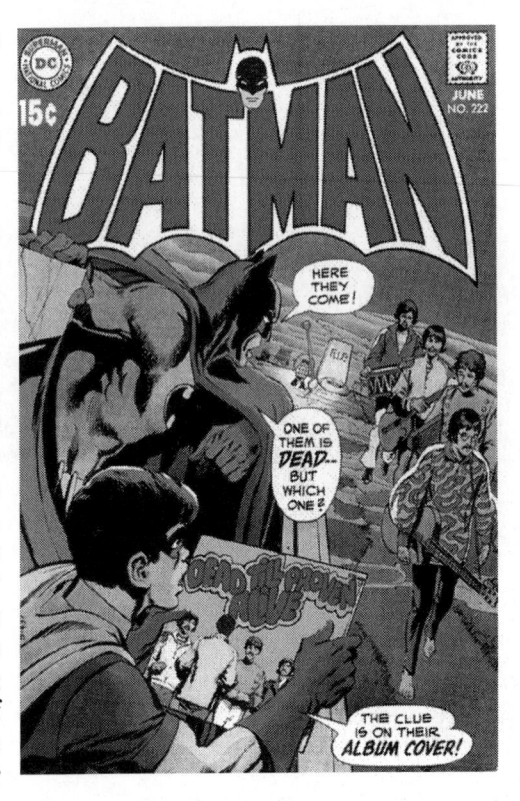

Playing a slowed-down track by the band they distinctly hear 'Sure was a ball, Saul, too bad it's over!'

Saul then shows up at in Gotham City but there is speculation he is just a double, a stand-in for the rumoured 'Dead Saul.' He is finding the rumours stressful: 'This death-role my nutty fans have dreamed up is getting to me!'

Grayson returns to his bat-cave, morphs back into Robin, and asks Batman to help him solve the mystery. Fortunately, the Bat-cave has got a 'sono-analyser' so they are able to compare some voice-pattern prints (echoing the work of Dr Truby, the voice recognition expert).

They finally discover that it's the other band members who died and were replaced, not Saul! Batman tells Saul:

> I believe now that you set up this cockeyed scheme with the noblest of motives, Saul – but like all dishonest put-ons, it BACK-FIRED! You realize now that the world has to learn the TRUE STORY, Saul! But if you face up to it and level with them, your fans will understand!

Hmm, that may not be quite the world we are living in... But the story ends happily as Saul and his band of phonies become the *Phoenix Trio* starring Sam Cartwright – an echo of *Wings* maybe? Conspiracy theorists mull over the issue of this comic 'Dead till Proven Alive,' being number 222 of the *Batman* series. Can it be mere chance ..? Yes, it probably can.

The story lingered on, as a humorous topic of conversation, a *dead* conspiracy theory. For example, McCartney appeared as a guest on *Saturday night Live* in 1993, interviewed by a Mr Chris Farley. He has such a knack of being persuasive:

> CHRIS: You remember when you were with the Beatles, and you were supposed to be dead? And .. uh .. there was all these clues that ... like ... you play some song backwards and it'd say ... like Paul is dead.' And ... uh ... everyone thought you were dead ... or somethin' ...
> PAUL: Yeah
> CHRIS: uh, that was a hoax, right?
> PAUL: Yeah, I wasn't really dead.
> CHRIS: Right.[21]

One is puzzled that he can be so relaxed. It would only need one hair from the head of Mike McGear, to compare its DNA with that of Faul (see Appendix 2), and presto! the game is up.[22]

---

21 Quoted in *Turn me on, Dead Man* by Andru Reeve, p.195.
22 see Appendix.

The Mirror Reveals

Here is a 1979 cover image of a Beatle fanzine, 'The Savage Young Beatles' and Paul's coffin, Circa 1961.[1] It recaptures the leather-clad lads as they used to appear in Hamburg. Epstein switched them into more middle-class suits for an English audience, because as he put it 'too many people would laugh' at the leathers.

The PID story died, and stayed dead for a decade, until a Mr Joel Glazier made a remarkable discovery. He discovered a *mirror* message on the Sgt. Pepper *drum*. *(Glazier, glass, mirror, get it?)*. It was he who first held up a mirror on the drum and read the amazing message. Now that is more than just a clue, it is an Opening of the Portal, once done there is no going back. Whoever could have designed so fiendish a code, and then how could they bear to not tell anyone about it?

Glazier wrote an article for the American Beatles Fanzine *Strawberry Fields Forever*, Issue 31 in January of 1979 of twenty-eight pages, entitled 'Paul Is Dead... Miss Him, Miss him'[2] which described this. It's not online

---
1 Photo ©Apple Corps./Peter Kaye: Reeve, *Turn me on Dead Man*, p.236; Iamaphoney, 'History Lesson – PID,' 5.4.08. PID-ers have not been able to find a story for this photo.
2 Hear these words on the *White Album* in between 'I'm so Tired' and 'Blackbird', if

and I have alas not been able to obtain a copy. It told of a Faustian pact whereby the Band could have total worldly success, but at the price, of their immortal souls. Mr Glazier has met all four of the Beatles, is an internationally known Beatles historian, and has appeared at many a Beatle Convention, such as the *Magical Mystery Tour* in Boston and the *Merseyside Convention* in England; where he would set up a booth and present clues to the fans.

The figure shows the haunting message Glazier saw, when a horizontal mirror is held up to the Sgt Pepper drum:

I ONE IX HE*DIE.

The arrowhead between HE DIE points upwards towards Faul in the picture. The message I ONE IX, if it were a date, would have to be 11 – 9 in Roman numerals, which would either mean September 11th to English readers or November 9th to Americans.[3]

Alternatively, the Roman-numeral sequence

I ONE I X HE*DIE

reads as three ones, I ONE I for the three remaining Beatles, plus 'X' for the one removed – X HE DIE. It was a chilling mirror message, something indeed to reflect upon.

An implosion of the Beatles band takes place around August/September 1966. Books tend to see this as taking place during the US tour in August, when the lads supposedly resolved never to perform again. John Lennon was shorn of his Beatle haircut on September 6th for a film. And yet, Paul McCartney's interview with *Disc and Music Echo* given in the first week of September gave no hint of the band in any way finishing or that anything

---

played backwards. Forwards, one hears only gibberish.
3 An early book on the subject, *The Walrus Was Paul* by Patterson 1996 allows both of these options. Gary Patterson describes holding the mirror up to the drum and seeing the message as if he were himself discovering it (p.56). The US PID book '*The Fifth Magician The Great Beatles Impostor Theory* by Forrest Dailey 2003 just gives November 9th; as likewise does the alleged 'Last Testament' by George Harrisson: 'Paul McCartney Really is Dead,' released in 2101.

The Mirror Reveals

was over[4]. He was asked about whether the US tour had been stressful. Ever the Beatle diplomat, he defended John's Jesus remark that had caused all of the trouble: 'People in America took what he had said as an arrogant remark. It wasn't.' (!)[5]

He explained that anticipating the US tour had been the worst bit, during the big storm of adverse publicity, however once it got going they were fine:

> The first few days were peculiar because it just wasn't a Beatles tour. We would have been more worried if we hadn't been working and so preoccupied. But after we'd been to Memphis – which we were most worried about - it was fine. We were in America as usual and that was that… Yes, we may still record in the States. What we would do is write some numbers especially, take them over, do them and see how it works out.

He added, concerning future prospects: 'We're not doing anything for a few weeks – then we'll be working on a new LP and single. I'm halfway through a song I started in Los Angeles but can't finish because they haven't moved my piano in here yet!' ('here' being his posh new home in Cavendish Avenue). There would be no British tour this year: 'No, I don't think we've really thought about doing a tour in Britain this year. You don't really miss touring. Really you rely on your audience for your act, which means that when you perform live it's difficult to keep control of what's going on.'

That, his last-ever interview, does not (I suggest) show any big change in direction, only that British fans wouldn't get their tour that year. A week later came the yearly *Melody Maker* awards ceremony, 13th September, where the Beatles had won various awards, and I here argue that the manner of reporting it indicates that the terrible thing had just happened: *Paul wasn't there.*

The Melody Maker Awards, 1966

In the very detailed *The Beatles an Intimate Day by Day History*, author Barry Miles makes no mention of any *Melody Maker* awards happening on 13th of September.[6] No newspaper anywhere showed any photo of that event within a couple of months after, nor did any journalist anywhere report as having been there. Hmm, that seems odd.

---

4 *Disc & Music Echo,* September 10th, Penny Valentine interview, A Beatle Talks about that US Trip.
5 My favourite part of Lennon's comment was: 'Jesus was all right but his disciples were thick and ordinary. Its them twisting it that ruins it for me.'
6 The beatlesbible.com has nothing for that day.

The report in the weekly *Melody Maker*, for 17th September, enthused about how the event had been attended by 'people from all sides of show business', including 'many representatives from Britain's press.' It was a lunchtime event, in the newly-opened restaurant at the top of London's Post Office Tower. *Melody Maker* commented:

> Beatles tighten grip on honours: The Beatles slipping? Forget it. British fans have once more given them an enormous vote of confidence and voted them winners of four sections in the MM poll. ...this year they have won the top group and best vocal disc sections in both the British and international sections of the poll.

Tom Jones won the top vocalist award and gave interviews, to journalists who had phoned him that day the 13th *at his home or place of work*:

> Said Tom at his home in Shepperton today: This is fantastic news. I thought I might be in the top ten, but I never dreamed I would take over from an established artist like Cliff.

- that's the *Evening Standard.* We get no hint that either the journo or Tom Jones had just been to the Post Office Tower for the luncheon – and wouldn't Londoners have enjoyed hearing about that? There isn't that much good news after all. All that the *Melody Maker* reported on Tom Jones' victory was:

> Tom excitedly rang the MM when he heard the news of his sweeping Pop Poll victory. 'I was thrilled to bits when I heard the news' said Tom during his lunch break while filming at Elstree Studios. He had just toppled Cliff Richard off his five-year reign as Britain's top male singer – and all we hear about is a phone call, with nothing about the event itself?

The *Daily Mail* ran a story on the 13th ('Beatles are still voted top') about the results, with no hint of any award ceremony. Certain newspapers were evidently given the results maybe the day before, so they could report them on the day. The *Mail* felt no urge to publish any follow-up the next day, about any award ceremony, if its journalist had been there – hardly a difficult place to reach. That restaurant had only opened up two months earlier, with its dizzy panorama of London town, it was an exciting new addition to Swinging London. Surely journalists would have been keen to attend.

A story about this made the front page of *The Mirror* on the 14th, but only as an anecdote concerning Dusty Springfield (who had won a female singer award) throwing a pie: 'Take that! Dusty hits waiter's boss with a pie.' The identical inane tale was reported in the *Daily Express* on that same day ('Dusty gets a 'Hit' and a 'Miss' with two cheese tarts'). For both papers, that was all they had to say – neither mentioning the Beatles. From this we infer

The Mirror Reveals

that neither paper had journalists present, i.e. they had only printed a syndicated story. Why weren't they there?

Paul scored well in the *Melody Maker's* Best Vocalist list. *When else had any 24 year old lad ever achieved so much, ever done so much for his country?* And yet we get no suggestion of anyone trying to contact him at this apogee of his career - with the Beatles album *Revolver* going platinum two days before this event, reaching number one on both sides of the Atlantic, their twentieth platinum disc. The Beatles won awards in both British and international sections for top group and top vocal disc – and nobody wants to interview him, or even photograph him at the awards ceremony? It's as if he *just wasn't there*.

George Harrison and Patti flew out to India on the 14th, and this is given as his reason for absence from the awards ceremony. I suggest that he swiftly booked up that flight to India after hearing of the catastrophe, he just needed to be far, far away. Had he wanted to be present at the ceremony - as always on previous years - he could easily have left a day later. Only one published photograph of the event appears in that year 1966, and that was *two months* later, in the November issue of the monthly *Beatles Book*. Under the picture a caption says

"It was all handshakes and smiles from Paul and Ringo when they received their Melody Maker award on behalf of the Beatles for being voted Britain's top group, from Johnny Mathis."

The picture shows a vacant-looking Paul McCartney lookalike not even making eye contact while shaking hands with Johnny Mathis. I suggest that character is not Paul – just a quickly-acquired lookalike stand-in.[7] *It* has now happened, and everything irreversibly alters.

There is an unpublished US photo floating around the web showing the cheerful winners Ringo, Paul, Tom Jones and Dusty Springfield, silhouetted against London behind them, seen through the big revolving windows of the

---

7 Some have expressed doubt whether that is really Ringo in the picture.

Post Office tower. The caption reads: 'with their awards at the *Melody Maker* Pop Poll luncheon in the GPO Tower restaurant.'[8] If this happy picture is by Getty images, co-owned by *The Express*' newspaper, then how come *The Express* never used it?

The four stars are all gazing in quite different directions, none with any shadow falling onto another. 'Paul' has a traced-ut shadow on the window behind, but none of the others do. Not only are the MM 'awards' they are holding totally different from those which appear in the previous pics, but 'Paul' isn't even holding his: he holds a glass of wine and a cigarette (if you look carefully), and this MM 'award' has been placed on top of his hands.

We here hold onto the historical approach taken in Chapter 5, where dated and published images are what count. Can one even show that that Getty image existed in the 20th century?[9]

Epstein's 'Star scene '66' party for the 13th of September was alas cancelled. He had a stable of different pop groups he managed, which meant that he could assemble top glitterati into his parties, and he loved these events. The year before, his Star Scene '65, at the Scotch of St James Club[10] had as guests the Everly Brothers, Ringo and Maureen, P.J.Proby, Eric Burdon, George and Pattie, Paul, Jimmy Tarbuck, Micky Most, Billy J.Kramer, the Dakotas and Cilla Black. A marvellous evening party was going to follow on from the award ceremony at lunchtime, what could possibly go wrong? But, it had to be cancelled.

As to what really happened on that day, the official Beatles History (online) recalled only that: 'The `Melody Maker' editor signs the certificate of the Beatles as winners in the 1966 poll in British and International Sections of the magazine.' I suggest that that, precisely, is what happened.

Paul was not there. The September 11th death-date is validated. The Beatles are now in a post-cataclysm world. Both the Stones and the Beatles survived death, they both rocked on after the death of their main star - for which we are grateful.

---

8 This image is registered as a 'Photo by Terry Disney/Express/Getty Images' and says 'Date created: September 13, 1966' http://www.gettyimages.co.uk/detail/news-photo/paul-mccartney-dusty-springfield-tom-jones-and-ringo-starr-news-photo/3205716 .
9 There is a video of this event on the web, showing Paul and Ringo with the awards, and a clapping audience. Notice that the camera does not pan from one to the other, as one might expect if they were in the same room, but it cuts: the awards are a different bit of film from the 'audience.'
10 The *Scotch of St James Club* was where Jimi Hendrix first played when he came to England. It was next to the *Indica Gallery* in Mason's Yard, Piccadilly.

November 9th

On the November 9th date Lennon recalled meeting Yoko Ono, at the Indica Gallery in 1966,[11] which came to signify a breakup of the Beatles 'Yoko took one look at John and attached herself to him like a limpet mine - with much the same destructive effect.' recalled Lennon's driver Les Anthony.[12]

Barry Miles, Indica gallery manager, confesses that 'had he set out to destroy John Lennon he could not have done better than to introduce him to Yoko Ono.'[13] Also on that date Epstein put out a statement that no future bookings were being accepted by the Band, reported next day in the press. As the PID story blossomed in America it focussed erroneously upon this date: which seems also to have some sort of meaning.

<u>Shakespeare play act (1965) Pyramus and Thisbe</u> (an act from Shakespeare's Midsummer Night's Dream) Paul as Pyramus draws his knife and exclaims, 'Thus I die!' and falls down onto the ground. As the camera comes close-up he says, "Now I am dead, now I am fled. Ah well, ya can't win 'em all." He then repeatedly stabs himself in the heart while shouting, "Now die, die, die, die!" over and over.[14]

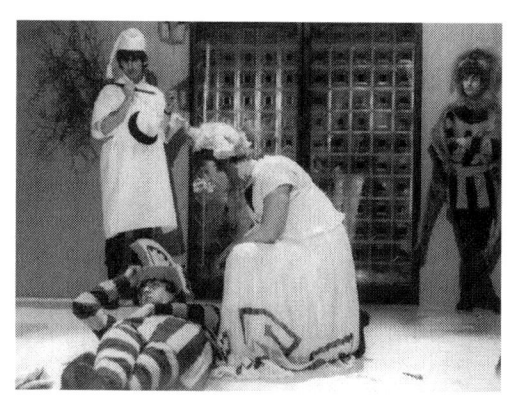

Paul called his cat Thisbe.

---

11 Or, Lennon remembers this date, whereas the opening of the exhibition was on the 7th.
12 Goldman, *Lives,* p243. Yoko Ono when Lennon met her was less than five feet tall, eight years older than him, and had twice been married with a child. Her then- husband had gone over to Japan and extracted her from the padded-cell of a mental hospital that her relatives had put her in (*Lives*, p.221). In 1965 she had starred in the film, *Satan's Bed*, as a Japanese mail-order bride, fianceé of a drug-smuggling government agent, featuring a succession of homicidal perverts.
13 Goldman, *Lives of John Lennon*, p.242.
14 For a sequence of this play, see '*The Last Testament of George Harrison*' (2010), at 19 mins.

Through a Glass Darkly

"How often have I said to you that when you have eliminated the impossible, whatever remains, however improbable, must be the truth? We know that he did not come through the door, the window, or the chimney. We also know that he could not have been concealed in the room, as there is no concealment possible. When, then, did he come?"

Sherlock Holmes to Watson, in *The Sign of the Four,* by Conan Doyle, Ch.6

Billy Pepper albums

Conjecture over where Faul might have come from has tended to focus upon two excruciating albums by *Billy Pepper and the Pepperpots* (*Sgt Pepper*, get it?). This was a band that never performed live, no-one sees their faces. The Pickwick recording studio where they made the albums nestles in an unappealing industrial estate, up the Cricklewood Road just north of Kilburn[1] and this, I discovered, happens to be *adjacent to* the premises where the monthly *Beatles Book*[2] was produced. The 'Pickwick' label is or was the Woolworths of the record industry, specialising in using unknown, cheap artists to cover better-known groups, and thereby produce rock-bottom price records, for a pound or so.

Merseymania Billy Pepper and the Pepperpots, Pickwick International, Cricklewood.
More Mersemania " Allegro Records 1964

Two such albums were produced, cashing in on the Beatlemania craze. The second, 'More Merseymania' is dated 1964 and covers the two Beatles

---

[1] Pickwick International: Victoria works, Edgware Road, Cricklewood. NW2
[2] Beat Publications Ltd. 244 Edgware Road NW2

songs 'Please Please Me' and 'She Loves You,' plus six other songs by 'Bill Shepherd' and two by 'Jimmy Frazer'. It's on an Allegro-Pickwick imprint. Bill or William Shepherd has long been a favoured name for the replacement - the story is that Lennon used to call him 'Beatles Bill.' The first album 'Merseymania' is undated, possibly produced in '63, with songs likewise credited to Bill Shepherd and Jimmy Frazer. The *Billy Shears Memoirs* avers that his friend Jimmy Fraser produced a few of the songs.

A few years later, that same UK recording studio produced the American-sounding 'Cowboy Favorites' by 'Bill Shepherd and the Ranch Hands' (1967), likewise on the Allegro imprint, 'A product of Pickwick International.' It too was made in Cricklewood. As with the *Pepperpots,* one finds very little on the web about this band, as to who they were, with no picture of them. Both Merseybeat and the Ranch Hands were released on the identical Allegro Pickwick International label.

The *Memoirs of Billy Shears* averred, 'Before I joined the Beatles ... I made albums that you have most likely never heard' and cited *Cowboy Favourites*, by the Maple Leaf Four, 'Bill Shepherd and the Ranch Hands' (p69), and claimed that his American accent then sounded similar to his 'Rocky Racoon' American-accent voice on *The White Album*; which would imply that the *Cowboy Favourite* songs were done a year or two before the album was released, 1967.

Did the versatility of this unknown session-musician earn him the title, 'man with a thousand voices' (MMT)? Some believe that the Bill Shepherd here employed in the Cricklewood studios was the composer of that name who worked with the Bee-Gees. I suggest this is a mistake. Quoting *Billy Shears* again:

> As the Pepperpots album label makes plain, Billy Pepper is Billy Shepherd. Billy pepper is the one and only Sgt Pepper... I should point out that even though I am "the one and only Billy Shears" in The Beatles act, it does not mean that I am the only Billy Shepherd in the music world. It would be very easy to get a few of us confused. *Memoirs*, p.148

I challenge anyone to listen to 'Maybe I will' on *Merseymania* and not hear a merry, Beatles-type sound.[3] Also, on its 2nd side, the version of 'I saw her standing there' sounds like Faul singing, does it not? Some listening to the sub-standard music on these albums have scoffed at the idea that they could be

---

[3] Here are two comments made about 'Maybe I will' on the first *MerseyMania* album: 'That high-pitched doo wop in the beginning. I don't know. It sounds to me like it could very well be Billy boy. He goes on like that in a lot of his songs (blogger 'Abbey');
'Yes it's Billy. The same typical Faul's "t".'('Sun King', 2004)

by 'him.' There is, let us admit a mystery here: comparing that voice with the lovely voice singing on Beatles albums, eg 'Let it Be' or 'The Long and Winding Road', or 'Eleanor Rigby', we are bound to make a dismissive comment.

But, we surely ought rather to be comparing it with songs on the *McCartney* (1970) or *Ram* (1971) albums when a very different voice there appears. Those latter two are really and unequivocally what Faul's voice sounds like. His voice first appears, in the cold light of day, on these post-Beatle albums – without the magic touch of George Martin. We hear a much rougher, less charming sound.[4] Suddenly, he's not half the man he used to be.

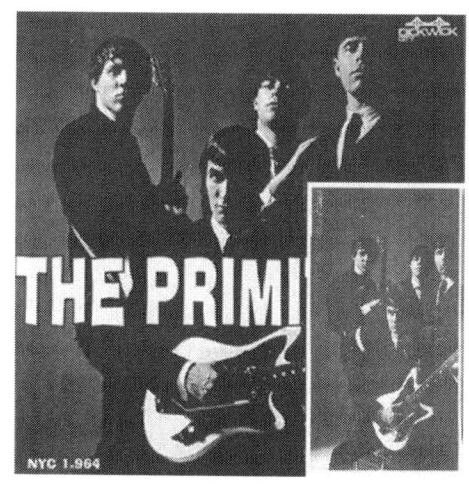

The front cover of the *Pepperpots* second album features dark images of four musicians, a picture strangely taken from an American Pickwick-label album cover, *The Primitives*' (featuring Lou Reed) after applying a 30% horizontal compression! Check it out, its easy to do on Photoshop. Thereby a quartet having a rather tough, thug-like appearance appear marginally more aesthetic, by having their faces made thinner. We are puzzled by the deceptive process thus applied, to avoid showing the faces of some English-studio singers.

One blogger ('Beatle Paul') commented: "I have a self-titled album by a Liverpool Merseybeat group from 1963 called *Billy Pepper and the Pepperpots*. I found it among a stack of old vinyl at a second hand shop one day"[5] while a Mr Anthony Gianotti was more puzzled about his *Pepperpots* album:

> What is really confusing is that the album I have has a pressing date of 1961, several years before the Beatles released anything in the US. The songwriters are not listed on any of the songs, and to be honest the

---

4 C. Salewicz: '*Ram*, miserably, was an even more marginal work than *McCartney*.' The first *Wings* album *Wild Life* 1971 'was Paul McCartney's least successful album ever…the real cause of the relative commercial failure of *Wild Life* was its unremitting mediocrity.' *McCartney The Biography*,p.225-6.
5 Some claim that "*The Pepperpots* released a single recorded in '63 " Don't Tell Me You Don't Know" but I haven't confirmed that.

version of 'I saw Her standing there' revivals the Beatles' version, while 'I want to Hold your Hand' is absolutely pathetic. Someone please give insight as to the 1961 pressing year, otherwise, the 'evidence' points to the fact that maybe this band actual wrote those. I am not the anti-christ, just looking for answers on this strange group.

No-one confirmed that story! That first *Pepperpot* album presently sells on both Amazon and eBay as dated 1962. Another blogger ('Reallyreallydead') noted, "It's interesting, all of the Bill Shepherd song-titles would be right at home on a 'Paul McCartney' album."

Concerning the brilliant period of creativity of the Band in the early sixties, when so many hits were apparently composed by Lennon and McCartney: quite a few have wondered whether there could have been somewhere a hidden cauldron a-brewing up the songs – maybe with the *Pepperpot* numbers emerging as sub-standard tunes that never made it? let's hear blogger 'Beatlies',

"I wonder if the *Pepperpots,* in addition to being a musical practice act for Phil Ackrill/"Neil Aspinall," may have been a kind of recycling bin for songs written for the Beatles that weren't good enough to make the cut as official "Lennon-McCartney"-written songs that would appear on Beatles or Cilla Black albums. "Maybe I Will" sung by "Billy Pepper" is basically a decent song, although copied from an earlier jazz classic "Maybe I Will or Maybe I Won't." If the Beatles had behind the scenes tin pan alley-type ghostwriters, and I think they did, these cadres must have also produced some also-ran "overflow" songs that could be used for specific functions elsewhere. I can see the Beatles recording the song "Maybe I Will" if it were musically improved and refined a little here and there."

One blogger 'Rubber Soul' commented, "It fits that the same Bill Shepherd who penned and possibly played on tracks for the Billy Pepper LPs is the same guy who recorded 'Cowboy Favourites' and those other records. So would that be Faul? I guess it does fit, because both albums were produced by Allegro records." Another 'Revolver' wondered, of the two *Pepperpot* albums: "Why are they unique in completely dropping out of the historical record and memory, as if there is an extensive cover-up?

Time of Decision

Let's come back to the crisis-moment, as we've so far apprehended it. Brian Epstein has to act quickly once the catastrophic death happens. As manager he had to reach a decision whether he could find a replacement and carry on. There was, on the story told in *Memoirs of Billy Shears*, one journalist who did recognise the crashed-car number-plate and realised that the mangled body must be that of Paul. Epstein had to apply persuasion so that his story did not appear ('Wednesday morning, papers didn't come'). On this view the replacement cannot be far away, cannot be out in Canada or up in Scotland. He has to be contacted right away. Epstein has to hear him sing and then make the biggest decision of his life.

Thus the *Billy Shears Memoirs,* for Monday 12th September, 1966 recollects: "Brian had discussed possible Paul imitators with his brother and with a few intimate friends. One of them, familiar with my Billy Pepper albums (which had covered Beatles songs), recommended me for the position. Having worked with me before, Brian already knew me, but did not know if I was up to the role. Besides, I did not fully look the part. ...He called me and asked me to meet him at the Abbey Road studio in an hour. He told me to bring my albums."

The newcomer plays his version of *She loves you*, then *I want to hold your hand*, then 'I played parts of a few songs I wrote.'

> He seemed nervously abrupt at first, but that lessened gradually and was replaced with a growing excitement. Finally, before Brian had told me a word about Paul's death, he asked, "How would you like to be Paul McCartney?"
> I thought he was asking me to fill in for Paul to help with a particular recording session. I said, "I'd be delighted to play on a Beatles album!" I would help with a song or two, I thought.
> "Even if it means you are not credited?" Brian asked, as if it mattered.
> "Certainly," I said, "That is standard for most of us session musicians I can play as anyone. I do it all the time."
> Brian slowly nodded his head as he studied my eyes. He smiled. "Marvellous!" he said. Then he told me the whole story.'[6]

That feels like an authentic snapshot of Brian Epstein. He was a decisive character, a man of discerning taste and fair with money. He was a fixer, a deal clincher. The story that here emerges may raise more questions than it answers, but it gives us a slight glimpse of an answer, as to where Faul emerged from.

The *Billy Shears Memoirs* were composed under the constraint that they would draw a veil over Faul's origin, ensuring that no spotlight could be thrown upon any still-living relatives. They had to claim to be fictional, and even to contain manifestly fictional material, so that in a court of law

---

6 *The Memoirs of Billy Shears*, p.159.

they could be plausibly argued to be such![7] Yet I feel that this part of the story, concerning his emergence from obscurity into the limelight, does not contravene that legal limitation and so may be reliable.

Other Bill Shepherds

The mystery author of the first Beatles biography 'Billy Shepherd' is all-to-easily identified as Neil Aspinall. By1964 Aspinall who had been training to be an accountant, had made the big decision of his life to become the Road Manager of the Band. If he had any such literary talents, he kept very quiet about it for the rest of his life.

From its first issue, the monthly *Beatles Book* had a historical-review column by 'Bill Shepherd'. Neil Aspinall had his own column in the *Beatles Book*, as did Mal Evans, so it's not at once evident why the busy Mr Aspinall would desire a separate anonymous column, but maybe he did. Both this mag and the book were published at a venue only yards from where the Pickwick recording studio was located, on the Edgware Road south of the North Circular.

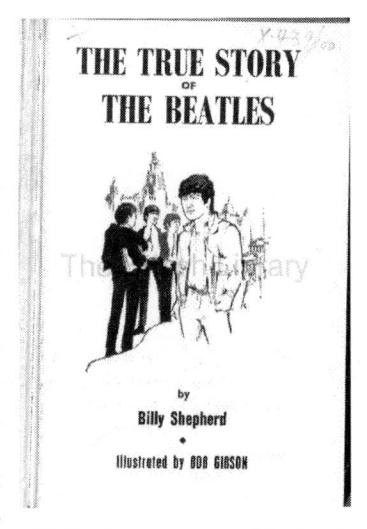

The Australian band the Bee-Gees had a producer Bill Shepherd, who managed them somewhat as George Martin did the Beatles. He was a composer of light-orchestral music who produced several such albums, and emigrated to Australia.

One of the Bee-Gees recalled, 'We always wanted strings on our albums. When we met Bill Shepherd and found out he was a string arranger, we said, Will you come back to England with us?' Bill Shepherd was part of the Bee Gees extended family for many years, arranging strings on their albums and conducting the orchestra in concert.[8]

Was this William Shepherd behind the *Pepperpot* albums? It is hard to find evidence that the Bee-Gees Bill Shepherd ever sang, or still less that he

---

7 This comes near the end, pp.598, 611: He [the lawyer] sternly said that the book must not be published without a significant thread of fiction running throughout the whole.' Chapter 14 deals with this.
8 *Bee Gees The Authorized Biography* B., R. & M. Gibb 'as told to David Leaf"

Through a Glass Darkly

wanted to be in a Merseybeat-type band.[9] Pickwick generally did not normally employ known, established artists who would charge a fee.

Big Mal's Mystery Friend

Here is an image, of roadie Mal Evans with a mystery friend. The year is 1966, and Mal Evans is looking very pleased with himself. His enigmatic smile says, "Who do you think this fellow is?" A toyboy, perhaps? He would seem to be one who entertains or performs in some way, as shown by his shirt.

A lot of people have taken the view, that it was the young Neil Aspinall. But, Mal Evans and Aspinall were the two Beatle roadies - would he really have such an expression being with his co-roadie? His mystery pal has the appearance of a dreamer, of one who could dream up songs and sing them, but hardly shift equipment around.

Here for comparison is a picture of the two roadies together. The two Beatle roadies were strong, sound and reliable characters, men of action.

---

9 See *Bill Shepherd, Artistic Biography* by Bruce Eder (online). Over the period that concerns us it states: 'He also worked with legendary producer Joe Meek during the early '60s and cut a song with Gene Vincent, conducting the orchestral accompaniment for the American rock legend in 1963 before emigrating to Australia in 1964.'

Here is another picture of the young Neil Aspinall: do you agree they are the same person? You might have a problem here: as with many of the central characters in our story, there is a degree of mutability in their appearance, they are *protean.* Surely, the dreamy, poetic-looking fellow shown earlier with Big Mal is *not* Neil Aspinall.

Did this unknown character morph into Faul[10]?

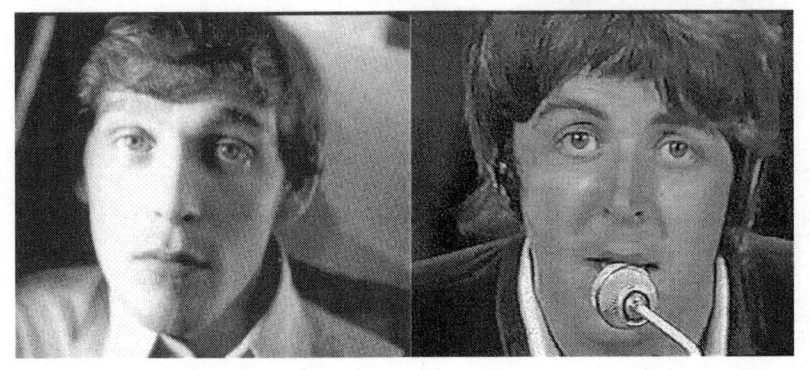

Presto! The right-hand image comes from the *Hey Jude* video. (That's the image with green eyes, which you can't see here). I am taking this argument (to acknowledge my source) from the Facebook page of Sun King, a generally well-respected source. The mystery character is widely averred to be Mr Phil Ackrill, he is called that on a lot of websites.

Mr Phil Ackrill – Trevor Philip Ackrill – was in the band *Denny Lane and the Diplomats.* All recordings, of *The Diplomats* with Denny Laine, recorded by EMI, are withheld from distribution, no-one can hear them. Scarcely any pictures of Ackrill are available, and he has no Wikipedia site. Even the school down my road has its Wiki site, so what is going on here?

Put in 'Phil Ackrill' and more or less all the posts coming up will be about the Faul identity! A credible case can furthermore be made out for him vanishing around the destined date, although inevitably one finds some claiming that he is still around. *No websites* describe the life of Phil Ackrill, of Trevor Philip Ackrill. The *Diplomats* began in 1962 and paired up with the Beatles now and then.

If that surmise is correct, then 'Denny Lane' (Brian Hines) could tell us a

---

10 Phil Ackrill: https://www.youtube.com/watch?v=bl3xnxartMk

thing or two about this character. Coming out of the *Moody Blues*, he joined *The Diplomats* – then later, in *Wings,* did he pair up with the same partner he had earlier played with in *The Diplomats?*

A rather unconvincing passage in the *Memoirs of Billy Shears* describes a concert where the *Diplomats* and *Beatles* performed together in the same Plaza Ballroom, and admits: some have surmised that 'I played then, not as the Beatles' Paul McCartney, but as The Diplomats' Phil Akrill.' They have indeed wondered that… He then strangely dismissed the Phil Ackrill story, on the grounds that: "Everyone ought to consider this question, "If I were Phil, why wouldn't I admit it now? He was a dandy singer and guitar player, and a fine person. Who would this Bill rather have been than Phil?" (p.287)

That does not sound at all convincing. There are all sorts of reasons why 'Billy Shears' would not want to admit the Phil Ackrill identity. Having read and re-read the *Billy Shears Memoirs* several times, this does seem to be a passage where some veil is being drawn over its author's identity. That *Billy Shears* text does however concede that Mr Phil Ackrill is in the past tense - he is no longer around.

From Jane to Linda

We come now to a story of true love, in fact two stories of true love, between Paul and Jane, and then between Faul and Linda. The first lasted three years, the second almost three decades.

The duality here involved is confusing and has baffled the world, so you may wish to start off with some major dates, and refer to them during the story.

Faul flies out to be with Jane on her 21st birthday	April 1967
Faul chats up Linda at Bag o' Nails pub	May '67
Jane and Faul engaged	December '67
They visit the Maharishi:	Feb-March '68
Jane breaks off with Faul (he's in bed with another):	July '68
Linda moves in to Cavendish Ave	September '68
Faul marries Linda	March '69
Jane's father found dead	April '69

This could be the first account you read which *almost* makes sense. The story can I suggest *only* do that, in the terms described in Chapter One, namely a 'Fractured identity.' The two different love-stories we shall here describe comprise decisive evidence for the PID hypothesis. Of the two women, one died of cancer aged fifty-seven, while the other is quite famous but lives in a depressed and traumatised condition. Jane becomes like a character in one of her films, pulverized by forces which she cannot comprehend.

Whether acting in *Dr Who* or Shakespeare at the Old vic, Jane charmed everyone. She had starred in 1961 in the *Greengage Summer* playing a 13 year-old girl on vacation with her siblings. The girl had a crush on a hotel errand-boy named Paul. The latter painted some fake blood on the wall with fake bullet holes, to attract guests looking for old hotels with war-history appeal. Jane in the play says, "Paul says blood makes good business." Alas he later falls to his death during a fight. Or, her 1964 film *The Masque of the Red Death* (Edgar Allen Poe) has Jane Asher's character forced to choose between the death of her father and the death of her lover. It features a Judgement Tarot card and the film sees much Tarot usage. The entire end-credit sequence is keyed over a Tarot reading, which ends with the Death card. At the end of the film, Death helps Gino (Asher) to escape.

Teen pictures of Jane remind us of the words Shakespeare put into the words of Romeo, upon first clapping eyes upon Juliette: 'O, she doth teach the very torches to burn bright!' She'd starred in six films by the time she met Paul, the most recent being *Alfie* with Michael Caine. In April '63 the seventeen year-old Jane Asher came to interview the Beatles for the *Radio Times* in Sloane Square. The group found themselves being quite affected by her presence: her sharp intelligence, the zing of her bright blue eyes, her fiery ginger hair and her lovely figure.

After a while the others, feeling a bit left out, pushed off and left Paul and Jane chatting. They returned after a few hours and found the couple in just the same position. It was then dawning on the world's most eligible bachelor that his free-as-a-bird days were drawing to a close. This time Paul definitely wasn't going to be giving any instructions as to how she should resemble Brigitte Bardot! This was soul-communion, and love-songs were going to be written about it - as his biographer observed, 'Jane's beauty was composed of an innocence that flowed from within her, a quality that entranced Paul, rather than from any sense of overt sexuality.'[1]

Six months later he moved into Jane Asher's home, a tall, 18th-century house in Wimpole Street, and met her distinguished family: Jane's aristocratic, musical mother a professional oboist, her father who was head of the psychiatric department at the Central Middlesex Hospital and her brother a founder of the trendy Indica gallery (named after *Cannabis indica*) off St James' street, and part of the pop music duo Peter and Gordon. That duo had a number one smash hit in 1964, a time when Paul and Jane were very close.

The situation suited Paul so well that he lodged there for three years, staying long after he had become a millionaire and the other Beatles had bought big country homes. Some of his best love-songs were written to her, Jane Asher, eg 'And I love her'[2] ('A love like ours could never die'), while his

---

1 Salewicz, p.150.
2 See the photo-montage of the two in video 'Paul McCartney and Jane Asher'.

'I'm looking through you' is said to reflect a bad patch in their relationship. She was a virgin when she met him.

She and Paul cruised around town as rock royalty, the beat elite, and mingled with the glitterati of swinging London. Jane helped him to furnish his new house on Cavendish Avenue which became ready to inhabit in the spring of '66, and gave him the gold ID bracelet he always wore. Paul had won a Prize for English literature and his teacher wanted him to go onto university,[3] so they had quite a bit to talk about. Jane was into reading Dostoevski. Paul absorbed *culture* from her and her family. The Beatles might not always have appreciated this: for example, they once visited the Greek Parthenon and Ringo grumbled: 'I remember going around the Parthenon three times - I think to keep Jane happy - and it was really tiring.'[4]

A Rising Star

The year 1966 saw doors of opportunity opening up for the twenty year old Jane: 'This is Jane Asher's year. We salute her,' gushed *Fabulous* magazine,[5] and thus described her dramatic talents:

> She may be in *The Saint, Love Story* or in any old kitchen sink drama on TV, but the moment she appears, there is something happening on the screen. She doesn't throw her limbs into theatrical poses or shrill out her lines. There is a quiet strength in her performances that makes them far more memorable than hammy histrionics.

> She has a pale, elfin face, dominated by deep-set blue eyes, rather serious and a little sad. There is a lot happening behind them. Her long hair looks like great flames leaping about her face. THE supreme test came this year, when Jane played the lead in a new play called *Cleo* for the Bristol Old Vic Company. She held the stage for two-and-a-half hours playing a mixed-up teenager with a sensitivity unusual in a girl of twenty.

---

3 Michael McCartney, *Remember*, p.101.
4 *The Beatles Anthology*, 2000, p.100.
5 Fabulous Magazine, 29 October 1966, 208 p.19 *Playin' Jane*

Jane took a dozen curtain calls on the first night. People pushed into her dressing-room to shake her hand, and tell her how much they had enjoyed seeing a star born. The star sat on the floor in her shaggy sweater and kneed blue jeans, and calmly drank champagne from a cracked mug. Jane is uncompromisingly down-to-earth and sensible. She can cut through hours of fancy discussion with one simple sentence of logic. It's her ability to separate the real from the superficial that makes her a good actress.

When she's in London, Jane is a loyal customer of *Indica Books,* of which Peter is a director. A bookshop was a natural business for Peter to establish, and for Jane to frequent, because they both read last thing at night, no matter how late the hour, and first thing on waking, preferring to rush about later to meet appointments.

Aside from qualifying for a discount at *Indica* because of her relationship to one of the directors, she also more than earned it by helping Peter, John Dunbar and Miles paint the shop and build bookshelves.

Jane did as she must have been asked to do, coping with the death of her beloved Paul and calmly accepting the replacement for company: no-one saw her shattered to the core. She did grow to like the new guy, after all they had to be seen together, and in return she was rewarded as her career took off that year.

A Farm in the Middle of Nowhere

Paul told *New Musical Express* in June 1966 that he had purchased a 200 acre farm 'up there at the tip of Scotland' so he could occasionally get some solitude. It was hardly near the tip of Scotland, it was far out on to the West and was 55 acres not 200, but we don't expect a twenty-four year old megastar to be bothered about such matters, he was probably advised to get it as tax-deductible.

The month before in May his ultra-smart Cavendish Avenue home had been furnished and acquired its piano. He and Jane chose the furniture and Moroccan rugs. He had a butler, and his Aston-Martin car.

Why did he also want the opposite - a muddy, run-down ramshackle farm way off the Scottish mainland, with a wet, cold climate and nothing much except fifty-five sheep, and not a tree in sight? How could the urban and urbane JPM - just getting into the London scene, the Indica gallery and all that - desire such a thing? He and Jane were urban trendsetters, would she appreciate the bare, windswept hills and the monotonous sound of sheep baa-ing?

From Jane to Linda

Figure: These two images, of Jane with Paul and then later on with Faul, shows the height difference.

Alistair Taylor (manager of Apple) recalls how he was with Paul and Jane quite a bit, and in his view Paul was faithful to Jane:

> He loved Jane and hadn't strayed.. Jane seemed to be the first woman that Paul took seriously.. If there was one Beatles romance that I thought would really last it was the love affair between Paul and Jane Asher. They did seem very much in love. I thought they were made for each other. Jane was just the most adorable woman you could expect to meet.'[6]

He claimed to have accompanied Paul and Jane to their Scottish residence: 'The farm hadn't been lived in for about five years. There were 400 acres of nothing but sheep and wind.' Paul wanted it to be done up in the most Spartan manner: 'he was absolutely sick of luxury.' The two of them were 'fervent vegetarians'[7]- this casts a *lot* of doubt over Mr Taylor's entire testimony, because it was Faul and Linda who both became vegetarians definitely not Paul. Paul brought up his big sheepdog Martha who liked the farm.

For both of them High Park was a 'wonderful escape.' Ian the neighbour looked after the sheep. Paul's estate had a little lake with a rowing boat. High Park 'was a super-magical place' (p134), not easy to believe. We're not given a year or date for these memories of Mr Taylor so we don't know whether its Paul or Faul he is talking about.

---

6 A Taylor, *A Secret History, an Inside story of the Beatles rise and fall*, 2003, p.132.
7 Ibid., p.131.

On Friday, January 13, 1967, Jane flew to the United States with the Bristol Old Vic for a four-and-a-half-month tour and Paul was not at Heathrow to see her off. We gain the impression that once the replacement took over, the affair was not intense but was a kind of formality. Accounts of the breakup put a lot of 'blame' on Faul's bed-hopping habit or on Jane not taking drugs but these comments may be missing the point. There is a deep duality here, and it is important for us not to miss the sweet love that did exist – a thing not that easy to come by – in this context. Later that year, the 21-year old Jane played Juliet in 1967 at the Bristol Old Vic.

Meeting Linda

Linda's family were lawyers and her family name Epstein was changed by her Father to Eastman to sound less Jewish. She had a fine figure, with the aid of which she is said to have notched up twenty lovers in two years, 1966-68, her preference being for rock stars. She enjoyed a 'Queen of the Groupies' reputation. Before she'd met any of the Beatles, she told Nat Weiss, the American business partner of The Beatles' manager Brian Epstein, that she was going to marry Paul McCartney. That seemed unlikely - after all, Linda lived in near-obscurity in new York while the already world-famous Paul lived in London with his beautiful redhead, the actress Jane Asher.

Faul well recalled when he first clapped eyes upon his future wife, at the *Bag of Nails* nightclub in London, On 15th of May, 1969:

I introduced myself, and said, ‹We›re going on to another club after this, would you like to join us?›

That was my big pulling line! Well, I›d never used it before, of course, but it worked this time! It was a fairly slim chance but it worked. She said, ‹Yes, okay, we›ll go on. How shall we do it?› I forget how we did it. ‹You come in our car› or whatever, and we all went on, the people I was with and the Animals, we went on to the Speakeasy.[8]

Linda also remembered this event, especially how they heard the new song *A Whiter Shade of Pale* by Procul Harum:

We flirted a bit, and then it was time for me to go back with them and Paul said, 'Well, we're going to another club. You want to come?' I remember everybody at the table heard *A Whiter Shade Of Pale* that night for the first time and we all thought, Who is that? Stevie Winwood? We all said Stevie. The minute that record came out, you just knew you loved it.

---

[8] Recollected in *Many Years from Now,* Barry Miles, quoted in The Beatles Bible on-line. See also *Fab: An Intimate Life Of Paul McCartney* by Howard Sounes 2014.

From Jane to Linda

That's when we actually met. Then we went back to his house. We were in the Mini with I think Lulu and Dudley Edwards, who painted Paul's piano; Paul was giving him a lift home. I was impressed to see his Magrittes.

<u>Figure:</u> Linda pulls the last unmarried Beatle

Faul narrated to his daughter this memorable moment of meeting her mother. Explaining why he decided to marry Linda he says: "At a certain age, you start to get serious, you think 'I can't just be a playboy all my life.'"[9] That does not *at all* sound as if he were in love with Jane, or as if he had been going steady with her for years. His daughter should then have asked, 'Thanks for that moving account of how you and Mom met and tuned into each other. Why then, seven months later, did you propose to Jane Asher?' – but, she didn't.

Readers may conclude from these accounts, which have no guilt associated with them, that Faul was *not* in any deep relationship with Jane. The two met again four days later at the *Sgt Pepper* launch party, a very exclusive event held at Brian Epstein's pad in Belgravia. Linda's entrée came through being a photographer co-producing a photo book *Rock and other Four-letter Words* with journalist Jay Marks. She had a brilliant portfolio of rock-star photos, and would hang around with people like Jimi Hendrix and Eric Burdon in the London clubs. She had photos of Janis Joplin from the legendary Fillmore East in New York. We can well appreciate that this is someone Faul would want to be with. That evening Linda found herself inside the home of one of the world's most eligible bachelors. She 'may' have spent the night there.

Jane, then in America with her acting company the Bristol Old Vic, returned on 29th of May. Earlier, Faul had flown out to Denver in April to be with Jane on her 21st birthday. I suggest this was an act of *friendship,* against the alternative view that Faul was deceiving or two-timing Jane by thus flirting with Linda.

Linda's chat-up line is said to have been, I know who you are, or rather who you are not, because I've been photographing the band.[10] 'I want you to

---

9 *Wingspan Paul and Linda McCartney Documentary*, 5 mins.
10 *Memoirs of Billy Shears*: 'When we met at the *Sgt Peppers* party, she let me know

marry me *and* have me in your group.' She had no musical talent, and yet this was the best thing that could have happened to him. It meant that someone really cared for him, *not* taking him for someone else. He could talk about the mysterious transformation he had been though to this savvy New Yorker. She would listen, as to how difficult it still was to step into someone else's shoes. She built up his confidence.

Jane's Mistake

Jane became engaged to Faul in December 1967, some months after this event, then it was called off six months later. It's not easy for *anyone* to explain what might have been going on here. Marianne Faithful who was around and spent time in Cavendish Avenue with them was never convinced by their liason: 'I never remember them getting on very well, Jane and him, it was sort of like an act almost, and I can quite see that he would be much happier with Linda because with Jane it would have been very difficult. .. I always thought Jane and Paul were very tense.[11]

A story concerning this comes from the New York rock 'n' roll journalist Jay Marks. The Paul-is-dead hysteria was peaking in late 1969, and people turned to him because of the excellent book on rock musicians in the swinging sixties he had just co-authored with Linda, published the year before.

In the *New York Times*, Marks recalled how in the autumn of '67 a party was being thrown in London by The Fool, a group of artists and clothes-designers working for Apple. Faul and Jane were present as were Jay and Linda. The former two were 'betrothed' and Linda was heard complaining that 'a chick didn't have much of a chance with bachelor McCartney because of Jane Asher.' This caused a friend of the Beatles (unnamed) to pipe up:

'Didn't you know that Paul was killed last year? That's just a double who's posing as Paul so sales aren't hurt by the tragedy. And, you see,' he went on as my mouth fell open, 'Jane is just going along with it to help out. The man she loves died last November. One day soon she will announce a break-up. Its just a matter of keeping up appearances until the appropriate time.'

Another source[12] has Jay Marks narrating the event, while standing on a street corner in New York, to the PID-investigator DJ Robey Younge.

---

that her eyes were open. She pulled me aside and asked me when and why I replaced Paul.' p550.
11 Miles, *Many Years from Now,* p.453.
12 Jay Marks, *New York Times*, 'No, no, No, Paul McCartney is not Dead,' 2.11.69, quoted in Reeve, *Turn me on Dead Man* pp.173-4.

From Jane to Linda

Marks recalled how had been at a cocktail party for Paul and Jane 'for their engagement situation' back in '67 and then -

'I noticed that Paul was not paying any attention to Jane but was being rather cozy with Linda Eastman. I asked 'What's this?' And I was told, 'Don't you know? That's not the boy she fell in live with, it's his replacement. It's all very hush-hush you know.'[13]

These two accounts, although rather different (for one its an engagement party, for the other its just a Beatles-Apple party) suggest a real memory behind them.[14] As a theatre-type Jane may have enjoyed the drama and excitement of being 'with the Beatles,' but she just was not into the drugs scene so they had different groups of friends.

In the beginning of 1968 Jane accepted an emerald-and-diamond engagement ring from Faul. In March the papers reported the two of them returning from the Maharishi's meditation centre in India, blissfully happy together. They planned to continue mediating for one hour a day. 'It was a wonderful experience' said Jane.[15] On Paul's birthday date of June 18th a feature on the two happy lovebirds entitled 'She loves you .. and you know it must be true' wondered about when their wedding date would be, and quoted Faul: 'We are waiting for the right time and place.'[16] That evening he went to see the opening of a new play starring Jane.

Visiting the US on June 20th he phoned Linda to come and join him, and on 22th in Los Angeles they sort of bonded:

Relieved at how well it (a business meeting) had gone we were ready to return to the hotel and leap into the swimming pool again. When we went into the bungalow to change, followed by the trail of girls, we were rather surprised to find Linda Eastman sitting there radiantly, totally spaced out, waiting for Paul. She had a joint in one hand and a beatific smile on her face.

Paul immediately detached himself from the circus surrounding him and took Linda aside. As I looked across the room, I suddenly saw something happen. Right before my eyes, they fell in love. It was like the thunderbolt that Sicilians speak of, the *coup-de-foudre* that the French speak of in

---

13 Patterson, *Walrus*, p.102: PID investigator Robey Younge related the story on New York WABC *Beatle Brunch* radio interview.
14 Hear the voice of Jay Marks recalling this incident, in *The Winged Beetle* 2010, 26 minutes; plus another version in RA77, at 3 minutes.
15 'Paul comes home to do some more meditating' Daily Express, 27.3.68.
16 Daily Express, 13.6.68

hushed tones, that once-in-a-lifetime feeling. Paul was struck almost dumb as he and Linda gazed at each other.

- or, that was Tony Bramwell's version in his *Magical Mystery Tours* (2006). That evening the couple went to an LA nightclub together and again we'll quote him:

> The club was hot, dark and crowded. Paul and Linda sat in a corner both while we acted as a kind of hedge. By a strange coincidence, both Eric Burdon and Georgie Fame were in the booth next to us, a fact not missed by Linda or Paul in their state of heightened awareness. Eric and Georgie had been at the Bag O'Nails on <u>the night they had met</u> some thirteen months ago. Now here they were on the night they had fallen in love. It was a sign.

Returning back home two days later, Faul jumped into bed with Francine Schwartz, in his Cavendish Avenue home. She wrote up her period with Faul in her steamy *Body Count.* He was running three different liasons that June! A British newspaper was cooing about him and Jane and wondering when the happy day would be, then a few days later Beatle expert Tony Bramwell was claiming to witness the once-in-a-lifetime thunderbolt of true love. Faul here is experiencing a somewhat dissociated mode of being, as if he were two different people. Linda will win because she doesn't want to be in love with 'Paul McCartney', she appreciates that he needs a different future and will help him find it.

Jane supposedly catches him in bed with Ms Schwartz, and then announced publicly (on TV) that the engagement was over: despite which Faul was quoted as saying, 'We will just have to see – but everything will be allright.'[17]

Then, a private wedding takes place of him and Linda. His 'stepmother', i.e. Angela McCartney, the wife of Paul's Father Jim, said: 'My husband and I have not been told about the wedding plans and certainly we have not been invited.' And the three other Beatles stayed away 'at the couple's request.' (*Express,* 12.3.69) Only big Mal was invited. Faul is here wanting to break free of the old Paul identity and start a new life. His 'parents' not even being told about the wedding may remind us of a later event, when he declined to attend his 'father' Jim McCartney's funeral in 1976. Mal Evans' presence reminds us of his having been close to Faul in the months after his first appearance (so to speak) in late '66.

The two Beatles John and Faul both married in the same month, March

---

17 The Express, 27 March, 13th June and 22nd July, 1968.

From Jane to Linda

1969, to wives Linda Eastman and Yoko Ono - both divorcees who had graduated from the *same* college in New York, the private Sarah-Lawrence Liberal Arts College (for parents loaded with cash). Neither were musicians or hardly even musical, yet both were included in their husbands' bands, *Wings* and the *Plastic Ono Band.*

Right through the 1970s Faul never played a Beatles' song - the nearest he would get to it was an occasional rendition of Little Richard's *Long Tall Sally*.

Murder

All the fun vanished for Jane a month after Faul got married, when her father was found dead in the basement of his own home, where Paul had spent such happy years. All those wonderful love-songs, had they really been written for her? She has to forget them and resign herself to the awful necessity of silence, she has to pack down her grief into the bottom of her soul and cannot ever talk about it.

On 30th of April, 1969 *The Express* reported:
Dr Richard Asher, 57-year old father of actress Jane Asher and her pop star brother Peter, has been missing from his Wimpole Street, London home. Dr Asher went out last Saturday to visit Marylebone library and failed to return. It is feared he is suffering from loss of memory.

'That was all.' Then a few days later came the bombshell: he was found dead on May 2nd in the cellar of his home. It added: 'crime is not suspected.' I find that ve-e-e-ry strange. Not suspected? He had been reported missing, then his corpse suddenly appears in the basement of his own home. 'Two bottles' were found near to the body: bottles of what? The family have to try and pretend that they had somehow not noticed his smelly corpse in the basement.

Then – I find this bit hard to believe – the journalist tries to insinuate that the late Richard Asher was not happy about what his children had been up to: 'It is known that Dr Asher, a controversial figure in medical circles, was not happy about his children's chosen professions.' The journo is trying by innuendo to imply that Dr Asher committed suicide, without giving any hint as to the cause of death. (*Express*, 3.5.69) That is not ethical journalism.

The body lay 'undiscovered for a week', according to a *Telegraph* journalist thirty years later.[18] Saturday 26th April he went missing, then his corpse was discovered a week later. Of course, 'crime is not suspected'!

The women remain so silent in this story. We've heard the history, but what about her-story? Ah, if only we had Jane's memoirs – of her Father, after

---
18 David Thomas, 'The Darkness Behind the Smile', *Telegraph* 19.8.04

whom a new psychiatric condition was named, of her mother, who taught music to George Martin at the Guildhall, and of her high-IQ musical brother, co-founder of the trendy Indica Gallery - and above all of her *feelings* of for example when she got engaged to Faul in December 1967, whatever did she think was going on?

How could her home, where the happy songs were composed, from 'I want to Hold your Hand' to 'Yesterday' - in the attic where Paul lived, and next door where Peter Asher lived– end up with the Father's dead body rotting in the basement? No-one ever tells the story, and Jane develops deep amnesia over that ancient pain. Paul had composed *Eleanor Rigby* on the upright piano in Mrs Asher's music room in the basement of Wimpole Street. Where the songs were made, the body was found.

Dr Richard Asher, author of a paper on hypnotism, has to have known about the swap, and what the Tavistock-type programming if any was involved to 'make' the replacement for Paul McCartney. When his adorable, famous daughter was humiliated by being dumped after receiving an engagement ring, it was the shock of her life, and he is disturbed by this, feeling it to be unfair. Was he then in danger of speaking to some people about the matter? That cannot be allowed to happen. Ditto for Jane, she has to have an example that will prevent her from ever talking about what she has been through.

Dorothy Rhone, Paul's girlfriend until 1962 (next chapter) never says a word. Jane shuts up. Heather Mills knows something awful (Chapter 3) but is paid to remain silent.

Ram

'After being with Jane five years, he suddenly he marries another woman and becomes a family man living on a farm in the middle of nowhere.'[19]

> Maybe I'm amazed at the way you pulled me out of time
> And hung me on a line
> Maybe I'm a man and maybe I'm a lonely man
> Who's in the middle of something
> That he doesn't really understand
>
> Maybe I'm a man and maybe you're the only woman
> Who could ever help me
> Baby won't you help me understand
> McCartney, *Maybe I'm Amazed,* 1970

---

19 Blogger 'Cherilyn7.' All blogger quotes are from www.invanddis.proboards.com.

From Jane to Linda

Linda helps Faul to understand himself, to seek for his post-Beatle identity, and become who he wants to be – someone who is five years older than the guy he's been acting. This could be a good time to listen to *Maybe I'm Amazed* ('You pulled me out of time') where the 1976 version on *Wings Over America* is recommended. Being with Jane always involved the strain of seeming to be, 'Paul.' Faul and Linda were attuned to each other and people remarked upon this.

His *Ram* album of 1971 co-produced with Linda has cover images of him *not* trying to be Paul. He's not pretty! We also see an image of him in a horrid mask, indicating the strain of having his face done over to make him resemble another. This is the first time we see Faul no longer trying to resemble another. He was *not* the Beautiful Boy and Linda could accept that and love him for who he was – provided only that she could be in his band.[20]

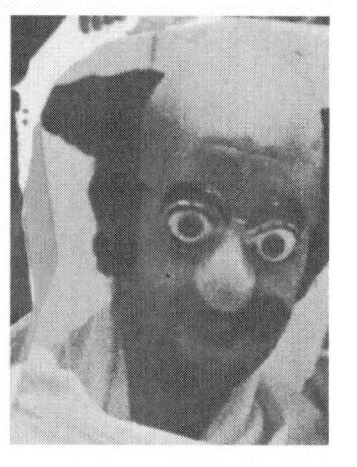

She Feels the Pain

For Jane, decades later, it still hurts. An interview with Ms Asher by a *Telegraph* journalist in 2004 describes her awesome achievements, the distinguished positions she holds, her still-radiant beauty[21]. Indeed, we are startled that one person can have done so many commendable things. But Jane then added rather abruptly: "Life is bloody dark and awful ... I don't think there's any meaning to anything. I have slightly more of an acceptance that you're hurtling towards the abyss [than I had before].'

The puzzled journalist cannot prise much out of her about where this *angst* came from, and makes even less progress when he tries to ask about

---

20 The two ladies are compared in the video, *Paul McCartney – Jane Asher or Linda?*
21 'At 58, she has not the faintest trace of a flabby arm, saggy jaw or baggy eye.' David Thomas 'The Darkness Behind the Smile' *Telegraph* 19.8.04

Paul, whom Jane's mother had invited to move into the family home (in itself a slightly odd situation). Years earlier in a *Sunday Times* article, she had explained how she suffered 'deep, black holes full of inexplicable panic' and worried about 'figures of death stalking my loved ones.' That *is* buried trauma.[22]

Thirty years after the catastrophe of 1966, Jane starts to write novels. She has to date written three best-selling novels: *The Longing, The Question* and *Losing It,* all concerned with trauma, loss and broken love-affairs - no happy endings, no redemption themes. As *The Telegraph* commented, Jane's novels 'reveal a perception of the human condition which is unusually bleak.

Her first two books, *The Longing* (1996) and *The Question* (1998), run through the gamut of human misery - bulimia, infertility, adultery, sexual obsession, revenge and madness. Her third, due to be published next spring, will tackle the issue of obesity.'[23] Thus her novel called *The Question* (1998) has 'John' *badly injured in a car crash.* A blogger ('pennylane') commented: 'It's kinda creepy.. it's about a woman named Eleanor and her husband named John who is very successful and wealthy and she finds out he has been cheating on her and their whole marriage has been a sham for 30 years.

'Then John, badly injured in a car crash, becomes a victim of PVS -- Persistent Vegetative State. Although he is capable of communicating by the tiniest of signals, he has no quality of life. And so arises the ultimate question - and the ultimate opportunity for revenge. Should he live, or should he die?' Her novels may express a bleak, unremitting pessimism, but at least she is still alive, which is more than can be said for quite a lot of characters in this story. One may contrast her present dire condition with the unforgettable love-songs composed about her in her youth.

She married Gerald Scarfe, the savagely satirical cartoonist. In her novels we come face to face with the deep trauma:

> I'd done it before in daylight, forcing myself to look away to the other side of the road as I approached the dreaded place-I-can't name. I even enjoyed the test sometimes: seeing just how much or little it took to trigger me into going back over it all; watching myself almost disinterestedly for signs of hysteria, regret or anger.
>
> But this was different. I hadn't realised how strongly it would make its presence felt once darkness had fallen. I turned away quickly as the

---

22 Jane Asher, *Sunday Times* 1987, quoted in *Telegraph, op.cit.*
23 *The Telegraph,* 8.11.99).

old panic began to churn in my stomach, and I looked back towards the way I had come and took deep breaths in an attempt to calm myself down enough to be able to walk on again ... I'm prepared to find my subconscious capable of plotting just about anything these days: it's taken me by surprise so many times over the last year or so while its been dealing with the unthinkable.

Funny, I thought, that here I am, looking with the same eyes, standing over the same legs, wearing – and I glanced down at myself – yes, even wearing the same coat as I did over a year ago, before it all started. Knowledge. Knowing what he did – what the two of them did. Knowing that ...he won't be there. *That he never will be again.* (my italics)

I can still picture him that evening. Or can I? Perhaps I'm imagining it. Maybe its another sign of this bloody crafty subconscious of mine inventing the bits that I have lost....God, it's fascinating how much I do remember: I suppose, as well as being the opening scene of the impending terrible drama, it was also the last scene of my other life.[24]

Her character remembers the catastrophic event, the last scene of her 'other life' before everything changed. The memories bubble up from her subconscious, after she has tried to forget them: 'He never will be again' - that was the terrible thing! She experiences her subconscious as some sort of 'other' which is 'capable of plotting just about anything' and 'it's taken me by surprise so many times.' It was Jane's Father's terrible and inscrutable death – where no hint of the cause of death was ever made public - that locked her into that deep silence.

But, looking on the bright side, the US fanzine *My Sweet Lady Jane* dedicated to Jane Asher has been coming out quarterly for the last 22 years! US readers want to hear about a real English Rose.

Today these two ladies are remembered for their food: 'Linda McCartney' vegetarian meals and Jane Asher's cakes. Munching our way through these, we may reflect upon the tremendous dramas which they went through. Nothing shows more clearly the replacement, in the wake of Paul's death, than these two separate love stories.

---

24 Jane Asher, *Losing It* pp.4-10

Glimpses of Paul

He's an evanescent character, whose image so easily gets lost behind that of the ever-garrulous Faul. No biographies of him exist. We try and avoid biographies based on Faul 'remembering'[1] impressive though this no doubt is.

A third-generation musician

Do not deny yourself the pleasure of watching the Shea Stadium performance (Volume Five of *The Anthology*) where fifty thousand people watched the Fab Four perform. Bigger audiences than that may nowadays be common, but using visual stage effects. At Shea there were no fancy effects, no electronic gizmos - only the Band. One should note how Paul sings overtones and harmonies while John holds onto the main melody: which may help us to become aware of the musical family he came from.

His grandfather Joe McCartney, Jim's father, liked opera and had played an E-flat tuba in the local Territorial Army band that played in Stanley Park, and the Copes' Tobacco factory Brass Band where he worked. He came from an Irish family, and yet was teetotal. He played the double bass at home and sang, hoping to interest his children in music.

Paul's father Jim McCartney reacted against this older Liverpudlian tradition and formed his own ragtime band when he was seventeen, the Masked Melody Makers, as later became 'Jim Mac's Jazz Band.' They would perform with dinner jackets and paper shirt fronts and cuffs.

At home he had a collection of old, 78 rpm records that he would often play, and he would perform his musical "party-pieces"—the hits of the time—on the piano. In that musical household, before Paul was born, Jim's sister Jin recalled that each day one would hear tunes 'wafting up the stairway' from the parlour.

---

[1] NB Chris Salewicz's commendable *McCartney the Biography* is three-quarters about Paul, i.e pre-'67.

Jim would point out the different instruments in songs on the radio to his sons Michael and Paul, and take them to local brass band concerts. He taught them a basic idea of harmony between instruments, and Paul credited his father's tuition as helpful when later singing harmonies with Lennon.

Asked at school to describe his Father's profession, Paul wrote down: 'Lead guitarist with Rory 'Shakin' Blackwell' but then crossed it out, and underneath that he wrote 'Or Cotton Salesman.'[2]

Jim would much enjoy evenings in the pub, and yet would avoid undue inebriation, and taught his concept of self-control to his sons.

Paul's father fixed up a radio earpiece with wires so that at night Paul and his brother could listen in bed via the overseas Radio Luxembourg to the new American sounds. As Britain's closest port to America, Liverpool was especially receptive to the exciting new trans-Atlantic sounds, from Bill Haley to Elvis. Scousers could get to hear the new R&B sounds never released in UK

'His main childhood memories are of writing back to front – a habit he's grown out of', cryptically explained 'Bill Shepherd' in the *Beatles Book*, concerning Paul, adding the inscrutable comment: 'He would also pedal his bicycle back to front.'[3] Presumably this had no connection to his re-stringing his famous Hofner bass guitar to play it left-handed.

But, it does sound quite relevant to him later on devising the private name for himself Ian Iachimoe, which is supposedly what his name sounds like backwards. There is an original manuscript of 'Paperback Writer' (1966) signed Ian Iachimoe. Friends could write to him with that name, and would stand a better chance of getting an answer through the pile of fan mail.[4]

Paul's mother Mary died in 1956, when Paul was fourteen, and she had been a forceful character who knew what was right and what was wrong: never would she have stood for the teenage racket that started up after her death at 20 Forthlin Road. Their next-door neighbour Tom Gaule who lived at number 18 would hear Jim complaining about the noise.

Quite frankly, if Paul's mother had been alive, there would have been no Beatles as far as Paul was concerned. She'd never have stood for that row. The lady was a real stickler, very much a You-do-as-I-say kind of person.

---

[2] Ibid, p.71
[3] Billy Shepherd, *A Tale of Four Beatles* September '63.
[4] Paul did contribute towards the Indica Gallery's journal, and advertised for a competition in its first issue, where he called himself a 'Polish filmaker' Ian Iachimoe.

Glimpses of Paul

She was the dominant factor next door – there was no nonsense with Mrs McCartney. She'd never have allowed it, all that argy-bargy.'(p76)

His dear mother had to die, whereby the first-beginnings of the Band grew in a male household where Father Jim did the cooking. We sense a deep fate in Paul's life, whereby everything had to be just as it was. His brother Mike McGear recalled how his fourteen year old brother had his interest in the guitar had greatly intensify following his Mother's death that year: 'As soon as Paul picked up the guitar, he'd go into a world of his own.'[5] He dreamed of a new music, burning with the sweet fires of youth:

Yet secretly, Jim knew he couldn't be prouder if Paul did become a musician, for it stirred up within him all the thrills he'd been forced to forget when he gave up Jim Mac's Jazz band.

And he realised that it was becoming increasingly likely that this might be Paul's destiny. After at first supplying cautious criticism, Jim McCartney came home one night at 5.30 and heard the three guitarists playing strong new chords. He still couldn't understand why they didn't want to play numbers like 'Stairway to Paradise' and 'When the Saints go Marching In'; he could have taught them such good arrangements. From time to time, Jim would even sit in with his son and his friends, playing the piano almost as easily as he had done twenty years before.'[6]

It's such a difficult balance for a father to see the genius and talent of the family blossoming in his son, and yet not seek to control or boss him around. Jim seems to have managed that, and therefore it was a happy household.

In July-August 1957 Paul joined John Lennon's skiffle band *The Quarrymen*. John used to bring his girlfriend Cynthia around, and her comment was, 'The warmth I experienced whenever I entered the modest home of this talented family was wonderful. Jim was a father in a million. The cheerful way he coped with a situation that many a man would have run away from was admirable.'

Aunty Jin and Aunt Milly would turn up in the week helping to cook tea and clean up etc. These sisters of Jim are very relevant for DNA sampling which one hopes will soon be feasible, using hair-samples from their relatives and comparing with for example the children of Linda's daughter, Stella McCartney.[7]

---

[5] McGear, *Remember*, p27.
[6] Chris Salewicz, *McCartney, The Biography*, p74
[7] Jin McCartney married Harry Harris, becoming Jin Harris, living in Huyton.

Paul's brother Mike recalls how his brother used to instruct him to bang a drum while walking down the street away from the house, and if he could not hear it a hundred yards away it was insufficiently offensive. Their neighbour Tom just had to put up with it!

It was a terrific row to our ears in those days – absolutely horrible. I like classical stuff, to be honest.[8]

A Shared Sorrow

In 1958 John's mother Julia was killed, in an absurd and meaningless car accident. The two lads drew closer together, sharing the deep, inexpressible pain. John would come over to Forthlin road while Jim McCartney was out at work and the two of them - smoking Typhoo tea in Jim's pipe - began their rehearsals. A mysterious melancholia lay at the back of everything they now composed, no matter how lively and up-tempo. The trio (including Stuart Sutcliffe) didn't really have a name in those days unless it was *Johnny and the Moondogs*. Paul showed John all the chords he had learned, but as Paul played left-handed guitar John had to go to the mirror in his bedroom and re-learn them.

All the bands in Liverpool had such names, featuring one lead singer plus the others, it was mandatory. For example Richard Starkey aka Ringo Starr was then drumming for the band *Rory Storm and the Hurricanes*. No way could that happen to John's band because he knew he could never be as good as Paul - or, if you like, he could never dream of being better than Paul. So an unheard-of thing happened when in 1960 they became just *The Beatles* –a kind of French term, les 'Beat'. There was no leader!

Paul's steady girlfriend was Dot or Dorothy Rhone, as John had his Cynthia. Dot loved visiting Forthlin Road, where brilliant parties used to happen, with music played by Paul on guitar and his father on piano. 'Paul was always writing songs and he would try them out on me,' she recalled, such as 'PS I love you' – released on the first Beatles EP in 1962, just months after the couple broke up. The poor girls came under awful pressure to look like Brigitte Bardot, having to go blonde and wear mini-skirts.

After Dot, Paul dated Iris Caldwell, and loved being round at their home and chatting to her mother there. Her brother Alan, 'Rory Storm' of the *Hurricanes* was also there. Years earlier Iris had dated a skinny young kid George Harrison. Paul couldn't do a love-song for Iris, he tactfully explained, because nothing rhymed with it! She recollected:

---

8 Salewicz, p.75

Glimpses of Paul

I never heard him say a bad word about anyone. The only person he was ruthless with was himself. ..The difference between Paul and my brother was his total dedication, which all the Beatles had...Paul was so determined, with a total belief in himself to an extent that some would think he was self-centred and in love with himself. But he wasn't – it was just that he wasn't ordinary, and knew that he wasn't. ..He never swore, he never told a dirty joke. Paul was the whole driving force of the group, he was the clever one. And he was all right, Paul, he worked for everything he got.'[9]

Here is a picture of the Caldwell household: we see Alan Caldwell (Rory Storm) to the left with his lady friend, 'Johnny Guitar' plus friend at centre, his arm round a happy Mrs Caldwell, then in the right-hand corner a blissed-out Paul with his eyes closed – dreaming of things to come, in the arms of his girlfriend Dot.[10] Both *Rory Storm and The Hurricanes* and the *Beatles* had come back from playing in Hamburg, so this is a close-knit group.

The picture is from 1960, a while before Ringo has been taken away from Rory Storm's group, *The Hurricanes*, where he used to sing and drum. The picture surely evokes these words of Paul's biographer: 'Paul became very attached to Iris' mother. Mrs Caldwell was never averse to staying up chatting and joking with the musicians her son would bring around after gigs. The Caldwells were a warm, loving family, bound together by a sense of humour that reached even beyond that which could reasonably be expected from Mereyside. Even when Iris and Paul stopped going out together, he continued to visit the house, having come to look on Mrs Caldwell as something of a substitute mother.

"Our house was an escape for him" says Iris, "My mother was so easy to get along with. So he'd escape back to our place and eat cheese sandwiches and drink tea, talking all night.'[11]

---

9 Salewicz, *The Biography*., p.131-2.
10 Image from *The Macs, Mike McCartney's Family album*, 1981, Chapter 'Early Days'.
11 Salewicz, *The Biography*, p.130.

In 1972, both Rory Storm and his mother Mrs Caldwell, 'commit suicide' – Uh oh, just another accident, too many pills. They die together.[12]

There are *a lot* of funny deaths that follow Paul's departure from this world, of people who were very close to him and who might have been difficult to silence. For many who knew the old Paul, their silence could be bought and was bought, but maybe this was not so for the Caldwells. Those two deaths would have been a signal to the wide circle of people in Liverpool who had known him, to keep quiet and accept the new guy.

Dot vanishes forever from the scene in 1962, going off to Canada.

Hamburg

Paul phoned up Pete Best, "'Ere Pete, 'owdja fancy comin' to 'Amburg with us as our drummer for a couple of months?" - an offer he couldn't refuse. They were due over in Hamburg for August, 1960. A new youth-culture was starting to blossom, fourteen years after the entire city had been reduced to rubble by a firestorm of British bombs. A Liverpool businessmen had cut the deal. The Indra Club was formerly strip-club, in a red-light area run by shady characters on the fringes of the underworld which made Liverpool's vice and violence seem quite tame by comparison. In Hamburg Paul played the piano, which didn't happen in England. The group were then a quintet, with Stu Sutcliffe on bass guitar, George and John on guitars and Pete Best on drums. Paul learnt from his idol Little Richard, at the nearby Star Club in Hamburg.

Stu's girlfriend Astrid cut his hair, getting rid of his teddy-boy squiff and combing his hair forward, and lo! the Beatle mop-top was born. Stu had mean and moody good looks but wasn't much good at the music. When he finally left them Paul was as he put it 'lumbered' with the bass guitar. Until Paul came along the bass guitar was a fairly boring instrument, something played by the fat guy in the background.

The Beatles avoided National Service by the skin of their teeth, after 1960 when the government abolished that compulsory two-year army training. Growing up in the Teddy-boy era, they heard as teenagers the siren song of

---

12 'Sadly, some years ago, after the death of Mr Caldwell, Rory and his Mum committed suicide together.' *Op. cit.,* Mike McCartney. As with Epstein, the inquest found evidence of sleeping pills and alcohol in both bodies, but hardly enough to cause death. As of 2012, *all* former members of the group (except Ringo) were dead. In 1967, Rory's lead guitarist Ty (Charles) O'Brien collapsed on stage during a concert, dying in hospital aged 26. That band knew too much. They played together with the Beatles at the KaiserKeller in Hamburg.

the raw, new beat from America. They had the leisure time to pursue their music without entering the army - as Elvis had had to in America, and as too had Jimi Hendrix, come to that.

When in 1961 Brian Epstein became manager of the Beatles, Paul would have sensed a family connection, because his Father Jim had purchased his upright piano from Harry Epstein, Brian's father at the North End Music Store. The Epstein family owned a furniture store in Liverpool, next door to which was the NEMS which Brian came to manage. He got the newly-named Beatles into an audition at the EMI studio at Abbey road with George Martin in April of 1962, after which the latter recalled: 'I thought the only one who could really play was Paul; John just stood there knocking out the chords, George's solos were not that impressive, and any average drummer could have done just as well.'[13] (NB this was before Ringo had joined the group).

Mike McCartney described the historic partnership as: '...the Rogers and Hammerstein of the musical world, John's musical hard edge merging with Paul's melodic feel, both creating genius.'[14] But, his biographer put it better:

While John would work out a rough chord structure, Paul would add the sense of sweet, lingering, somehow archetypal melody that he had inherited from his father and from his own catholic appreciation of music. (Salewicz, p.62)

In his last, sorrowful interview a few months before his death[15], John described the partnership as: "Well, you could say that he [Paul] provided a lightness, an optimism, while I would always go for the sadness, the discords, a certain bluesy edge. There was a period when I thought I didn't write melodies, that Paul wrote those and I just wrote straight, shouting rock 'n roll.'

Moving into the Asher residence in Wimpole Street, Paul would have been reassured to learn that Jane Asher's mother Margaret had taught George Martin, at the Guildhall School of Music. Peter Asher lived in the room next to Paul on the top floor: he like Jane had been a child star. His ginger hair did not have quite the flaming brightness of Jane's, but it was close. Paul wrote for him the song 'World without Love' which became the big hit for the 'Peter and Gordon' duo. Later on, after Paul died, Peter acquired a senior position in Apple Corps.

In his interview with David Frost in 1964 (online), Paul was asked what

---

13 Salewicz, *The Biography*, p.129.
14 Mike McGear, *Remember, the Recollections and Photographs of Michael McCartney*,1992, p.106.
15 September 1980 *Playboy* interview, online (See Appendix for discussion).

ambitions he still had, and he said, 'retire.' Asked to clarify when, he added: 'The way things are going, maybe a couple of years or so.'

There is a touching scene of Paul being tempted by two beauties, while filming 'Help' on Paradise Island in the Bahamas, in February 1965, viewed by the filmmaker Richard Lester: 'Two of the most beautiful women he [Lester] had ever seen, dressed in identical stunning black swimsuits' were attempting to persuade Paul to take some heroin, but Paul managed to decline this offer.'[16] We are impressed by such remarkable inner strength, to resist temptation.

A Chipped tooth

Paul had an accident, while visiting his father and step-mother at their Cheshire home, just South of Liverpool, on his moped. From a *New Musical Express* interview in the last months of his life:

> "He started to finger his lip, almost without thinking, and I asked him about the reports that he'd broken a tooth. "You're right," he admitted candidly. "I did it not long ago when I came off a moped. Now I've had it capped... Look." I looked but I couldn't see anything. A perfect mend. Only a small scar remains on his lip as a souvenir. "It was quite a serious accident at the time. It probably sounds daft, having a serious accident on a motorized bicycle, but I came off it hard and I got knocked about a bit. My head and lip were cut and I broke the tooth. I was only doing about 30 at the time, but it was dark and I hit a stone and went flyin' through the air. It was my fault... it was a nice night and I was looking at the moon."

He sipped his tea and reached for a cigarette (16.6.66).

'Not long ago' here meant six months earlier! Various sources eg *The Beatles' Bible* put the date of this event at 26th December, 1965. Here is Brian Epstein's account:

> Last mid-December, Paul injured his lip and chipped his tooth in the moped accident. He honestly thought no one would notice the chip, for it is so small. I told him three times he should do something about it. It is in a place where there are no nerve ends, so there is no pain. Paul assured me that he would have the tooth capped, but - unfortunately - he has not done so. Could he be afraid of the dentist? It is my opinion that he will just let it be.'[17]

It seems that he did let it be, from December 1965 to May-June 1966,

---

16 Andrew Yule, *The Man who 'Framed' the Beatles, a Biography of Richard Lester*,1994, p.99
17 Interviewed by the US teen mag *16*.

Glimpses of Paul

just before the above interview. He had it fixed before the group flew off to Japan. Faul normally manages a credible 'memory' of what life was like for James Paul McCartney - as if guided by some divine inner voice - but here his 'recollection' failed completely. Here is the story he told on *Anthology:*

> I had an accident when I came off a moped in Wirral, near Liverpool. I had a very good friend who lived in London called Tara Browne, a Guinness heir - a nice Irish guy, very sensitive bloke. I'd see him from time to time, and enjoyed being around him. He came up to visit me in Liverpool once when I was there seeing my dad and brother. I had a couple of mopeds on hire, so we hit upon the bright idea of going to my cousin Bett's house.
>
> We were riding along on the mopeds. I was showing Tara the scenery. He was behind me, and it was an incredible full moon; it really was huge. I said something about the moon and he said 'yeah', and I suddenly had a freeze-frame image of myself at that angle to the ground when it's too late to pull back up again: I was still looking at the moon and then I looked at the ground, and it seemed to take a few minutes to think, 'Ah, too bad - I'm going to smack that pavement with my face!' Bang! ...
>
> In fact that was why I started to grow a moustache ... It caught on with the guys in the group: if one of us did something like growing his hair long and we liked the idea, we'd all tend to do it. And then it became seen as a kind of revolutionary idea, that young men of our age definitely ought to grow a moustache!

The moustache is a year too early, nor was there any Full moon anywhere near the date of the accident, and no mopeds had been hired, plus it is most unlikely that Tara Browne was around! The Full Moon arrived on December 8th, followed by a New Moon on 22nd, so in mid-December there was no Moon at all in the sky. By 26th there was a fairly young Moon which set at 8 o'clock, which would have hung quite low in the sky, hardly visible in an urban environment. Faul's 'memory' that "it was an incredible full moon; it really was huge" would put it near to the 8th of December, *however* the Beatles then had a punishing schedule of tour-dates[18] -

   3 December 1965 - Glasgow - Scotland - Odeon
   4 December 1965 - Newcastle - England - Newcastle City Hall
   5 December 1965 - Liverpool - Liverpool Empire Theatre
   7 December 1965 - Manchester - Manchester Apollo
   8 December 1965 - Sheffield - Sheffield City Hall
   9 December 1965 - Birmingham - Odeon

---

18 pointed out on drtomoculus' blogspot: 'Postings and musings on the thing called Beatles'.

10 December 1965 - London - Hammersmith Odeon
11 December 1965 - Finsbury Park - Astoria
12 December 1965 - Cardiff - Wales - Capitol Centre

-which left no time at all to visit his folks. A bruised, chipped-tooth Paul would then have been big news. The only newspaper report of this accident around that period, was that of the *Mirror* on 31st December: 'He said he had fallen off his moped during his Christmas stay with his family near Liverpool' - which really does not sound like driving out with Tara Browne.

Paul actually had two mopeds, one for him and one for Jane. We get this story from a Mr John Cameron, who was then helping his father to run a moped and motorcycle shop not far from where Paul's father and stepmother were living in Wirrall. They received an order from a Mr McCartney living in Baskervylle Road (The house that Paul had bought for his Father in 1964) for two Raleigh mopeds, and he was asked by his father to return from school early to help with the delivery that afternoon. Neither realized who was the buyer, then on arriving at the house they were startled to see Paul and Jane Asher come out to meet them. (post on *The Beatles Bible*)

Nor would Tara Browne have been around over December 26th, being expected at his stately home in Ireland (his family beingt heirs to the Guinness fortune) over the festive season, to be together with his wife and their newborn child. There is no record of Tara Browne visiting Liverpool, or knowing Faul's father and stepmother. This is a clear glitch in Faul's 'memory' whereby Tara's fatal car-crash a year later, on 17th December 1966 (see Appendix) has become associated with the moped-accident, just as he 'remembered' growing a moustache a year too early.

Kennedy

Mark Lane met Paul in early '66 when working on his magnum opus exposing the truth about the Kennedy assassination, *Rush to Judgement*, which became a bestseller. He recalled: 'He [Paul] seemed very young and remarkably modest. That was because he was twenty-two years old, and he was not impressed by his accomplishments.' Paul asked to see the manuscript and Mark Lane kindly lent him his only UK copy: a

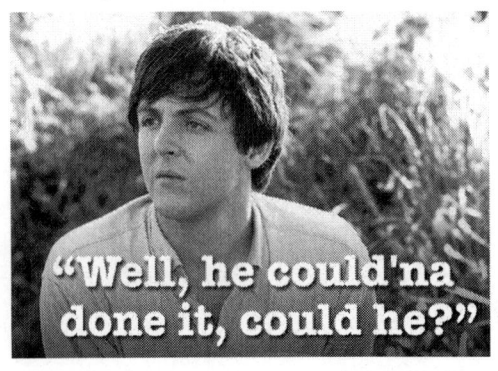

"Well, he could'na done it, could he?"

'man in a chauffeur's outfit' came to collect it the next day, then returned it a few days later.

Then Mr Lane was startled to receive a phone call out of the blue saying "Well he could'na done it, could he?" Irritated, he replied, "Who is this? And who could not have done what?" Paul quickly introduced himself, and explained, "I meant that Oswald could not have killed President Kennedy."[19] The two then met up for dinner, and had a long discussion of the matter. Mark Lane mentioned that a film version was being prepared:

> '(McCartney) asked if there was going to be any music, and I said that the director and I had not even thought about that yet.
>
> "Well," he said, "I would like to write a musical score for the film, as a present for you."
>
> I was astonished by that generous offer and speechless for a moment, but then I cautioned him that the subject matter was very controversial in the United States and that he might be jeopardizing his future.
>
> He added, "One day my children are going to ask me what I did with my life, and I can't just answer that I was a Beatle."[20]

This was written up nearly half a century later so we need to take it with a large grain of salt, but it may have a ring of authenticity. It would be unthinkable for Mark Lane's film to have had a Paul McCartney soundtrack – why, youngsters might have come to realise that the official version of the JFK assassination was a total pack of lies. Even information that Paul was intending to do such a thing would have put his life in jeopardy.[21] Mark Lane recalled that Paul then played a new song he had just composed, *Eleanor Rigby*, whereby he became one of the first people to hear about 'the lonely people' and 'some father darning his socks at night.' That memory, if reliable, would put the events in June '66, after which Mark Lane's book emerged in October.

Brother Mike

Paul's younger brother Mike does not at all resemble him, though he seems to be Paul's one and only real bother; whereas Ruth, Paul's step-sister, the lovely Ruth, does in some degree resemble him (her mother Angela

---

19 Mark Lane, *Citizen Kane, Defending our rights*, 2012, p.168.
20 Ibid, p.178; sounds rather doubtful as Paul then had no (legitimate) children.
21 Plastic.macca.co.uk, 'JPM Hoped to Expose JFK Assassination Lies' quoting from Mark Lane's autobiography, *Citizen Lane* 2012.

married Alf McCartney in '64) even though she is not one gathers a blood-relative. Mike 'McGear' as he calls himself – not wishing to be burdened with the McCartney name[22] – formed the group 'Scaffold' known for its hit 'Lily the Pink'. Inevitably he keeps being asked the Question – as to whether his brother had died, or been replaced - and we here listen to an answer he gave on a US TV show in October '69, just as the whole issue was hitting the headlines.

A Mike Douglas chat show was featuring the three members of the group *Scaffold* who were doing a US tour, performing some humorous skits. Then they took front seats in the audience, as a PID 'conspiracy theorist' Christopher Glenn strode onto the stage, armed with a pile of Beatle albums. He gave a brief but colourful exposition on the topic, not committing himself either way as regards the veracity of the rumour. Invited to respond, Mike McGear said quite angrily: "First off, I find it really embarrassing what you were saying" - pointing an accusatory finger at Glenn - "but the worst thing was that it was boring. For the last – however long that took – was a very boring piece of television…. You've got nothing at all to base it on. It's all a fantastically-contrived piece of press material of which you're making a television debut." Clearly, no word of that was true.

The host Mike Douglas tried to steer the conversation away from personal attack, asking: "Do you call that a hoax, Michael?" McCartney replied, "No, I think he's dead, alright," causing a ripple of laughter. Then looking at Mr Glenn He cruelly added, "I think its terrifying how you get away with it." Later when Douglas asked him "When was the last time you saw your brother?" McCartney replied, "The last time? Was his funeral." [23] But Douglas persisted: 'No really when was the last time?' to which McGear replied 'I don't know.'

Watching the online video, we note how Mike McGear as the Englishman was able to get one up on the American: he puts down Chris Glenn, accusing him of having a scurrilous motive, viz. making money out of it (an absurd accusation). While he does this, we are startled to hear him switch into a BBC English accent. His Scouse (Liverpool accent) quite vanishes while he chastises Glenn in upper-crust English about how his presentation was 'boring' etc., causing an out-witted Mr Glenn to back down and concede that the whole thing was just a story. Was not that immensely strange? While trying to remember about his brother, one would surely expect to hear a native Liverpool accent. The reply he gave has been described as 'convoluted.' He could have responded with something like 'It's not true,' but instead made a statement whose clear untruth was evident to everyone in the room, i.e. that

---

22 But his family picture-album 'Remember' 1992 is subtitled, 'the recollections and photographs of Michael McCartney.'
23 Reeve *Turn me on Dead Man* pp.139-142.

Glimpses of Paul

Chris Glen was propounding the currently-prevalent PID theory in order to make money. Years later, when his family memoir *The Macs* (1981) describes the event, it has changed somewhat:

> I pointed out that apart from it being too silly to waste valuable air time for me, the *Scaffold* and the American public, it was also a gigantic, well-planned hoax [by whom?], based on groundless innuendo and straight lies [by whom?], but most of all how could you, Mr. DJ, condone, or live with, the precise moment in time when millions of young loving trusting teenagers heard that their biggest pop hero was ... dead! (It was as though the Kennedy and Martin Luther King murders were a hoax!)

That creative recollection - penned before a video of the original interview went up onto the Web - implied, as one conspiracy theorist concluded: "he is saying that his brother's death is a hoax in the same manner as the King and Kennedy murders were a hoax. Their murders are fact and Paul's death (murder) is a fact."[24] Whether or not Mike McGear intended to express that view, he in fact has. His reply, and his later written account of it, are opaque like some gnostic text, and differ totally one from the other.

Paul wrote an Introduction to Lennon's *In his own Write* which appeared alas posthumously. We can still chuckle over what the *Disc and Music Echo*[25] called his 'classy Introduction:'

> Is he deep? Is he arty, with it, or cultured? There are bound to be thickheads who will wonder why some of it doesn't make sense, and others who will search for hidden meanings...

Paul was an all-rounder with no formal training, who could play bass and rhythm guitar, the piano, trumpet and drums – though, there is room for debate as to how good he was on the piano as he recorded nothing on it. Modern popular music has the straight-from-the-heart quality of not using a written score. He was a perfectionist and he knew it.

As he told *Disc* a couple of months before he passed away: 'If is its possible, I'd like us to be remembered when we are dead, as four people who made music that stood up to being remembered.'[26] Paul could stand up before an audience of fifty thousand without a tremor, because he knew there was nothing he loved more than his Art.

How do people remember him? 'Anonymous' found, writing on the *Plastic Macca* site, that he was remembered for –

---

24 Guest on 'Mike McCartney's book', invanddis proboards.
25 Oct 29 1977 p.7 'LENNON is his own write again'
26 *Disc and Music Echo,* interview, 11.6.66

135

his LOVE,
his HEART,
his KINDNESS,
his GENTLENESS,
his COMPASSION,
his EMPATHY,
his GENIUS,
his TALENT,
his GENTILITY,
his RESPECTFULNESS,
his GENEROSITY,
his BRILLIANCE,
his UNIQUENESS,
his CREATIVITY,
his WISDOM,
his ABILITY TO BE A FANTASTIC SHOWMAN,
his INCREDIBLE BEAUTY (INSIDE AND OUT),
his APPRECIATION FOR LIFE,
his HUMBLENESS,
his FAITH,
his DRIVE,
his DEDICATION,
his SACRIFICES,
his WORK ETHIC,
his INCREDIBLE ABILITY TO MOVE THE SOUL,
his LAUGH,
his SMILE,
his BEAUTIFUL EYES,
his VOICE,
his YOUTHFUL ENTHUSIASM,
his OPTIMISM,
his SINCERITY,
his SOUL,
his VISION,
his UNMATCHABLE SPIRIT,
his INSATIABLE NEED FOR PERFECTION,
his DESIRE TO BRING JOY AND HAPPINESS TO OTHERS,
his PERSISTENCE,
his STRENGTH,
and his COURAGE.

One thing that could be added to that list, I'd say, is the very rare trait, of his lacking any desire to cause harm to another.

Clue-Bearing Albums

Well, here's another clue for y'all
                    Lennon, *Glass Onion* 1968

There are eight *clue-bearing albums* made by the Beatles, three of which have clues only on their covers, here shown in italics.

	Released
The Butcher Album	June '66
Golden Oldies [1]	December '66
Sgt Pepper	June '67
The Magical Mystery Tour	November '67
The White Album	November '68
Abbey Road	September '69
Let it Be	May '70
The Beatles/ 1967-70 ('Blue' album).	April '73

Online images of these covers are alas of low resolution, for legal reasons, and so may not be very helpful in evaluating the clues. You need the vinyl covers! Apart from a few lucky old-timers this means modern album re-issues, to see the 'clues.'[2] So I hope the following discussion won't be too frustrating.

The so-called 'Butcher's album', otherwise known as *The Beatles Yesterday and Today*, was produced in the USA in June '66. A decapitated head and bloody arms, broken dolls and butcher's meat, hang around the lads wearing white coats. Two decapitated dolls both sit on Paul's shoulders. Clues such as these which turn up *before* the crash are called 'pre-clues'. It is my personal view that not one of the shady characters on this hideous cover are actually the Fab Four: but not many agree with me on this matter.

---

[1] Some believe that the titles of songs selected on this album are pertinent: *Drive my Car, I'm Only Sleeping, Yesterday* ('I'm not half the man I used to be') *Act Naturally* and *Nowhere Man.* Many of them could hardly be called 'oldies' by December 1966.
[2] *Yellow Submarine* released in January '69, has not here been included.

After protests this cover was soon recalled and replaced by a more innocuous design, of three Beatles gathered around a trunk and Paul inside it, which PID-ers felt indicated that he was being packed away! It may not be clear why this album was allowed to rip off unpublished tracks from the brilliant *Revolver* album.

Images of the *Butcher's* cover appeared in the June issue of *Disc and Music Echo,* just when Paul was giving some interviews saying how the Band eschewed gimmicks, leading to angry readers' comments and denunciations. Paul's interviews were in two issues, the 11th and 18th of June, with the Butcher's cover featuring in the 3rd and 11th issues, and it's as if the two went in parallel without any interaction, except by the nauseated fans.

On the 18th, Paul was explaining to *Melody Maker* about the forthcoming *Revolver* album: 'Its sort of verging on the electronic. When I tell friends that the LP has a different sound, they never believe me. But when I play it to them, they say "this is like nothing we've ever heard before."' The album was almost finished: 'I'm just writing one more number.' Paul added, 'There are sounds that nobody has done yet. I mean nobody,...ever.' On June 18th they also appeared on Top of the Pops, virtually their first public appearance of '66.

The week after featured a *Melody Maker* interview with George in a serious mood: 'I've increasingly become aware that there are other things in life than being a Beatle. I'm not fed up with being a Beatle, far from it, but I am fed up with all the trivial things that go with it.' Of photographs, 'I suppose I have consciously been backing away from this side of Beatle life. In fact, it wouldn't worry me at all if nobody ever took my photograph again. He expressed optimism about their music: 'Musically, we're only just starting.' I'm just suggesting (I may be wrong) that these don't sound like the comments of young men who have just posed for the obscene *Butcher's Album* photo-shoot.

Such 'pre-clues' appearing before the event had happened remind us of Goethe's saying, 'Coming events cast their shadow before;' or as the seer lady tells Neo in *The Matrix,* 'That's really gonna do your noodle in.' If you feel events are compelling you to believe in a predestination and intention to the death of Paul McCartney - that it was more than just a tragic accident - then you may feel obliged to view this album cover as part of such an intent. The Empire is supposed to announce in advance what it intends to do, isn't it?

Six months later, clues a-plenty were appearing on the *Golden Oldies* album. On its front cover there reclined a long, tall stranger, a lover of music but no Beatle, the *newcomer.* We are puzzled to see him wearing women's shoes as if he has been though some strange transformation. To the left the Fab

Four gather round an old, vintage car, beside which the words are written on the wall 'To the original,' somewhat covered up. Three of them are gathered round while one of them is in the car, about to drive off. The one behind the car lifts off his hat as if saying farewell.

That same car is then seen in the background driving with its lights on (i.e., at night) and coming off the road, as if out of control, maybe approaching the head of the reclining stranger. The back cover consists of a photo of the Four, with Paul in the background having a shirt painted totally black (He usually wore white shirts). But what is the uncanny mist of 'ectoplasm' seething around his arms, as if he were an apparition? He lurks in the background, appearing at a bit of a distance from the others.

The Sgt Pepper Album Cover

Sgt Pepper had a burial scene on its cover, with dark, newly-dug earth in its foreground. A resurrection theme is here being portrayed. The Swinging Sixties got the message without knowing what it was about. Its front, centre and back are drenched in primary red colours, sometimes said to represent the blood of Paul, or maybe the colour of the resurrection mantle of the Risen One, as shown in old paintings.

At the centre, impeccably costumed in the regalia of a turn-of-the-century brass band, we have the Fab Four. Paul's father Jim had played a tuba in his local Territorial Army band, also at a tobacco factory brass band where he worked in Liverpool; as too his father before him had played in a brass band. Father Jim used to take his two sons to local brass band concerts; then after their mother Mary›s death he bought Paul a nickel-plated trumpet as a birthday present. These very instruments are here shown, to honour Paul's musical family.

This cover shows the Beatles mysteriously assuming a new identity, laying to rest their earlier image. The name being buried 'BEATLES' was written in flowers. *Hyacinthus* was a slain Greek deity, so the hyacinth flower was somewhat associated with death. These flowers spelt out that name – or, as some saw it, BE AT LES$_o$ 'Leso' being, or so rumour had it, the mystery Greek island where Paul was buried.

The old Beatles' band was shown by the group of waxwork statues from Madam Tussauds. The head of Paul is here faithfully depicted as fairly round in shape, whereas Faul - dazzlingly portrayed in the centre - has a more elongated head; plus he is also shown a few inches taller than Lennon, whereas in the waxworks group they have the same height.

The ultimate clue, the drumskin, was said in the album to have been designed by 'Joe Ephgrave,' evidently a fictional character.[3] After all, Jos*eph Eph*grave hardly sounds like a real name does it? No such person has ever been heard of, despite the unprecedented interest in the album cover - not even when one of the two original drumskin designs was auctioned at Christie's in 2008 for over a million dollars.

Some saw Paul's crashed Aston-Martin car depicted (though very small) on the right leg of the child-actress Shirley Temple, shown to the far-right. She is covered in blood, especially the bloody glove to her left worn by the woman on whose lap she sits. Alistair Crowley appears at the top left and also as we'll see later, on the far-right just beneath Bob Dylan, lurking only partly visible behind the statuesque Diana Dors.

It was around the time of *Sgt Pepper* that 'Paul' switched from using a Hoffner bass to a Rickenbacher. Paul had been famous for using that Hoffner during the touring years. He still used it in the spring of '66 during the 'Paperback writer' promo film. His Hoffner bass had been strung to be left-handed, and this is said to be depicted in the yellow flowers on the grave. We can discern within this guitar shape, the letters 'PAUL?' in the flowers, though only the top part of the first two letters may be visible. The strings of the guitar are shown by three fine wooden sticks, signifying the three remaining Beatles.

Above the yellow guitar shape and amongst the red hyacinths is placed Paul's rugby trophy from his school days, such that its vertical structure may here resemble the letter 'I': placed in-between the L and E, it enables us to read 'LIES,' and as that is directly above 'Paul,' it reads 'LIES PAUL' or 'Paul lies' here. The Beatles had to lie about Paul. He lies there, and they lied about him - the layered Beatle-meanings.

Just behind and above Faul on the front cover we glimpse the American novelist Stephen Crane. His *The Open Boat* featured a group of four fishermen, where one died and the others had to carry on as if nothing had happened. A hand in front of this character is held over Faul's head by a comic actor.

Three Beatles face the camera at different angles whereas Paul is facing us straight on maybe as if he were being propped up by Ringo and George. He holds a black *cor anglaise* wooden instrument, while the others hold gleaming instruments of brass. He is the only one with a hand over his head—a symbol some have suggested of death representing the hand of a religious leader who blesses the body before it's interned, or maybe it is more about the Band's

---

3 George Martin fibbed that Joe Ephgrave was a 'fairground artist': *Making of Sgt Pepper*, Martin, p116.

Clue-Bearing Albums

respect for the being or being-ness of Paul somehow being with Faul. We compare that with subsequent such images, in MMT and *Yellow Submarine:*

Figures: 'Paul' shown with hand over his head on (1) *Sgt Pepper* cover, (2) Scene of rejoicing in MMT (with Mal Evans beside him, putting his hand above) and (3) in the *Yellow Submarine* film, with Lennon putting hand above.

No other Beatle is ever shown with a hand over his head anywhere in *Magical Mystery Tour* or, for that matter, on any other Beatles album

To the right we see the small child-actress Shirley Temple, the only figure appearing thrice on this album cover. On the left she is barely visible just below Marlon Brando. The line here drawn in black goes though the tops of the heads of the three Shirley Temples and through Faul's heart.[4] At right-angles to this is a line made by the musical instrument held by Faul, a cor anglais, and that is passing through the centre of the drum-skin. 'Cor anglais' means, we might reasonably say, 'English heart'.

Then we draw a line from the top of Jung's head to the same

---

4 Diagram drawn by 'Jarface,' in 'Solution to Sgt Pepper Enigma', Invanddis.

position in the sculpture on the ground (who might be Lawrence of Arabia, no-one is sure) which likewise passes through Faul's heart. Thus a structure begins to appear focussed as it were upon the centre of the drumskin and the position of Faul's heart. The 'Shirley Temple' line we started off with goes through the heads of the four old Beatles and also touches the head of Sonny Liston the boxing champ on the far-left. He is dressed in regal gold attire and we may here take his name as Sun-Lion, Son(ny) Li(st)on.

Let's quote here the *Memoirs of Billy Shears*:

> Notice the symmetry on the Sgt Pepper's cover. All of it passes right through me, representing the departed Paul. Seeing him as me, consider how all is centred in his heart. All is in the heart of Paul. Seeing it this way, get out your compass and square to see how everything lines up through me, the new queen or king of the game ...
>
> Everything crosses through Paul's heart – which is represented by my own heart. For example, use a square or other straight edge to see that the top of all three of the heads of Shirley Temple form a line right through my heart.(p.97)

Of the Carl Jung figure, 'From the shadow of his glasses that rest on his forehead, it looks as though he has a third eye. A ray from his third eye through my heart points to the third eye on a statue from John's house.'...

Here is an image of these criss-cross lines that went up on the Invanddis. proboard site in March 2009, explaining the mystical meaning of the cover. That is six months before the above words were published. It has the central cross, and we can also see how a line from Jung's forehead would go down through Faul's heart to the forehead of the stone statue.

The *Memoirs* comment on the red slippers of the Shirley Temple doll on the right echoing the blood dripping from her clothes, and the bloody driving

Clue-Bearing Albums

glove. This theme is said to connect with the wizard of Oz story. W.C.Fields, who was the original actor in the 1939 version of the classic Wizard of Oz film, can be seen on the top row with a yellow hat.

On the lap of this 'bleeding doll' we see a white car, said to be Paul's white Aston-Martin he crashed in. A line from that goes to Oscar Wilde: 'wild car.' You get the general idea. A brilliant exposition of the Sgt Pepper 'hidden structure' was given on a PID site, then discussed and explained a mere six months later in the *Memoirs of Billy Shears.*

They are different enough that it does not look as if one had copied from the other: the *Memoirs* for example do not describe that line made by the Cor anglais instrument held by Faul, through the drum centre - tilted at twelve degrees to the vertical - as being at right-angles to the major 'Shirley-Temple' line.

The *Sgt Pepper* centrefold shows the famous face which is a *composite image* of Paul and Faul, and that was centrally important in enabling the world to accept the identity-swap. It blurred the differences, in a happy portrait that blended the two identities. The figure had 'OPD' stitched onto his right armband, which English readers took as 'Officially Pronounced Dead.' Faul here told a story about the Ontario Police Department in Canada. Somebody just gave it to him, he said...

The new Fab Four wear saches on the right-hand side of their chests - whereas on the blood-red back cover this appears as being mirror-reversed. While Faul strangely has his back to the audience, as if no longer part of the group, the others are earing the sashes on their left chest, which is military dress code at a funeral.

Abbey Road and Let it Be

Most of *Let It Be* was recorded in January 1969, before the recording and release of the album *Abbey Road.* For this reason, some have argued that *Abbey Road* should be considered the group's final album and *Let It Be* the penultimate. Does this really matter?

On the famous album cover of Abbey road, the Beetle car parked at the side of the road has a number-plate which says '28if.' Was that the age Paul McCartney would have been 'if' he were still alive, or was one year out, as he would then have been only 27? Some say that, had the band not broken up, the Abbey Road album would have appeared a year later when this 'clue' would have been correct.

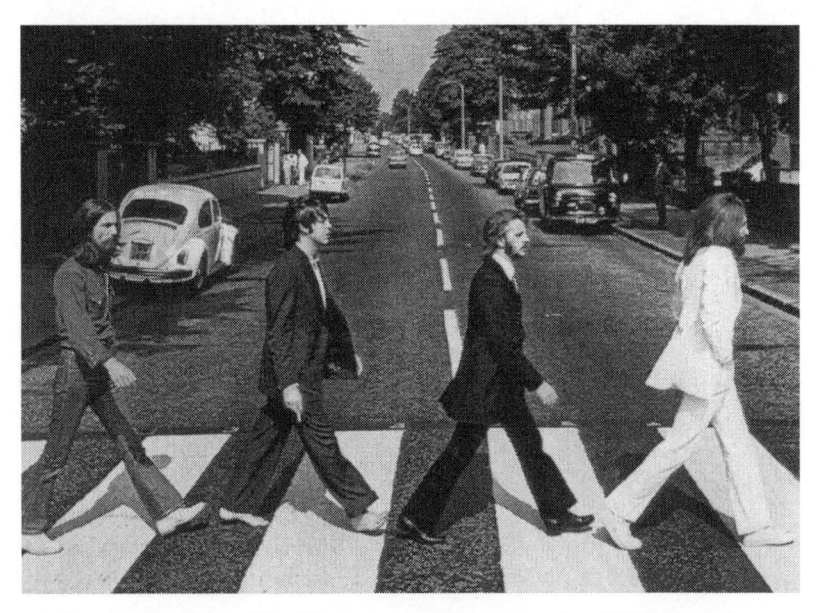

Here is the view of Fred Labour, a PID pioneer, in a TV interview:

A. Well, the license plate says 28 IF, and if Paul McCartney were alive today, he would be in his 28th year of existence.
Q. In other words, he would be 27, looking toward his 28th birthday?
A. That's correct. That's correct.[5]

Abbey Road remains the Beatles best-selling album. Its cover shows what is famously seen to be, a funeral procession. Each of the Four represent the crucial participants in a funeral: the minister, the undertaker, the corpse and the grave digger. Lennon dressed all in white signifies the minister, Ringo in black is the undertaker, George wearing denims is the gravedigger while Faul barefoot and out of step with the others represents the corpse.

Today that Abbey Road zebra crossing is quite worn out and seems to have a permanent crowd of Japanese tourists a-buzzing around it.

The *Let it Be* cover had 'Paul' photographed differently from the others. The Four were shown, three against white backgrounds while Faul was portrayed against a blood-red background. He had lots of black hair, much darker than Paul's, making the two dominant colours for Faul's photo red and black.

---

5 Brian Moriarty, 'Who Buried Paul?' San Jose convention 1999.

The Beatles' Book

The official fanzine *Beatles' Book* monthly kept going right through 1966 as if nothing had happened, as likewise it did for January '67, using old pictures of Paul. Then, in February 1967, it weirdly started drawing a moustache onto Paul's face. It was the old and real Paul, but they added a moustache! It also contained a one-paragraph denial of any accident:

FALSE RUMOUR

"The seventh of January was very icy, with dangerous conditions on the M1 motorway linking London with the midlands, and towards the end of the day, a rumour swept London that Paul McCartney had been killed in a car crash on the M1. But of course, there was absolutely no truth in it at all, as the Beatles' press officer found out when he telephoned Paul's St. Johns Wood home, and was answered by Paul himself ..."

This reminds one of the journalist's motto "Never believe anything until it has been officially denied."

On the next page, a paradoxical image was displayed, of George shaving, showing a 'moustache' present in the mirror but not on the real George. This is a clue, made by people who may not have liked deception but have abruptly been forced into it.

Not until the April edition do we discern the point of the false-moustaches, when the new smart-looking Faul is abruptly introduced, with a real moustache. The April issue had to be quite diplomatic, explaining why there have been no more tours but also reassuring fans that the next album 'should contain the best Beatles songs ever.' Thus gradually did the official Beatle 'zine accustom its readers to the vanishing of their darling Paul.

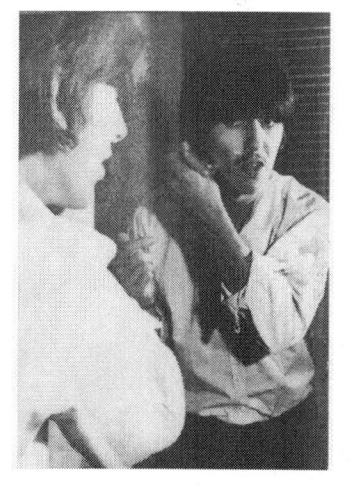

Post-Beatle Faul albums

When the magic had gone and the Beatles were history, Faul with help from his wife Linda started to produce some rather tuneless songs. These strain our credulity that it was the same singer as before. Dave Barry in his *Book of Worst Songs* has expressed the baffling dilemma. He had asked listeners to write in with their 'worst song' vote and received a huge mailbag, so he wrote a little book on the subject:

> *There are a lot more bad songs, but in my opinion one of the worst, when you consider who wrote it, is 'Silly Love songs' by Paul McCartney because it ... it ... how do I find the words .. it just sucks.[6] And so does 'My love,' wherein Paul, apparently too busy to write actual words, goes with:*

> *wo wo wo wo*
> *Wo wo wo wo*
> *My love does it good!*

> *The big question is: What happened to Paul? Did his brain get taken over by aliens from the planet Twinkie? I mean, he was a Beatle, for goshsakes, a certified genius, a man who wrote dozens of truly great songs, including such butt-kicking rockers as 'I'm Down,' and then for some mysterious reason he began cranking out songs like, 'Uncle Albert/Admiral Halsey,' 'Listen to what the Man Said,' and 'Let 'Em In,' which expresses this powerful and universal theme:*

> *Someone's knockin' at the door*
> *Somebody's ringin' the bell*
> *Someone's knockin' at the door*
> *Somebody's ringin' the bell*
> *Do me a favour, open the door*
> *And let 'em in[7]*

That well sums up the situation. Has not Dave Barry intuited that two different people were here involved?

Like a mask when it slips, Faul's face can go badly wrong: while he was singing 'Silly Love songs' it produced three double chins (see 1976 concert with *Wings*, at 1:50).

.

---

6 But, NB, this *Wings* hit held the Number One position for five weeks in the US charts, being the biggest US chart hit of his post-Beatle career.
7 The song alludes to Faul's alleged family members: 'Sister Suzie, Brother John, Martin Luther, Phil And Don, Brother Michael, Auntie Gin.'

Doom of Lennon

If such a replacement had occurred, people say to me incredulously, would not John Lennon have spoken out about it, as he became in later years bitter and angry towards Faul? However, after the PID story broke in '69, Lennon was the person who would categorically deny all of the 'clues;' after which he was 'locked in' to the drama, since it would hardly have been possible for him to deny all of his earlier denials.

Owing to Lennon's fearless reputation as the truth-sayer - one who would challenge heaven and earth with his fearless words - people therefore wanted to hear his view more than anyone else's, concerning the strange rumour. Was there anything in it? No, he replied, very simply, and would dismiss every 'clue'. Why, he even claimed to baffled fans, he had said 'cranberry sauce' at the end of Strawberry Fields. Why would he have said that?

As diverse 'clues' were alluded to, he kept replying that, no, they didn't mean anything. This may have had a bad effect upon his psyche, but he really had no option: precisely that honesty-of-soul which people admired in him compelled him to insert the clues, but alas! He then had to deny them all: which left him emotionally rather paralysed. You can listen to him denying that the clues meant anything on the Rotten Apple video 72 – although, he does at one point admit 'It was too far-out for any of us to have thought of it.'

The remaining Beatles gave their names to the newcomer: first he was Billy Shears, then 'Beatle Bill' and 'Faul', and finally 'Boogaloo' – four names! The first of these we associate with glowing enthusiasm, when the good times were a-rolling, the second and third indicate a degree of sarcasm and distress, while the third was an outright insult.

Let's start off with a New York domestic scene (RA 13, at 0:50-1:10) in 1971, while the *Imagine* album was being composed. It's being filmed. A dapper-looking Lennon and a hairy George were being served tea by Yoko Ono.

John "This is actually a Beatle wife, fixing the tea for one of the Fab Four ex-Beatles."
George "Fab three,
John "Fab three"
George "I see Beatle Bill making a pig of himself."
John "Not doing so well these days is he, Beatle Bill?"
George "Well,, he's number five in Sweden."
John "Oh in Sweden, that's it."
John then gives a knowing-wink to the camera.

George is here unfairly claiming that Faul was not fab or less so than the other three: we leave it to futurity to decide, whether that was the case. The film here made was called *Gimme some truth* and the above excerpt appears just before the scathing song 'How do you Sleep?' in which terrible accusations were levelled against Faul.

That song was recorded in July of 1971. It displays the condition of moral and spiritual bankuptcy to which Lennon had sunk, when he hissed his unfair accusations against Faul. In December 1970 his song 'God' had appeared, in which he really threw all of his toys out of the pram, attaining a final state of nihilistic solipsism. Indeed we may here quote from his biographer Mr Albert Goldman:

'But what John Lennon presents as his reborn self is merely his primalled-out self, that sad little boy, destined not many years hence to retire to his bedroom, where, with the aid of his drugs and his toys, he will dream away the rest of his life. Having reduced the world and himself through the irresistible power of his negativity to his solipsistic essence, John Lennon is obliged to lay down his Magical Minstrel's wand and confess that he can no longer lead his people because he no longer knows where he or they are going.'[1]

In 'How do you Sleep?' Lennon starts off by saying that Faul is *not* who he appears to be, because somehow Paul has died:

---

1 Goldman, *The Lives of John Lennon*, p.395.

> You better see right through that mother's eyes. Those freaks
> was right when they said you was dead.

This is generally read as alluding to some notional artistic death. Then, as if Faul had done something terribly wrong, the accusation is hurled:

> How do you sleep?
> How do you sleep at night?

He is surely talking about himself here, as becomes evident in the next line:

> Jump when your momma tell you anything

Lennon allowed himself to become greatly controlled by Ms Ono, which condition he needed to gain a sense of security. (He had addressed her as 'Mother Superior' on his anti-love song *Happiness is a Warm Gun* on the 'White Album') A couple of years later in 1973 Lennon admitted: 'I'm talking about myself in that song, I just know it.'[2]

Different 'yous' are here alluded to:

> The only thing you done was *Yesterday*
> And since you've gone you're just another day

Here it's the old Paul who is being accused, that he did nothing but compose *Yesterday* and then '*since you've gone*' it's just another day. Lennon is thus saying that the old Paul has gone and the new one is somehow deceptive or not real. What more could he have said?

He finally denounces Faul's music:

> The sound you make is muzak to my ears
> You must have learned something in all those years

George Harrison played guitar suggesting that he was in agreement over the song's sentiments. (*Rolling Stone's* review of the album called this song "horrifying and indefensible") The two of them should have been asked: if Paul's music sounded like Muzak to their ears, then where on Earth did the Beatle sound come from?' Two years later, Lennon composed the satirical 'I'm the Greatest' for Ringo to sing, which as we've seen reiterates the name Billy Shears.

---

2 Doggett, *You Never Give me your Money*, p.170: Crawdaddy interview Nov. '73.

George alluded to 'Faul' twice[3] in an interview he gave after John's death. Asked why the three remaining Beatles didn't get on, he alluded to 'The personal problem Faul had...' and explained, 'as soon as we do that, Faul will be free of any problem he may have..' George appears as quite stressed out by ongoing financial haggles and as an honest man cannot bring himself to say 'Paul' any more.

Antithesis

Is there any definite, firm proof that Paul McCartney was replaced? If that exists, then here it is. There is a mysterious principle of balance in the universe whereby light and darkness, joy and sorrow, are intertwined. After the wonderful glory of the Beatles music, those chords of youthful harmony, whereby the band founded by John Lennon brought happiness to the world, he then turned to a total antithesis, one which negated everything Paul McCartney had stood for: of an atonal, infernal racket; this being I suggest a proof of his passing.

Sonic torture is nowadays used in Guantanamo Bay, which involves playing Yoko Ono records to captives. Apparently, any of her records will do. That must be a dire torture: waterboarding is bad enough, but being forced to listen to Ms Ono! One may here be reminded of comments following her solo performance at a 1975 Japanese peace festival, where critics compared the sound of her voice to "a drunk throwing up in the gutter" and "the stomach pumping of a suicide attempt."[4]

Or, to comments made after her performance at the 2014 Glastonbury Festival: 'like a hyena dying on-stage,' 'like a goat with a sore throat,' 'You've got to be kidding, PLEASE tell me this is a joke,' and 'I would rather have my testicles tied to a moving vehicle than listen to this talentless crap ever again,' or 'This has got to be the WORST thing I've ever heard in my life' - and so forth. Her performance was soon voted the 'worst live performance ever'. At 81 years she had lost none of her ability to inflict real pain.

Lennon insisted on bringing her into the Apple studio and the others had to put up with her sitting around, or lying on a bed in the studio, distracting them, and occasionally doing her screeching. 'Revolution 9' by Ono and Lennon, allegedly an 'avant-garde' sound, consistently voted the worst

---

3 The video is entitled 'Paul McCartney Dead' uploaded 27.6.12, with George being interviewed on Ray Martin's "The Midday Show", 10.2.88. Some claim that the soundtrack has been edited however as blogger Rich Ryan commented, George's lips don't appear to come together when the 'f' sound is made, as they would have had to for a 'p' sound.
4 Goldman, p.536.

Beatles track, was recorded in June 1968 and put onto the *White Album* despite protests by the other three.

The 'avant garde music' made by Lennon and Ms Ono was described by Rolling Stone as sounding 'like a severely retarded child being tortured.' Our sympathies are with George when he found himself driven out of the Beatles' recording studio because 'Yoko's just screaming, doing her screeching number.'[5] What the hell was she doing in the studio anyway? It gave him a headache and he went home and composed 'Wah-Wah' (on All Things Must Pass), sadly alluding to how much Lennon used to mean to him, in terms of his whole life, and what things had now come to. If you really want to hear Ms Ono doing her stuff, screaming like a banshee, checkout the Rolling Stones Rock and Roll Circus of December 1966.

In 1965 she had starred in the film, Satan's Bed, as a Japanese mail-order bride who came to the U.S. as the fianceé of a drug-smuggling government agent. A succession of homicidal perverts rape and kill their way through the film, with Ms Ono being subject to frequent nonconsensual sexual attentions of a portly, greasy-looking fellow. The films she made like 'Fly' about the life-cycle of a fly and 'Bottoms' and 'Up your Legs Forever' have a generally sub-human character.

It is often said that John and Yoko met on the 9th of November, 1966, eg that is the date given by Brown in his Beatle-Bio The Love you Make (p83), although it may have been a day or two earlier (at the Indica gallery). That date has been the most frequently-inferred from the Sgt Pepper drumskin (See chapter 8) with its eerie mirror-image HE * DIE code.

Also on that date, Brown has Epstein make a statement to the effect that no future bookings are being accepted by the Band, reported the next day in the papers – almost but not quite the same as saying they will never perform again in public. He gives those dated with no allusion to the Sgt Pepper drumskin! People have wondered whether there was some sort of doom or death omen on that date?

A year after their meeting, the 'Two Virgins' album cover appeared. Here were two people, both married to others and both with children in those marriages, appearing totally naked together. Ms Ono was then three months pregnant. Could Lennon not even have waited for his divorce from Cynthia to go through before appearing thus? We admire Neil Aspinall for doing his best to stop it: 'I don't like it, and Paul doesn't like it, and none of the others are going to like it, and I don't care what the f*** [John] says, I don't want

---

5 A February 1977 *Crawdaddy* interview with George Harrisson: Patterson, *The Walrus Was Paul* p.126.

it coming out,' (Doggett p.54) however the contract allowed Lennon to push it through. The atonal sounds in the album resembled the wailing of the souls of the damned. The album generated a level of public nausea which was, as Lennon said, the reason for the couple deciding to leave England and going to New York. Many balloons were released and drifted over London in July, 1968 from 'John and Yoko' which invited a message to be sent back, and back came the messages of anger and nausea. It would have been out of the question for such a disruption of the Band to have happened, while Paul was alive. It was a negation of everything he had stood for, a proof of his passing.

Instant Karma

In 1970, Lennon's Instant Karma became the first solo single by a member of the band to sell a million copies.

> Instant Karma's gonna get you
> Gonna knock you right on the head
> You better get yourself together
> Pretty soon you're gonna be dead

In this song, Lennon may be describing what he feels his fate to be, and how afterwards his name will shine on, like a star: 'We all shine on, like the Sun and Moon and stars.' In the video Ms Ono quietly sits and knits, like one of the Fates, she looks after the *Moira* of his fate.

Lennon believed he would die a violent death owing to his violent past, it was his 'karmic destiny.'[6] He may have caused the death of his best friend Stuart Sutcliffe in a vicious fight[7] - part of his tough rocker image (He was 'Ron Nasty' in the Ruttles' spoof of the Beatles).

Lennon composed his album Imagine in 1971, and soon after left England for New York. An old friend of his remarked, 'Once John had got involved with Yoko One, apart from Imagine, John Lennon to me, the real John Lennon, died, the creative genius was finished, he became Lennon Ono...'[8] We may agree with the fan who wrote: 'His entire legacy – that is what he will forever

---

6 Ibid, p107.
7 Albert Goldman, *The lives of John Lennon,* p.119: Story told by Lennon, about him beating up Stuart Sutcliffe, and kicking him in the temple with his pointed shoes, where he later on developed a brain tumour; Goldman is unsure whether to believe it, but argues that Lennon himself told that story, eg to Yoko Ono. For beating up an English sailor in Hamburg, with help from drummer Pete Best, to rob his wallet, see p.106. For peeing over nuns from a balcony on a Sunday morning in Hamburg, see p.120; Philip Norman, *Shout! The Beatles in Their Generation*, p. 152.
8 Video The Real John Lennon 2000 (Full documentary), Bill Harry a college friend, at 45 mins.

be remembered for – lies basically with what he created from 1962 (The Beatles' first single) through 1971 (release of Imagine). Everything thereafter was devoid of the innovation, creativity, wit, charm and extraordinary talent that he evinced during his unbelievably fertile younger years. Photos of John during the last years of his life depict an almost-cadaverous, hollow-eyed wastrel -- hardly the picture of someone who was "rejuvenated" by living in America.'[9]

1974 *Scared.*

From album *Walls and Bridges* by John Lennon, released on September 1974:

>*I'm scared, I'm scared, I'm scared*
>*I'm scared, so scared*
>*I'm scared, I'm scared, I'm scared*
>*As the years roll away*
>*And that I paid the price*
>*And the straws slip away*
>*You don't have to suffer*
>*It is what it is.*
>
>*No bell book or candle*
>*Can get you out of this, oh no!*
>*I'm scarred, I'm scarred, I'm scarred*
>*I'm scarred, uh huh*
>*I'm scarred, I'm scarred, I'm scarred*
>**Every day of my life**
>**I just manage to survive**
>**I just wanna stay alive**
>*You don't have to worry*
>*In heaven or hell*
>*Just dance to the music*
>*You do it so well, well, well!*
>
>**Hatred and jealousy, gonna be the death of me**
>*I guess I knew it right from the start*
>*Sing out about love and peace*
>**Do not wanna see the red raw meat**
>**The green-eyed goddamn straight from your heart**
>*I'm tired, I'm tired, I'm tired*
>*Of being so alone*

---

[9] Palash Ghosh, in *International Business Times* 8.12.11: 'John Lennon died long before his official passing.'

No place to call my own
Like a rollin' 'stone

Lennon here seems scared as if some voodoo curse were chasing him. Is there some price he has to pay? He alludes to the Catholic Church's excommunication ritual, cursing by Bell, Book and Candle; as if something demonic were out to get him and rip him apart!

'Do not wanna see the red raw meat / the green eyed goddam straight from your heart / I'm tired, I'm tired, I'm tired...' Is he suffering from having abandoned his wife, child and country: '... so alone / No place to call my own / Like a rolling stone'? Would a home have protected him, from whatever it is that is coming to get him? Paul's death was no doubt still preying on his mind.

He had then been living on the 7th floor of the Dakota building in New York[10]: in the *same apartment* where the *Rosemary's Baby* horror-film classic by Polanski was shot (he knew Roman Polanski). The Dakota was a Gothic-looking New York building where a lot of eminent people had lived. In 1973 when Yoko Ono and Lennon were married, and were *planning* to have a baby together, they *chose* to move into that same flat where ...

On October 9 1975 Ms Ono was *cut open* so a caesarean birth could take place of her child one month early on Lennon's birthday, her voodoo belief being that thereby the son would inherit his father's *manas* or spirit-power when he died. After such dirty magic it's understandable that Lennon should feel apprehensive. You don't need a crystal ball to see why he could feel in trouble – if you believe in all that stuff.

Shortly before his violent death in 1980, he sung or rather croaked '*Help me to Help Myself*' -

Well, I tried so hard to stay alive,
But the angel of destruction keeps on houndin' me all around

These awful words were kept a secret from his fans for twenty years, only released on the 2000 *Double Fantasy* remastered album (The original had emerged three weeks before his murder in 1980). It's as if Lennon were searching for a way out of some fatal pact.

Ms Ono had been given complete charge of his finances so his death was

---

10 Over that summer he was estranged from Ms Ono: who instructed him to have an affair with her assistant Mae Pang as she needed go get him out of her hair for a bit, which he did (Oct '73). Eventually Ms Ono was running out of money for her $5,000 a week heroin habit and had to take him back again (February '75): Goldman, *Lives of John Lennon*, pp.456, 12.

no problem to her, in fact it was rather convenient. She stopped Lennon's English family from coming to the funeral. She almost managed to disinherit his son Julian from the will. Lennon's death enabled her to emerge from under his 'shadow.'

She spliced tracks of Lennon's voice onto the B-side of her next album, i.e. she exploited his death to promote it; nor did she shirk from putting an image of Lennon's broken, bloodstained glasses on the front cover of her next album. Within a few months of the death, Ms Ono was being seen out with her new lover, who had moved in. They remained living in that same flat.

There was a light/darkness polarity between Paul McCartney and Lennon, maybe the secret of their creativity: Paul didn't really have a 'dark side' that one knows of, but Lennon did.

The Disclosure Process

Neil Aspinall set up the company *Standby Films,* and Apple paid it up to £500,000 per annum from the mid-nineties to produce the *Anthology* project,[1] which emerged in 1996. It may have started way back in in 1970 when the long-time Apple Corps manager Aspinall had compiled footage from various sources around the world of concert, interview and television appearances, from which he assembled a 90 minute feature film tentatively entitled *The Long and Winding Road* completed in 1971.

Years later that saw the light of day as the *Anthology* project. Some surmise that he became frustrated with McCartney's constant attempts to re-write history and to obscure the immense contributions from people like Mal Evans and Aspinall himself and so, once the McCartney approved *Anthology* was finally released, he set about trying to get the hidden truth into the public domain via agents such as Iamaphoney. Another version is, that he was uneasy about the staggering deception perpetrated upon the world, however good the motives, and wished before he departed from this world to do something about it.

In 2006 'Iamaphoney' appeared, as an insider who had access to a mass of archive material some quite private. We don't know who he was, but it was surmised that he could be Neil Aspinall, Sir Paul or the son of George Martin. The *Rotten Apple* series featured continually fragmented, unconnected images. There is an old thread about the *Rotten Apple* series which first appeared in 2006, on 'invandis.proboards.com' as 'The Rotten Apple 2', which conveys the sense of excitement of these first disclosures. Somebody called 'Bill' commented:

Glad you guys likes it...
There is so much more on its way...
trying to get some investers to help me out.

---

[1] Peter Doggett, *You Never Give me Your Money, The Battle for the Soul of the Beatles,* 2009, p.316.

...hopefully it will be the big revelation film,
The film that tells the true, and the final answer from the dead man himself

Phew, who's bothered about spelling with a message like that? No wonder that thread went up to 238 pages and over five thousand posts!

On the web, an avatar called 'Apollo' (or, 'Apollo C. Vermouth') belonged to a highly-regarded PID-investigator who was some sort of insider - alleged in certain quarters to have been Neil Aspinall. The concept of 'disclosure' involves the idea that key insiders in their last years of life wanted to help the truth to emerge.[2] Aspinall had run *Apple Corps Ltd* and, as such, managed all Beatle-related matters.

To everyone's surprise he left Apple in April of 2007, and then alas died in March of 2008. Could he have spent that year, knowing that his end was near, on getting some kind of truth out into the world? His passing was midway between the birth of the *Rotten Apple* series of videos and the magnificent *Winged Beetle* film of 2010. The latter was published nine years after the 9/11 event, on 11th September, 2010 and lasted an hour – with a 50% longer version appearing in 2012.

There is a video, which I reckon is part of the Rotten Apple series, put out in November 2007, about Heather Mills (called, 'Heathers secrets and the Media Lies'), as her sensational divorce case synchronized with the emergence of this remarkable series. It was noticed that a 'very sensitive document regarding Linda McCartney's primary physicians and treatment center' was printed on Sloan-Kettering Cancer Center headed notepaper.

One really needs some software for slowing down the RA videos because they make things flash up very quickly (at 1:01). I wouldn't like to say what connection that had to the Heather Mills story on this video. People have inferred that Sir Paul himself has to be involved in making such sensitive material available. Who else could have got such a document, or would not expect to be sued for putting it up?

A normal viewer might not notice that document as it flashes by in a tiny fraction of a second: which in turn causes one to reflect upon the purpose of the RA series. It contains *a lot* of such brief almost subliminal messages – as bewildered bloggers have complained. The RA has in effect put out an encyclopaedia of information on this topic, in the form of visual images,

---

2 The blogger 'Guitargaz' claimed to be the son Gary of Bill Shepherd, and averred that his father had done the Pepperpots albums, but produced no backup for such a claim. He could not even produce a picture of his Father! One may doubt whether the Bee-Gees Bill Shepherd had a son Gary, who 'Guitargaz' claimed to be.

clearly made by insiders of the Apple/Beatle enterprise, selecting from their vast data-archives.

To give an example, a letter from Faul to 'Isla' flashes up for half a second in RA 73 (1:51):

To Isla
love from that famous
actor!!, and pal
the late Paul McCartney
(illegible in brackets)
with Faul's unmistakeable
signature of 'Paul McCartney.'

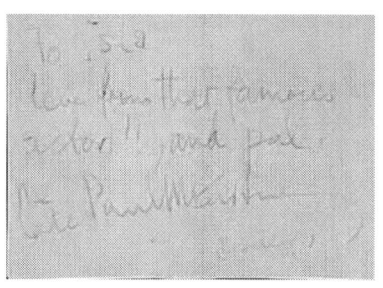

Maybe that note has by now been thrown away, only remembered in the video.

Emilo Lari

We are thereby led into Emilo Lari's view that somebody 'left the possibility of discovering the truth to the next generation.' Lari was a photographer for the Beatles film *Help!* The *Rotten Apple* videos have an interview with him, and some feel that is the most remarkable thing in the whole RA series. (See his interview released in 2014, 'Emilio Lari – TheIamaphoneyInterview')

He is indisputably one who was around at the time and speaks with authentic memory. He claims to have heard about the story in late '66, making this the earliest authentic memory of the event by someone who was around at the time, and describes the legendary car-crash as if it were a fact: 'The car was completely destroyed you know, nobody could have survived in that car-crash,' and then he adds, 'Everything is so f****** strange, let me tell you!'

We are hearing a man haunted and alarmed by the sheer number of people who have died, who had known the story: 'They died' he keeps reiterating. One can't hear all he is saying, with his thick Italian accent. Concerning what happened, 'We cannot even imagine what is behind it.' For comparison, earlier on RA 76 (August 2009) Emilo Lari's image was not visible, but was held out of focus: he there declared he was told in '66 that Paul had 'died in a car-crash on the M-I'. Evidently, when first interviewed, in a brief and fragmentary manner, he had only agreed on condition that he was not named, and a very blurred image of him appeared. Then in RA 81 we get a more coherent talk by him, now clearly in focus. 'But it's very complicated. Whoever is behind this, must be a genius.'

His words are easier to hear in this 2014 video than in the earlier RA disclosures. 'He left the possibility to discover the truth to the next generation' – those words are so important! It was alas less than clear who the 'he' was, here alluded to. 'You find the organizer of all this, you will find the secret of the, of Paul's death, you know.' Uh-huh.

He still has his beautiful pictures, and shows us his favourite one of Paul, saying: 'Look at the eyes of this one, this angel, you know.' Alluding to Faul he says: 'This guy's a *sosia* (in Italian this means "double"). I mean he is the devil, he's not a human being.' No comment!

As to why his home was raided, he shows a photo showing how Paul was fairly short (we're here arguing that he was some 5'8" high, much the same as Lennon). 'Then the Apple Society, the Paul McCartney society, they tried to stop those pictures to go in circulation, they got into the house, they put everything upside down, but they didn't steal anything at all, you know' – Lari anyway had the negatives. They were his films so 'I had total rights to sell it, no restriction whatsoever; but they tried to stop it, Paul McCartney tried to buy everything, that is concerning the Beatles, you know, but he could not buy my picture.' (NB, by 'Paul McCartney' Lari here alludes to the replacement, Faul).

Peter Trabant, author of *The Beatles Book of Revelations,* as well as *The Sgt Pepper Code*, does not endorse the PID story, however he does support the prevalent notion that Aspinall funded the Iamaphoney project. A look at the board of directors for Apple will reveal that the company secretary is listed as 'Standby Films Ltd.' Standby Films continues to exist, and could be the source whereby Iamaphoney's project developed.

None or hardly any of Iamaphoney's YouTube material has been hit with a copyright infringement by Apple. The motive was presumably the same as drove the author of *Memoirs of Billy Shears* to tell his story: Standby Films appear on its website as an Apple-fronted organisation. This process or initiative is balanced between on the one hand wanting to make some disclosure, to help the truth come out, and on the other fearing huge lawsuits that would transpire if things were spelt out too clearly or too soon.

Billy Martin is a name sometimes used by Iamaphoney. Mr Trabant managed to contact a 'Billy Martin' on Linkedin (a business–contact setup) asking about Standby Films and received a startling reply.[3] 'Billy Martin' is producer at Cosmania Vision, A Paulcorps Ltd., (Reminder: *Apple Corps Ltd.* was the company set up in 1968) and previously of Standup Films. He is 'director' of APaul corps Ltd. Mr Trabant has a 'sensible' non-PID reputation, which may be why he got the reply.

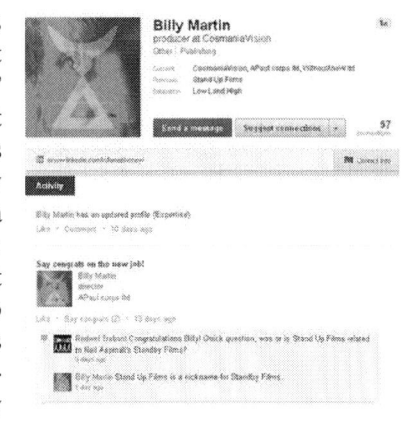

To reiterate, a Director of 'APaul corps ltd' is called Billy Martin.

The name of the Beatle company APaul corps is humorously poised midway between Apple Core and A Paul Corpse: the meaning is there, but deniable.

Apple core
Apple Corps
A Paul corpse
APaul corps

The Quiet Beatle

We were talking about the space between us all.
And the people who hide themselves behind a wall of illusion
Never glimpse the truth, then it's far too late, when they pass away

George Harrison, *Within you, Without you*, 1967

An amicable letter from George was sent to the Beatle's former roadie Mal Evans, who has evidently written to George asking his permission, to describe the Beatle story in a forthcoming book. Writing from his Henley estate, on 25th February 1975, George was happy to give that permission, for 'a book about our experience.' Eleven months later, Mal Evans' manuscript *Living the Beatles' Legend* was due to be delivered to the publisher Grosset and Dunlap on January the 12th. (a Mr John Hoernie had been collaborating on this opus). He was murdered in L.A. on 5th of January '76[4] and his suitcase containing

---

3 beaconfilms2011, 'Iamaphoney, Neil Aspinall and Apple,' 28.3.13: the logo is from the cover of TheRightAlbum by 'Iamaphoney': http://therevelation2012.weebly.com/.
4 Evans was shot by LAPD officer Charles Higby, who had FBI connections and was

that manuscript vanished – as too did the ashes, after his cremation!

According to *The Times*, "For years now, an ever-growing number of Beatles historians have regarded the Mal Evans archive as the holy grail[5]. On some accounts, that legendary lost archive ended up with Yoko Ono in the Dakota building, New York. That doom befalling Mal Evans would have conveyed forcefully to George, the danger which anyone likely to speak out could be facing.

John Lennon's death in December, 1980 devastated George. He became unable to leave his stately neo-Gothic home in Henley, as fear gripped a hold of him. He surrounded it with safety features, fortifying it and shutting himself away, limiting his public appearances for some time. It was not a simple fear but more like panic - his house was called "Fort Knox" by his neighbours, because it was like a bunker. George had spent thousands of dollars to install walls, fences, cameras, etc.

'George was always worried that somebody would try to kill him' recalled Colin Harris who had worked for him since 1975. 'He kept himself hidden and was even afraid to go for a walk in the garden. There was a time – a few years after Lennon was shot – when he wouldn't go out. We didn't see him for three months. He brought in security men and they patrolled the grounds day and night. One went everywhere with George.'[6] That seems odd behaviour for a gentle musician who had never harmed a flea, and whose life was dedicated to spreading peace, love and Eastern music.

In 1987 George's merrily nostalgic 'When we was Fab' appeared, accompanied by an innovative music video. We see George playing while Ringo potters around, being helpful here and there, but what about the other two? John is after all dead, however a distinctly Lennonesque character strolls across the screen at 2:00 minutes, holding an album; followed by a wobbly shapeshifting character, whom we cannot identify. Enough said.

---

involved in the Robert Kennedy assassination case.
5 The Times 25.3.05; NB, this was the issue which carried a partial and censored text of Mal Evans' diaries – missing out the entire year 1966!
6 Doggett, *You Never give me your Money* p.280.

The Disclosure Process

In 1988 there came the moment when the Beatles were inducted into the Rock and Roll Hall of Fame. Ringo, George and Yoko Ono attended - but Faul refused to come. The latter put out a staggering press release which made newspaper headlines, stating he would not come because he needed to avoid the company of his two old bandmates: " *I would feel like a complete hypocrite waving and smiling with (Harrison and Starr) at a fake reunion.*"

One of the Beach Boys who also was being inducted that evening, made a dig at McCartney 'who couldn't be here tonight because he's in a lawsuit with Ringo and Yoko . That's a bummer because we're talking about harmony.' One appreciates that Faul did not want to be defined as a Beatle any more, that he was endeavouring to form a new identity (and succeeding very well) and perhaps we also appreciate that his height difference would have stood out rather starkly, had the three been gathered together on that stage. But, the sharp malevolence of his note may have prompted George and Ringo to hint a little - as far as was possible - at its cause.

The two ex-Beatles were introduced by Mick Jagger, whose fine speech to the assembled showbiz millionaires displayed, as we would expect, a glad eloquence, with his warm smile and his rich, English accent – but, what a contrast this made with the few, stumbling words that Ringo and George managed to come out with, while staring sheepishly down at the floor or up at the ceiling! At this historic moment, their brief comments – we can hardly call them speeches - seemed more remarkable for what they could not say, for what they avoided saying, than what they did.

We are far from confident that these two characters even liked each other - George had after all taken Ringo's wife Maureen, all those years ago. In vain George's wife Pattie Boyd had tried to warn Ringo, who just refused to believe that such a thing could be happening - until finally George told him. The Starkey's marriage then collapsed, with Maureen so upset that she deliberately drove her motor bike into a brick wall, after which she required extensive plastic surgery.[7] George's marriage with the lovely Pattie Boyd then fell apart. Such memories of horror do not quickly fade away. But, here were the two together again, overshadowed as ever by their 'glorious past'.

Ringo spoke first, saying 'There were four of us in that band, and [now] there just seems to be George and I ... [then pointing] Yoko, Sean and Julian.' He was here alluding to Faul's absence from the ceremony, while also managing to imply rather more. George then made a diffident and too-short speech, introducing himself as 'the quiet Beatle.' He started by saying how hard it was to represent the Beatles without John: 'We all know why John can't be here, and I'm sure he would be, and it's hard really to stand here

---

7 This was in 1973: Ibid, p.209.

supposedly representing the Beatles ... it's what's left, I'm afraid, but um, *we all loved him so much, and we all loved Paul very much.*' That is the key passage – it's as far as George can go. I hear it as 'we all loved Paul' but it could be in the present tense.

It is unthinkable that George could here have been alluding to the band member who had refused to be present and had derided the invitation with his scornful comment. George has to have been here alluding to the two dead Beatles.

Despite all the security measures installed around his house, in 1999 a Michael Abram breached its security *without* setting off any of the alarms, and then further continued to breach the security by getting inside the heavily-fortified home without triggering the system. He pleaded insane but must have been quite intelligent, with such ability to gain access to the security system and its codes. He went to great lengths to penetrate what was a kind of fortress. Or, were the alarms switched off by someone who knew the system? More than one person would have been required to arrange such a break-in.[8]

George thereby had a *very* near-death experience, being repeatedly stabbed by Abram, who was knocked out just in time by Harrison's wife with a fire poker. At his trial the 35-year-old Abram pleaded insanity, with a clearly absurd claim that he was on a "mission from God" but that defence somehow worked and he was acquitted of attempted murder on grounds of insanity.

After being detained for treatment in a secure hospital, he was then released after only 19 months detention. How can it happen, that a famous pop musician gets hospitalised with forty stab wounds by a killer having no discernable motive – who is then let out after less than two years? After this incident George became a recluse. The gentle George died of cancer a month or two after his attacker was released.

The murder attempts on two Beatles by 'lone nuts' many years after the height of their fame should not be ignored. One does not see these kind of attacks on other superstars. We could add in here the bizarre death of Mal Evans in Los Angeles where so many mysterious deaths have occurred: could these have been three threats to outing Paul conveniently dying, or almost dying in George's case, or dying soon after - by random, unexplained violence?

And how was it, that for years *before* these attacks transpired, these two great heroes suffered from deep anxiety that just such a fate was in store for them? There was surely nothing paranoid about George's deep fear, after

---

8 Facebook, The true story of the Beatles / on George Harrison second part, Lady Ruth.

John's assassination. After all, the two of them did share the awful secret. In contrast, Faul never had anything resembling such anxiety, he knew his life was protected by British intelligence - James Bond was looking after him. He was strangely blasé when Lennon died, just saying in the street, 'Yeah it's a drag.'

Nicholas Kollerstrom

A Magic Touch

Vortex of Power

I've seen religion from Jesus to Paul
Lennon *I found out* 1970

King Charles II the Merry Monarch would touch people with the effect or so it was believed of healing them. Huge crowds would gather at sessions where the public could be so touched and cripples etc would be brought forward. There are even reports of people being crushed to death in such a crowd. He was the last English monarch to be able to do this. Nobody wanted to be touched by the Hanoverian Georges – yuk! After the so-called 'Glorious Revolution' of 1688 any 'divine' status of the British monarchy had gone.

I suggest that, since then, this phenomenon may not have appeared again in England, until the arrival of the Beatles. No other pop group had lines of sick people and cripples brought forth, to try and touch them, or had such healing power accredited to them. Consider the following account by Derek Tayler:

The Beatles wonder about themselves and draw no answers. "It's incredible, absolutely incredible," says Derek Tayler, the Beatles Press Officer. "Here are these four boys from Liverpool. They're rude, they're profane, they're vulgar and they've taken over the world. It's as if they'd founded a new religion. They're completely anti-Christ. I mean I'm anti-Christ as well, but they're so anti-Christ they shock me, which isn't an easy thing. But I'm obsessed with them. Isn't everybody? I'm obsessed with their honesty. And the people who like them most are the people who should be outraged most. In Australia for example each time we'd arrive at an airport, it was as if De Gaulle had landed, or better yet, the Messiah.

The routes were lined solid, cripples threw away their sticks, sick people rushed up to the car as if a touch from one of the boys would make them well again, old women stood watching with their grandchildren, and as we'd pass by, I could see the look on their faces.

It was as if some saviour had arrived and all these people were happy and relieved, as if things somehow were going to be better now."(*Saturday Evening Post* 8.8.64, 'The Return of the Beatles' by A. Aronowitz)

As to what life was like at the centre of the vortex:

"Look if you weren't there you can't begin to understand the pressures they were under and their way of life. I don't give a damn how many books you've read or how many people you interview; even I can't convey to you what it was like! I was very close to them, and I was under a lot of pressure. But I was not even remotely in their league. (Derek Taylor, Schultze p.16)

Lennon did find the rows of cripples along the corridors etc quite distressing and hard to handle. And once Paul had gone of course that aura of power just vanished like a dream forgotten, it just vanished like the morning dew: their *manas,* spirit-power or aura, whatever you want to call, it did not survive his departure.

Lennon came to lose his memory of those years, and in the mid-seventies recalled: "I can see the Beatles from a new point of view. Can't remember much of what happened, little bits and pieces here and there, and I've started taking an interest in what went on while I was in that fish tank. It must have been incredible." (Doggett p.222) Was there a deep pain that he needed to forget?

Asked in 1980 the perennial question, would the Beatles re-form, Lennon replied in terms of getting himself re-crucified: "Do we have to get crucified again? Do we have to do the walking on the water again, because a whole lot of dummies didn't see it the first time or didn't believe it when they saw it? That's what they're asking. 'Get off the cross, I didn't understand it the first time. Can you do it again?' No way, You can't do things twice.' (Turner *The Gospel According to The Beatles*, p.17)

What could it have been, that we didn't *believe* that we had *seen*? During the 1970s, all the world wanted the Beatles to re-form. In 1976 they were offered fifty million dollars for a single show, they would just have had to perform together for a minimum of twenty minutes! They didn't accept so the offer (by Bill Sargeant) was doubled! (Doggett p.242) All sorts of people pleaded with them, could they not re-form just once?

What would have been so terrible about making their fans happy all around the world? What was so awful about the Beatle-identity that the ex-Fab Four could never endure to meet up? Readers will by now be able to construct their own answer here. *The Eagles* could re-form in 2005 in Sydney Australia after three decades and be better than ever! However the remaining Beatles were too inwardly tortured by what they had gone through, and the stress of not being able to tell anyone the truth. Had people heard the sound they would or could make when together again, they would have had cause to wonder, as to where on Earth the original Beatles sound had come from?

Two Interviews

'I'm not just the great wizard who's going to sort it all out...'
Faul, IT interview with Barry Miles, 20.1.67

In April of 1964, Paul McCartney was interviewed by David Frost for his famous 'A Degree of Frost' program, which can now be viewed on Youtube. We can compare his replies then to an interview he gave later on, to *Melody Maker* in January 1966, here shown. His answers were in both cases quite simple and direct. The replies shown in the Melody Maker are the sort of thing teeny-boppers would have expected to read. They are a world apart from the first interview given by Faul, one year later.

In January 1967, Barry Miles interviewed Faul for the *International Times* which had just started, of which he was the Editor. (*IT* January 20th). This was a spontaneous, stream-of-consciousness rap, and the first philosophical statement by the Newcomer. I believe that Barry Miles was fully aware of

Glamour, films, Eppy — Paul leads off in the Beatle's pop think-in month

FILMS
I love them, but I can't stand westerns. But I love going to the pictures. Peanuts.

POTS
Never had all that many and I was thankful to the building forces.

VIETNAM
Bombs and shooting and killing and people doing things they shouldn't.

FRANCE
Paris. A great looking city. One of my favourite countries. The language sounds great. Maybe because I didn't do it at school and I can't speak a word.

WIMPOLE STREET
Dentists . . . and friendly faces.

PLAYBOY
You couldn't print it.

GLAMOUR GIRLS
Most are so unglamorous, isn't true. Girls with Brillo pad hair who shouldn't bother.

BUSES
I love buses.

STRING BASSES
They hurt your fingers, especially if you're a two-pound weakling like me.

EPPY
Someone who's learned a lot in a very short time and is as straight as they come.

TITO BURNS
While Rome fiddles.

CIGGIES
I seem to smoke them all the time and get great pleasure from it, so there.

GEORGE MARTIN
Great fellow who's very good at his job.

PHOTOGRAPHERS
They've got a hell of a job because if the editor says go and get a picture of someone in his bath, they have to do it. They probably realise it's a dirty trick but they do it just the same. It's a good thing they realise it's a low trick, but they still have to do it.

PSYCHIATRY
It helps but it's not the whole answer.

DRESSING GOWNS
I like them. I like the backing. Good to dance to.

LIVERPOOL
Home.

CARS
I like them, but mainly because they get you from place to place.

RHODESIA
Colour prejudice, I suppose.

DOGS
The only ones I don't like are those without a sense of proportion.

CATS
I like them but my dad hates them because they pee on the lavender.

ITALY
I like Rome. It's another fantastic looking place. It's one of the greatest looking cities in the world.

DE GAULLE
De Gerrieri

COWBOYS
I don't like them but I liked pretending to be one in America last year.

CHILDREN
Up to a certain age, I love all of them. After that, some of them get wrecked, mainly by parents.

COUNT BASIE
I haven't heard enough of him to know if I like him or not.

TOOTH PASTE
Fab. Gear. Madison. Twist. Crazy. Dig. Most.

a changeover – he knew both of them![1] This statement is important and worth reading in its entirety, but here are some fragments. The Band had just recorded *Strawberry Fields* and *Penny Lane*, and are a-brewing up *Sgt Pepper*:

> I'd prefer it if there was such a thing as magic, if magic things happened. So that magic happened in music. It used to happen a lot more in music for me until I started looking at it objectively after having written a bit. Then, what is still magic for other people, for me, it's a hit. "Well OK, I see why he's done that, and how he's done that and I'll learn from it, …

> … to take a note and wreck it and see in that note what else there is in it, that a simple act like distorting it has caused. ..I'd like a lot more things to happen like they did when you were kids, when you didn't know how the conjuror did it, and were happy to just sit there and say, 'Well its magic.' I use magic instead of 'spiritual' because spiritual sounds as if it fits into too many of the other categories. If something unbelievable happens to most people, at the moment they'd explain it by taking a little cross-filing out of their brain and saying, Well of course that doesn't happen you know, there aren't ghosts. And they just explain it with a great 20th century explanation for ghosts, which is that there aren't ghosts. Which is no f**** explanation at all! 'That couldn't have been a magic vision that just happened then, I must have been a bit drunk. I must have just been high there.' I don't believe that it ends with our Western logical thought, it can't do, because that's so messed up anyway, most of it, that you have got to allow for the possibility of their being a lot more than we know about. …

> There's so much going on in one note, but you never listen to it. so many harmonics buzzing around, that if that's all happening in one note and if in one frame or picture all that's happening. The thing is, it could take a bit of looking into.

> Miles: In the last few thousand years, only the materialistic side of man has developed and built up.

> Paul: The drag about this is that everybody has realised there aren't such things as ghosts, there isn't such a thing as God, and there is no such thing as a soul, and when you die you die. Which is great, it's fine, it's a brave thought really. The only trouble is, that you don't have the bit you did when you were a kid of innocently accepting things. for instance, if a film comes on that's superimposed and doesn't seem to mean anything, immediately its weird or its strange or it's a bit funny to most people, and they tend to laugh at it. The immediate reaction would be a laugh.

---

1 For Barry Miles (IMO) saying, 'Yes I knew both of them,' see RA 71, 3:00 minutes.

A Magic Touch

And that's wrong. That's the first mistake. And that's the big mistake that everybody makes, to immediately discount anything that they don't understand they're not sure of, and to say 'Well of course we'll never know about that...

The thing that's grown up out of this materialistic scene that everyone's grown into, is that for everything to exist on a material level you've got to be able to discount things that happen which don't fit in with it. And they're all very neatly disposed of these days...

It can make it difficult because if you say a thing according to the new book of the prophet, they say things in reply according to the old testament, and you find yourself saying, Well, yes, but I don't quite mean that. I know it sounds like that but its not. What I mean is, working on a new assumption of everything being fluid,' you find yourself getting into cock-ups with words. It's a big battle at the moment. Trying not to say too many words, and if there's a pregnant pause in the conversation, not feeling that I've got to fill it.

But let someone else, who fears the silence, fill it. I don't fear it anymore. Of course it will need a bit of training. But the good thing about it is that if you are prepared to accept that things aren't just broad and wide, they are infinitely broad and wide, then there's a great amount to be learned. And the change over .. it can be done. It just takes a bit of time, but it will be done, I think.[2]

It could cross one's mind here, that the 'new book of the prophet' was Crowley's 1929 opus on *Magick,* a copy of which which *Rotten Apple* have tried to persuade us was owned by either Lennon or Faul (or both). It's hard to think what else it could have been. As a general comment, I suggest that of these two interviews, the former with Paul shows a simpler soul, a less complex young man.

The Image of Crowley

On the cover of *Sgt Pepper*, the head of Aleister Crowley (1875-1947) appears *twice*, and a line between his two heads would pass through that of Faul. On the top left corner of the cover he is adjacent to the Indian guru Sri Yukteswar, who George Harrison would have wanted (he was author of *The Holy Science*) – and Sri Yukteswar must be turning in his grave to have the child-sacrificing black-magic "I am the Great Beast 666" satanist right next to him. To the right he lurks behind the statuesque figure of Diana Dors, who

---

[2] This interview, the first Barry Miles had done 'got picked up by the Underground Press syndicate all around the world' but it's not online. (*In the Sixties,* Barry Miles, 2003 p.159)

is resembling Lennon's 'pornographic priestess:' the Lennon on the left-hand side of the cover is not looking down, as are the other Band members at the grave, but may be staring across at her breasts. The *Sgt Pepper* cover has a lot of cardboard-cutout figures plus wax models (from Madame Tussuards), that of Ms Dors being one of these.

In front of Crowley is the child-actress Shirley Temple, and as we've seen she is the only figure appearing thrice on this album. Her eyes in each of these three appearances lie on a straight line with the middle of these three being in front of Crowley. Thus *the Magician* lurks behind 'doors' and a 'temple.' Just above Crowley is Lewis Carroll, echoing Lennon's interest in writing backwards or in backward-masking, as he cited Carroll as an influence in this respect. Summarising, to the left-hand side of the album cover Crowley stands beside a stern ascetic who has renounced worldly pleasures, while to the right he lurks behind the 'pornographic priestess.' The Magician is doubled, as are the Beatles, and no-one else is, which has to be deliberate.[3]

Magick

Faul will sometimes perform with an image of Aleister Crowley projected up behind him.[4] Not many musicians do that.

Allusions to Crowleyite Magick keep turning up in PID disclosures. To confess my prejudice in this matter, in an early debate with Clare Kuehn on Jim Fetzer's *Real Deal* on the PID topic (February 19th, 2014), she was talking about Aleister Crowley and I threatened to pull out of the discussion if she continued! I didn't want to talk about that black magician. It seems however that I may have been greatly in error here. The *Rotten Apple* series (2006-201?) and the *Winged Beetle* (2010, 2012) appear to be drawing from the same source and produced by much the same people, and continually allude to this topic in a cryptic manner.

Much of the evidence we here review comes from these 'disclosures,' presumably parts from the massive archive collected by Aspinall of the Fab Four not included in the *Anthology,* normally undated. They are surely authentic. Thus *The Rotten Apple* has an extremely strange quote from the Beatle biographer Phillip Norman, who wrote *Shout:*

> The Beatles is not a normal story, it's a supernatural story. ...McCartney won't tell you. Ringo can't tell you. John isn't here.
> Asked what he meant by saying Paul 'won't tell you' he replied, 'He

---

[3] Ms Temple's name is also linked to that of the founder of the Church of Satan, Colonel Michael Aquino, and Kenneth Anger.
[4] *The Rotten Apple* 72, 5:01.

rewrites history, all the time' (RA 27 3:40-3:55). Nothing in his biography helps us to make sense of that extraordinary claim! We may hope he will elucidate this in times to come. Here is Faul speaking:

> I believe in magic. There is such a thing as magic. And the Beatles was magic. It's an energy field...What we humans call magic. Something metaphysical, something very alchemic .. magic with a 'k'[5]

That is a core statement about his philosophy and belief. Magick with a 'k' does inexorably mean Crowleyite magic: it was he who added the 'k'. Elsewhere Faul said: "The whole thing was Crowley saying, Do what Thou wilt, you know, we're all sons of the Magickian." (*Winged Beetle* 2010 at 21.50; or 2012 at 23:40)).

Lennon made the cryptic, hard-to-hear comment: "Paul's so skilled people don't see it, but he can do whatever he wants in his world. We're all lined up to please him. He's not just daft, he's a bit daemonic." (*Winged Beatle* 2010, 45:50-46:00).

Crowley's advice about reading and speaking backwards, to destroy ingrained habits, and detach oneself from the habitual flux of events, specifically alluded to 'I am he' being spoken backwards as 'Eh ma I.' (1929 *Magick*, p.260) Here the reader may listen to Lennon singing 'I am the walrus' which goes: I am he and eeh may I' (*Winged Beetle* 2012 27:25-27)

Crowley's 1929 opus on Magick described a technique of doing things backwards to overcome routine habits, such as writing backwards or "listen to phonograph records, reversed." There certainly is quite a lot of this in the Beatles story - and it starts with 'Ian Iachimoe'. Crowley claimed to have received inspiration from a being 'Aiwaz' dictating some book to him, and we here recall the image of Faul in MMT sitting at a desk in an army uniform, with 'I WAS' written enigmatically in front of him.

As evidence for this inspiration, Crowley cited: 'his power to conceal a coherent system of number and letters in the text of a rapidly-written document, containing riddles and ciphers.' One could say that *Billy Shears Memoirs* has tried to do this in various ways. Crowley did feel a special connection to the number 666, and we find this number curiously emphasised in that opus.

---

[5] Interview with Anthony DeCurtis of *Rolling Stone* magazine: *Rotten Apple* 73, 0:40-0:50.

Concerning *Strawberry Fields Forever*, recorded in November-December 1966, we heard earlier (in Chapter 5) Big Mal's written account of his astonishment upon hearing it played backwards at the meeting in Cavendish Avenue on November 20th, when Faul and the other Beatles first met up: 'It blew my mind when he [Lennon] played it backwards. What a way to tell a story. Paul really gave him a new direction, a new way of art. Good and bad. Black and white'. – this is from what we have inferred to be a page of Mal Evans' 'read 'em and weep' unpublished and now lost manuscript. Here is a comment made recently (29.6.15) upon that song from the 'CosmaniaVision' Facebook page:

… in the beginning of the chorus, 'Strawberry Fields, Nothing is real' . Play that backwards and what you will hear loud and clear is; 'We will sing it now. We will be reverse' - The first deliberate backwards message ever recorded.[6]

Backwards-played versions of these Beatle songs seem to be available on Youtube. 'Loud and clear' may not be quite the appropriate phrase here, but one can assuredly hear something of that nature: something good enough to take us right back to that electrifying moment when the new Beatles first assembled, remembered on that Big Mal typewriter-written page. The text seems to give the credit for the idea to Faul: 'Paul really gave him a new direction' and you my care to notice that it throws in a comment about the dualities of light and darkness, good and evil – a reference to the Crowley book, perhaps?

After the grandiose finale of *Sgt Pepper,* the needle winds into the centre groove, and starts to make a chirpy, repeating sound as the disc revolves. Turning the disc to revolve backwards one hears this with total clarity, 'We'll all be magic supermen' – that is the final *Sgt Pepper* message! We are here reminded of the Four dressed up as magicians in MMT, later that same year.

Crowley published his book of poems *The Winged Beetle* in 1910, using an Egyptian scarab- motif with outstretched wings. The one hour long *The Winged Beetle* video that appeared in 2010 simply used a scanned-in version of this Crowley book cover design for its title – but didn't say so! The appearance of this weighty video, the definitive insider-revelation, was thus a *100th anniversary event*. It was resonating to several different dates - the date of 9/11, being nine years after it to the day, to the death of Paul being forty-four years later (if you accept the 9/11 date) *and* last but not least the year-period of a century.

---

6 http://beaconfilms2011.blogspot.dk/2015/07/phoney-ponderings.html Phoney Conspiracy, 'Beatle Ponderings' by Redwell Trabant, 17.7.15.

A Magic Touch

The Winged Beetle video *The Rotten Apple 2010 The Winged Beetle* (and the longer 2012 film the *Winged Beatle Extended Version* lasting for one hour and forty minutes.) tells how Paul put a humorous advert into the first issue of an 'Indica Gallery journal' in the spring of '66, just as the Indica Gallery was being set up[7]; alluding to himself as 'Ian Iachimoe the Polish 'new wave' film producer.' That's fine, however we are then disturbed to hear that in the next issue, the same fellow put in an advert saying: 'FILMAKER seeks genuine black magic group. Fakes will be sacrificed' (followed by a contact address in Tufnell Park).

I suggest these are *not* similar enough to warrant the inference of being by the same person. It then avers that this same person Ian Iachimoe contributed to the *Process, Church of the Final Judgement*' which again I suggest was not the case (11 – 11:30 mins). That magazine did not start up until 1967 which is far too late, and I checked the issue whose cover it shows, it was that of 1972 (in which various people including Faul were interviewed very briefly about what they feared most).

Worse, the *Winged Beatle* then avers that Paul introduced John to Ms Ono. Is nothing sacred? These two were antitheses, the opposite ends of John's universe. There is no evidence that they ever met. A chronology of that autumn of '66 around the Indica Gallery might want to include the arrival of the greatest rock'n'roll guitarist of all time - playing in the club next door!

Paul and Jane assisted the formation of *Indica* in Mason's Yard in the spring of '66. then, two weeks after Paul's death, on 23 September, Jimi Hendrix first played in England at the *Scotch of St James,* before a spellbound audience of the beat elite. On the 15th October, IT was launched at the Round House in Chalk Farm, with Ms Ono making a 'happening' and Faul 'disguised as an Arab'.

On November 7th Ms Ono's 'art' exhibition opened up at Indica and Lennon ~~like a fly going into a spider's web~~ there met her. Faul will occasionally make coy remarks about how he had met Ms Ono before John. The *Scotch of St James* remains but the *Indica* is long gone. Mason's Yard today is a grey, bleak place, one walks out of it quickly - hardly believing that it was once a focus of the London swinging scene.

The King of Cosmania

The *Rotten Apple* series started up in November 2006, and then in February 2007 its Number 28 argued a strange case, as regards where Faul

---

7 This was the precursor of *International Times,* which started later that year.

had come from - that he was some kind of 'son' of Alistair Crowley. What on Earth could that mean?

In June 2007, Sir Paul McCartney's album 'Memory Almost Full' had on its back the imperious acknowledgement, 'His Royal Highness the *King of Cosmania* and Surrounding Regions deigns to give thanks to the following people ...' His list of credits ends with 'not forgetting my beautiful family' - the mind boggles as to who that might be.

That was the year in which he proposed the London Eye be renamed after him, at least for a while, to promote his new album! He is not short of self-esteem. But then, he is listed in the *Guinness Book of Records* as the most successful musician and composer in popular music history, with 60 gold discs and sales of 100 million singles, as having the most records sold, most #1s (shared), the most covered song, "Yesterday" and the largest paid audience for a solo concert (350,000), etc. So we can allow him the 'Royal Highness' self-appellation!

PID enthusiasts pretty soon figured out that 'King of Cosmania' was an anagram:

The King of Cosmania = Son of the Magickian

That is a very strange coincidence, which has to indicate that RA and Faul are here collaborating. After the anagram had appeared in June on the album cover, the RA 36 of August that year explained it, *and* added that the title 'Memory almost full' was an anagram for 'For my soulmate LLM', i.e., Linda Louise McCartney. Again this must surely mean that Faul has pointed out this anagram to *Rotten Apple*. The album has a clear backwards-masking message. It keeps asking 'Who is this now?' several times, as a kind of refrain, followed by: 'I was Willie Campbell.'[8]

The *Rotten Apple* series appeared mainly around the death of Neil Aspinall in 2008, viz 2007-9, however there are one or two latecomers around 2011.[9] The last few seem even more fragmented and refractory than the others, as if uneasy at being unable to reach any conclusion. The series had the air of looking forward to the year 2012, of which if you remember

---

8 In the song 'gratitude': see video 'Paul is dead: a 'gratitude' clue,' March 2008. Played backwards, at 2:57 he says 'I was William Campbell,' and all the way thru he sings 'Who is this now?'
9 Summary of Dates: November 1966 – First RA; Feb 2007 - RA 27 says Faul is somehow the Son of Crowley; April - Aspinall retires from Apple; June - *Memory almost Full* album has 'King of Cosmania;' August RA 36 explains the anagram, as 'Son of the Magickian'; March 2008, Aspinall dies.

much was expected, but then nothing did happen, it was an anti-climax. Generally speaking the *Rotten Apple* initiative was finished by the time the *Winged Beetle* film appeared.

> I long to know
> All your secrets
> I want to walk
> Through your fire …
>
> I was awakened
> By magic
> I was alone
> In this world …

My Soul, McCartney, 2007

Nine Nine O Nine

And when the time comes around
We will be duty bound
To tell the truth of what we've seen
McCartney, *From a Lover to a Friend,* 2001

One book started me off on this journey, unexpectedly given to me by my pal Frank McGillion. It's expensive so I was rather awed at him giving it to me. In sixty-six chapters with just 666 pages it was published on 9-9-09, so it was numerically quite mysterious.

The book's high price, where even the kindle sells at $33 (actually $33.33, yes OK we get the message), indicates a motive, of writing a transformative and detailed book, but then pricing it out of the common market: to keep it 'underground' until its author has passed away.

It declares it was published by 'Peppers Press', a 'subsidiary of MACCA Corp,' and whether or not you reckon these publishing houses exist, there is no way such names could have been used unless the McCartney empire had approved. Ditto the book's dedication, 'A most special thanks to Sir J. Paul McCartney for providing such fantastic material.'

Amazon delivered that volume to me in mid-February,

2014. Its first chapter entitled 'Dreams of Paul' starts off with a dream which he, William (out of respect, we won't call him Faul in this chapter) had, where he heard 'You will be released on the twenty-first of February, 2104.' Was I here being summoned into the story? William had replied asking for a life-extension! (he doesn't say how…)

A few months later, I was in a pub *The Bell* where I live in Walthamstow, with a pal Mark who works in the music business, and I was explaining the strange tale to him, including Viv Stanshall and the *Bonzo Dog Band.* The book did at one point make a preposterous claim that he had been a persona of Faul, as if Viven Stanshall had not lived. 'No way', Mark replied, adding that the *Bonzo Dog Band* used to play in that very pub. Verily, I felt the Hand of Fate upon me.

An Encoded Text

The book starts by saying, "Opinions presented herein are solely those of Billy Shears and do not necessarily represent the views or values of the Encoder." Here the Encoder (Uharriet) is saying he has agreed to do the job, but may not agree with the views he is here recording, as expressed by 'Billy Shears' i.e. Sir Paul.

Each chapter of the *Memoirs of Billy Shears* is encoded such that the first letter of each alternate line puts together a message, one which echoes the content of the chapter. Thus, taking the first paragraph of the first chapter:

Almost everything about me taking Paul's place
was made possible because of the series of dreams
that Paul had, showing his death and me replacing
him – and by my dreams of Paul, showing me how.

First, let me, William Shepherd ("Billy Shears"),
tell you of a more recent dream. I want it told before
I die so that you will know I knew. After discussing
my undertakings in his name, Paul Said, "You will be
released on the twenty-first of February, 2014."

I asked for a nine-year extension for more tours.
Since I needed to see my Utah-based encoder one
last time, a tour would include it. Until I am done,
this book will be distributed on a level that will keep
it down. We will keep it underground until I am.

Nine Nine O Nine

The above encoding reads 'At first'. Proceeding right through Chapter One, taking each first letter of alternate lines and separating them into words and adding in punctuation, gives:

At first, you may say Paul is a dreamer but he is not the only one. From the time I joined him our dreams have made us together, as one dream sweet dreams. For me, I was introduced to LSD and other drugs by John and George, it's a trip from L.C. Dream of me; be happy, hello, hello, mum, Julia.[1]

This text wanders around rather like a channelled message! It's the sort of thing that one might expect to come off from a ouija board. A lot of it makes sense but he cannot quite hold it all the time. That chapter concerned his dreams and how John and George turned him onto taking LSD, and the song 'Let it Be' and his memory of his own mother.

Let's try Chapter Three, called 'Paul worked it out'. Taking the first letter from each alternate line and inserting punctuation:

Paul worked it out: Life is very short, and there's no time for fussing and fighting, my friend. I have always thought that it's a crime. So I will ask you once again to work it out.

That comes from the whole chapter, and it alludes to Paul's very song discussed in that chapter. The message encoded echoes the chapter content. The encoding is perfect, it does not break up as the first chapter did. One does not notice lines of different lengths, to accommodate this process.

Chapter Twelve 'Billy Shakespeare' is short, and concerns two Shakespearean allusions in Beatles songs: 'Lend me your ears' as we saw in *Sgt Pepper*, then the King Lear quote at the ending of 'I am the Walrus;' so as, William explains, 'to underpin the death message of the song.' ('O, untimely death! ... What, is he dead? Sit you down, father, rest you')

Its encrypted message is simple but eloquent: 'Shakespeare in song speaks of Paul's death.'

Chapter 13 'What's in a Name?' reviews different aliases used by Faul, as well as the early names of the Beatles. He wrote 'I'm the Urban spaceman' for the *Bonzo Dog Band* under the pseudonym Apollo C. Vermouth, then co-wrote Death Cab for Cutie with Neil Innes, singing it using his Elvis-voice at the end of MMT. More recently he has released incognito albums as *The*

---

[1] The booklet *Billy Shears Acrostical Decoding* by Thomas Uharriet gives these for each chapter.

Fireman but it became fairly evident that, 'twas he. The end of the chapter takes us back to Detroit on October 1969, when a certain PID theorist Fred Labour made up Faul's name, as William Campell – and it stuck!

The flawless acrostic message embedded in this Chapter 13 quotes Romeo and Juliet, some of the most famous lines of English poetry, when Juliet was wishing her lover was not of the Capulet family: 'O, be some other name! / What's in a name? That which we call a rose / By any other name would smell as sweet.' It is surely rather touching that anyone would want to compose a chapter that encodes such lines. I cannot remotely imagine how he managed to do it. The words echo the theme of the chapter and link up to the previous one.

Chapter 21, entitled 'Thursday Night, Your Stockings needed Mending' (a quote from *Lady Madonna*) reveals his feelings as he stepped into the new identity, and alludes to the songs Eleanor Rigby and Dear Prudence. Here is its first paragraph,

> **I**nspiration and serendipity always play a part in song writing. My favourite ones, those most worth **r**ecording, are given to me. They are channelled from another dimension like a gift. Suddenly I get the **e**ssence, as though a whole creation were beamed down. My talent or gift is to be able to receive fine **m**usic. I sit down at a piano, or pick up a guitar, and play a few chords. then often very effortlessly, **e**verything comes together. As the tune comes into my head, I plug in some silly gibberish words to **m**atch the rhythm, then keep laying until the words complete themselves. I started doing that at the **b**eginning of my Beatle career.

Taking as before the alternate first letters gives: 'I remember my painful loneliness, it hurt. Dear Prudence, open up your eyes. We transformed it. I entertained the world as Paul could not. Bye Jane Asher, "Honey pie".' He apologises for not having fulfilled whatever it was that Jane Asher wanted.

And who is Prudence? Chapter Four didn't comment on this *White Album* song. The group are begging her to 'open her eyes' and come out and enjoy the sunshine. One can read it as a poignant invocation to the dead Paul, to 'come out to play'?

> Dear Prudence, open up your eyes
> Dear Prudence, see the sunny skies

> The wind is low, the birds will sing
> That you are part of everything
> Dear Prudence, won't you open up your eyes?

During a radio interview on the subject of this book, the compere Richie Allen told me he could never believe that the family of Paul would have accepted the newcomer, that was the sticking-point for him. A meetup with the family was the first thing Brian Epstein arranged, according to this chapter, after finding the newcomer and deciding he was satisfactory. There was an urgency owing to the strain of withholding the terrible news from the press. After that meeting there followed swiftly a visit to the Asher household. These key people had to agree before a decision could be made, to go ahead. Quoting further from this chapter:

Through the Bathroom Window

During a visit with Jim and Angie McCartney's family on Monday 12th September 1966, when they

all took me to Paul's St John's Wood home for documents, the thing that won them over was that I

sang for them...

Just as we were ready to leave Paul's house, Ruth (Paul's half-sister) excitedly telephoned Jane

Asher. We waited for her at Paul's house. That first impression also went well. They had me sing again.

Next, Jane and I went to her house. She showed me their guestroom, that had become Paul's own for

evenings that went on too late to drive home. We were there less than an hour before we went back

again to Paul's. Jane wanted to collect her things.

The McCartneys had locked the door. Jane

Said that there was a ladder in the garden, and that she had used it before on one occasion. I followed

her through the yard, retrieved the ladder, and set it up to the bathroom window. It was already open

enough for Jane to reach her hands in to open it the rest of the way. She climbed in and then soon

returned to the front door to let me in. That
made her seem more fun than I had expected.

We have here been given a key to the song 'She Came in Through the Bathroom Window.' It's on the *Abbey Road* album, nowadays the best-selling of all Beatle albums:

She came in through the bathroom window
Protected by a silver spoon

His new lady comes from a privileged and somewhat upper-class background, that is the 'silver spoon' reference. The song next recalls the rush of those few days, seared forever into his memory – his first meeting with Jane being on Monday 12th September:

Sunday's on the phone to Monday
Tuesday's on the phone to me

A big problem with this relationship turned out to be, that Jane was away much of the time, off rehearsing with her acting friends:

She said she'd always been a dancer
She worked at 15 clubs a day

(This is quite naughty, to imagine Jane the actress as working in clubs!)

And though she thought I knew the answer
Well I knew what I could not say

This alludes to the very complicated business of taking over someone else's life –and girl!

And so I quit the police department
And got myself a steady job

He gets a steady job, i.e joins the Beatles. I'm not suggesting he actually worked in a police department – though quite a few have![2] Then alas,

And though she tried her best to help me
She could steal but she could not rob

---

[2] The story here has William Campbell in Canada selected in a Paul lookalike contest, leaving a police department.

The pair were a couple of actors who became too immersed in their roles. It was no doubt a thrill for Jane to have a Beatle with his arm around her, but it wasn't *real*: 'she could steal but she could not rob.'

She greatly helped him, by getting people to accept him as Paul McCartney, however it had to break - after which Jane could not heal her own anguish, her broken reputation. There was just nothing William could do:

> Didn't anybody tell her?
> Didn't anybody see?

Poor Jane was emotionally lost and seared: her Father could no doubt have consoled her, but had mysteriously died a month after Faul got married, his body found rotting in his own basement!

> But now she sucks her thumb and wanders
> By the banks of her own lagoon

-a piteous conclusion. What's the answer? There was none. But I honestly don't think Faul has anything to feel guilty about. They were two confused young people, Faul more so than Jane. He is feeling the pain in this song, which contrasts the happy girl he met who climbed into a bathroom window, and the lost girl he had to leave who cannot even explain to people what her problem is.

The relatives had to make a decision while they listened to William play. People can be motivated to keep an exciting secret if it is for the good, and in this case the good outcome was to prevent a rash of young girls committing suicide and also to allow Britain's best band to carry on.

As regards the wide, extended family which Paul had (as Richie Allen explained to me), did they really need to know? By the next spring William could manage a very good Paul, and especially with Jane by his side was well able to convince people.

Moving on (for no reason) to Chapter 32, entitled 'The Parting on the Left is now .. on the right' – which is from *The Who's* song, 'Won't Get Fooled Again' - it describes Faul's struggle to play the guitar left-handed, and how he would sometimes forget; and how people tried to change his hair, which parted naturally on his right:

Left is right, making it harder to remember even phen I'm wrong I'm right where I belong. I'm right where I belong with the Beatles. I'm right but am left to tell it right. See my ear shape.

The acrostic code is again almost perfect, just one letter going wrong, 'phen' for 'when'. I am awestruck that anyone could compose a 666-page book in this manner.

This alludes to William's song, *Fixing a Hole*, singing 'When I'm wrong I'm right.' The chapter ends by contrasting their ear shapes, which unlike other facial characteristics could not be changed by plastic surgery: "Human earlobes come in two basic styles. Based on one's genetic dominance, earlobes are either both detached, hanging free from the head, like you can see mine are, or they are both attached, joined to the head, like Paul's...also notice that our ears are of entirely different shapes. He had more rounded, monkey-like ears that pop out. ...notice that I have less space between my eyes.' There is a lot up on the web about these differing ear-shapes and I don't have much to add to it.

I Am

The book has a staggering sequence of 'I am' affirmations running through it –

> **I'm the urban spaceman**
> **I am the core of the Apple**
> **I am Billy Shears**
> **I am the most successful songwriter in history**
> **I am that one and only Sgt Pepper**
> **I am the man of a thousand voices**
> **I was transformed to mend that broken band**
> **I am the true messenger of Paul.**

(pages 109, 299, 236, 511, 246, 140, 245) which may remind one of Jesus Christ in the Fourth Gospel: 'I am the bread of life,' etc. I have kind permission from Tom Uharriet to reproduce these bits from his book.

Earlier we looked at the 9-11 date, which kept echoing through events, starting in the first Beatles recording session at EMI in 1962, and climaxing on the release of the *Winged Beetle* film, by Iamaphoney, in 2010 September 11th - nine years after the catalytic, new millenium event of 9/11. A 14-album box set of complete Beatle CDs was released 9-9-09 in the USA.[3] Ostensibly there is no connection between these two events, on different sides of the Atlantic, but it would seem that somebody takes these number-patterns quite seriously. Thus the book appears as part of an ongoing disclosure process.

---

3 Some years later on the same date 9.9.14 the complete vinyl set of 14 Beatle Albums was re-released.

A Picture

William (Billy Shears) claims that John Lennon gave him a picture, shown here (p.90). Let's suppose for the sake of argument that that is an authentic Lennon drawing of the Fab Four, although it has not featured in collections of John Lennon's artwork. Wherever it is now, it would be good evidence for the authenticity of the present narrative.

It is composed with multi-layer meaning as Lennon was wont to do. Its fourfold Beatle symbolism works as in the suits of a pack of cards (Hearts, spades, diamonds and clubs), pieces of chess (castle, bishop, king and knight) and last but not least the Book of Revelation (Bull, Man, Lion and Eagle).

Quoting from the *Billy Shears Memoirs,* the last of these is 'based on Revelation 4:7. But, John drew a horse for George instead of a calf,' George is the 'dark horse' or 'black knight' of our game: he was with John in the beginning playing in clubs, and clubs are drawn in as the horse's eyes. George called his music company *Dark Horse* in the 1970s. He is slightly in the background, behind the main figures.

Paul is the ace of spades and has a hat that reaches higher than anyone else's: 'Cards sold with the Yellow Submarine storybook in 2004 featured Paul as the ace of spades.' We recognise Paul's face and he plays his left-handed bass guitar. John is diamonds, 'think of him singing 'Lucy in the Sky with Diamonds,' but also he is the fierce lion, whose roar was heard around the world. Also he is the Bishop, with bishop's mitre, maybe like his role on the Abbey Road cover. He's at the centre, because it's his band. The suit of hearts goes to Ringo 'John never did see him as the brains of the outfit, but always loved his heart. Ringo has a good heart. The R and O of Ringo also ties in with the rook in chess. Besides being a rook in chess, a rook is a bird…' – rather strained symbolism but we'll let it go. We're here reminded of Mick Jagger alluding to the Beatles as the 'Four-headed monster.'[4]

'Checkmate' is the name Lennon gave to the image, signifying 'the king is captured' or dead, i.e. Paul is gone. The remaining four had to learn how to play the game once the king (Paul) had departed. Maybe also the image shows the agony of four young men being bound *too close* together,

---
4 Jagger's speech at the Beatles Hall of Fame induction ceremony,1988.

held by huge financial contracts, such that Lennon could in the 1970s not ever bear to re-form his band. All the world cried out for them to re-form, but they never could.

The Deal

A deal was worked out: 'Before long, we were discussing particulars such as my role in providing timely material, his role in encoding my messages, my guaruntee of historical accuracy, his work standardizing the language as American English, my commitment to reveal all without reservation, the restricted extent of his creative licence, my right to override any changes he makes while lining up words to fit the allotted spaces, his methods of transferring chapters to me (via e-mail) for approval, my turnabout time, and finally, his payment for aiding me in this extraordinary mammoth undertaking .. Hiring a collaborator on this project is similar to what I have always done with projects. Whenever I slap the McCartney name on a label, I might have hired all sorts of people to help me make the sounds that I have in my head.' (p.338)

Just claiming it was fictional, his lawyer explained, would not be enough; 'He sternly said that the book must not be published without a significant thread of fiction running throughout the whole.' (p.598)[5] There had to be 'enough that the fictional element can be shown to be recognizably made-up'. A huge financial empire could be at stake here: 'By a signed contract, I stand to lose everything if I confess that I am not Paul.' So various bits had to be deleted and changed; Uharriet included a message from his sponsor about his deadline:

'*Otherwise the project is looking good. Will you still have it finished by 09.09.09? ~ PM*'

What more proof does anyone want? The lawyer expresses concern over the death of William/Sir Paul, as to whether he will be cremated, to prevent DNA sampling, as could be a basis for lawsuits. In other words, when Sir Paul dies, it will be important whether his will can prevent DNA sampling by cremating the body.

The book discloses his celtic Scottish-Irish great-grandparents John and Arlene Crawford and their daughter Helen, William's grandmother (Chapter 44, 'Sir William'). His name is *William Wallace Shepherd,* entered into the

---

[5] I only found one clearly fictional part of the text: William claims to have been Viv Stanshall, implying that the man Vivien Stanshall did not live (pp108-9). Quite obviously he did - see his biography *Ginger Geezer* by Chris Welch.

family bible, as a descendent from William Wallace. William is presumably confident that no-one can thereby trace his identity.

Nicholas Kollerstrom

Endgame

Sir Paul has had around seventy hits to his name, if we include the Beatles *oevre,* and that is probably as much as any other musician or pop artist.[1] But is he real? *'I married a legend and there's a machine behind.* I can't really go into it, but, you know, you have to read between the lines' Heather Mills opined (Chapter 3).

Whatever it was she found out, or believed that she had, we are unlikely to hear about it anytime soon. These days (2015) Sir Paul gives huge music concerts, with a highly talented backing band, and big firework displays, which cannot altogether disguise his somewhat faint and croaky voice. While admiring the fact that anyone in their mid-seventies can perform thus, we venture to quote a couple of critiques of a concert he gave in Denmark.

'The wild rumour that refuses to die'

The old, Danish Viking centre called Roskilde nowadays hosts giant rock-concerts. On July 4th 'Paul McCartney' played there. Like a genii escaped from the bottle, the PID story here went mainstream – or, it tried to. The following story was deleted about a week after it appeared, and I believe nothing now remains of it except the English translation which I posted up onto the 'invanddis' website.

SCANDAL - THE WRONG McCARTNEY by Tomas Treo[2]
- Harmless doppelganger stole the show from the legend, who was only seen in glimpses.

---

1 Other artists such as Elvis or Cliff Richard have more, but those were not songs which they had themselves composed.
2 The two Roskilde July 4th Danish articles are 'Skandale: Den forkerte McCartney, Harmløs dobbeltgænger stjal showet fra legenden, der kun var på Orange i glimt' and 'Er det den ægte McCartney der spiller i aften?' They were both on the http://ekstrabladet.dk/musik website.

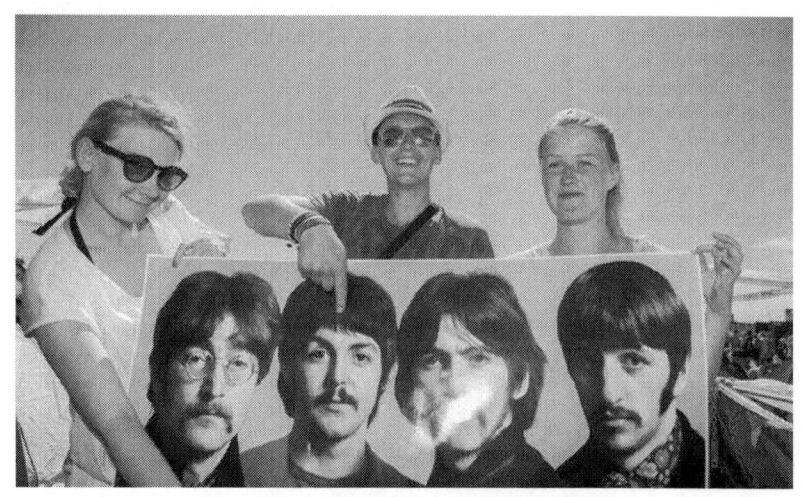

Figure: Doubtful Fans at Roskilde

Paul McCartney did not have to show ID to enter the festival-area. This turned out to be a fatal mistake. Instead of seeing the icon from the Beatles the audience was met by a wax figure from Madam Tussauds - nothing but a really bad forgery was headlining the festival.

The real Sir Paul was only observed in glimpses. Both he and the audience had problems staying awake until the final song *Golden Slumbers* was done at almost one o clock in the morning.

It all started at 10.05 pm with a weak version of *The Magical Mystery Tour,* which left the audience with more disappointment than any form of magic. The performance as a whole left McCartney's song treasure dull and sad in the Roskilde dust. It was certainly quite an achievement to get such good songs to sound so trivial, irrelevant and weak.

The impostor threw his jacket off after the fifth number, and it did help a little bit - Let me roll it - but only briefly, after which everything fell back into mediocrity. The audience seemed generally to applaud more out of politeness than enthusiasm , and we were left with a very sobering and strangely apathetic mood over the festival square.

Let us hope Roskilde have saved the receipt on the two-digit million amount, which they reportedly paid for the fraud. If the Roskilde Festival gets a refund on some of the money which they spent on the fraudster, these can be appropriately invested it in having *'John Lennon'* perform next year.

That trenchant comment vanished - perhaps not surprisingly - but a milder account was allowed to remain. Entitled, 'Is that the real McCartney playing tonight?' it featured a humorous interview with its musical director. Translating from the Danish:

> According to a persistent rumour he [JPM] died in 1966. Roskilde Festival is, however, confident that they can present the real thing. At Roskilde Festival, music director Donald Wahren takes the persistent rumors with serenity and a twinkle in his eye. Asked, "What have you done to ensure you that it actually is the real Paul McCartney, who shows up tonight?" He replied:
>
>> I have to admit that we actually have not done anything. However, we are 100% confident that this is the real Paul McCartney, who can be seen at the festival tonight. Instead we spent our energy to work vigorously to give the show the best possible conditions..
>
> Asked, 'What do you think about the wild rumour that apparently refuses to die?' he replied:
>
>> Of course I know it well. It pops up from time to time. I choose to see it as a sign that we have a genuine music legend to deal with. You must be of a certain calibre, before people begin to invent such stories.
>
> Should Sir Paul show ID, check in and have the ID bracelet that everyone else has to wear?
>
>> The short answer to that question is 'no'.

It concluded with the helpful advice:

> 'If you are a conspiracy theory fan and are getting a little tired of 9/11 and the moon landing, you can spend hours investigating the 'Paul is dead' theory online.'

Such articles would be unthinkable in the UK – this is, after all, where the Fab Four lived. And yet, earlier that year, *The Mirror* had featured articles reviewing the PID case for two days in succession (March 2-3) - although being careful to conclude with a firm dismissal of the story.

Some kind of disclosure process is definitely happening, and may even be unstoppable. Faul is said to dread the prospect of passing away before

Ms Ono, leaving her to have the final say. One can indeed appreciate the fear of so dire a prospect. But he gave indications in the *Memoirs of Billy Shears* that he hoped to pass away before the 'true' story emerged. We have reviewed how he has to have been collaborating with the *Winged Beetle* for what there emerged; whereby the *Rotten Apple* series was not banned despite all the copyrighted material it contained.

I may not have explained anything much in this book. Everything remains a mystery – maybe, more so than when we started. It has been a success *if* it leads you to a deeper appreciation of those old Beatle songs. Sir Paul's extraordinary genius may have blossomed because he is free of a mundane identity, and thereby can rise above ordinary self-pity etc. He is a character who at some deep level believes in magic, and that has appeared as a persistent theme.

The best account of the PID story has to be that given by Andru Reeves in 2004: his *Turn me on, Dead Man, The Beatles and the "Paul-is-dead" Hoax*. After taking us through three hundred pages of careful and in-depth scrutiny, from his many years of research, he then concludes that the whole thing had not been intended or planned by anyone, but 'has all the hallmarks of a giant cosmic coincidence – nothing more.' How one might detect 'hallmarks' of a 'giant cosmic coincidence' he did not specify. So, as regards the greatest urban legend in the history of rock'n'roll - nobody did it, it just happened, all by itself! At times one feels that Chance is given far too much credit.

Had the whole story been *designed* to sell Beatle records? John Lennon was pressed to comment in late 1969 once the PID story exploded, and we saw how he denied everything, maybe not too convincingly.

Lennon and Ms Ono appeared on the Dick Cavett Show on September 11th 1971 – a date which, as we've seen, keeps turning up in this story. It's online so one can enjoy the witty repartee between Lennon and Cavett. Thirty years before the towers crumbled, on that show on that day the video was premiered, of his biggest ever hit *Imagine*. A bleakly materialistic vision of a rootless proletariat wandering around and living from day to day, it soon became Number One around the world. But it was Lennon's call for world peace – on September 11th!

We've earlier quoted his response to a question from the audience on that show, concerning the PID rumour, where he replied:

It was too far-out for any of us to have thought of it.
(See *Rotten Apple* 72, at 1:08, also RA 73, 1:50)

That is, as such, absolutely true. The fate of the event had gripped all of the remaining Beatles and they may have felt they had little choice.

Or, does John here appear as being unaware of everything that he had done, and of the consequences of his actions? Had he not initially agreed that his broken band could be taken over by the imperious newcomer? Did not he and the others leave a massive trail of clues about what had happened, both on the album covers and in the music?

Did he feel it was all a destiny imposed upon him, which he had not caused to happen? Or was he becoming amnesiac from all the drugs and booze? His own psyche had been shattered to the core by losing his closest soulmate and he turned instead to an antithesis, producing anti-music resembling the wailing of the souls of the damned with his partner Ms Ono, until protests from his shocked fans persuaded him to emigrate to New York.

Someone has to have intended so colossal an event which pivoted around September 11th, a date which cannot be coincidental. We saw how John and Paul decided to have their *Magical Mystery Tour* start off on the morning of 9/11 - thirty-four years to the day (and hour!) before the Towers came down. His 'Glass Onion' song about his lost Paul was recorded on that very same date a year later.

How strange that anonymous histories should begin and end the epic tale: the first one in 1964, a *True History* of the Beatles, by 'Billy Shepherd' – did not fans ask who this author was? – then, in 2010 on September 11th the grandiose *Winged Beetle* video with its fearful magic message, as if there is something deep we're supposed to grasp. Ah yes I remember, Faul was the son of Alisteir Crowley, then in his sixties. That video was made by *somebody* with a considerable skill, sizeable budget and access to a vast archive.

Here is a young-Paul picture, while he was still at school at the Liverpool Institute. That is the fellow whom Dot (Dorothy Rhone) dated. Then, here is an image of the star, the Genius of Beatlemania – when 'he has arrived'.

His face is rounder, yet without too much trouble we can believe these are the same person. Both show a raised left eyebrow, a characteristic feature.

But, turning to a later appearance, at the last Beatle interview, given in Los Angeles on August 24th of 1966: is this really the same person? One can quite easily end up believing that there were various different doubles or replacements who were slotted in at short notice. Indeed some people believe this was and is quite normal in the world of showbiz.

We saw how the appearance of such doubles need not imply that the star has been replaced, it could just be that they are too tired or whatever to perform on that day. But, *if* you wished to believe that the fellow who there appeared in LA was a double – I'm not guiding you here – then you might wish to consider what very clearly is a double appearing as the Beatles got off the plane at San Francisco on 29th August, 1966 (see image).

Some PID-ers surmise that this character was Dino Danelli (of the band, *The Rascals*). He has a distinctly flat chin,[3] and wears a wig. Neither of these characters sing. It would be shall we say an omen, a very bad one, for these two doubles to have appeared within days of each other, in the US, at the conclusion of the last-ever Beatle tour. Some have taken the view that Paul was already dead or removed by this time, because of these doubles, and one may assocate this view with the *PlasticMacca*

---

[3] The same character turns up in the *Magical Mystery Tour* at ten minutes, we just see him briefly.

website. However (Chapter 6) the interview Paul gave a week later when he was back home, to Penny Valentine published of the *Disc and Music Echo* (10.9.66) shows that he was still very much alive and kicking.

'A new Bob Dylan'

At the risk of treading on sacred ground, we may draw an analogy here with Bob Dylan. The documentary about his career *No Direction Home* by Bob Scorsese shows us the career of this fiery poet *with a beautiful smile* (did that surprise you?), from 1961 to June 1966. That person then vanishes from the scene and then eight years later – after *various studio albums* have appeared - 'Dylan' starts touring again. There may be some deep analogies here, with our present theme.

The last few minutes of the Scorsese video shows Dylan and his people backstage somewhere in Europe, and they have each just done a line of speed. Dylan uses his fingers to get the last bits, then says: "I'm gonna get me a new Bob Dylan next week. I'm gonna get me a new Bob Dylan, use him, and see how long HE lasts."

After his mysterious motorcycle accident in June 1966 (with no medical or police documentation on public record), Dylan remained out of the public eye for over a year and a half, which synchronized with Paul's demise. Some felt it was convenient that, at the height of the anti-Vietnam war protests, when his persona could have been a powerful leader-inspiration to the left and to youth, he just vanished.

Never again would we hear his fiery anti-war protest songs! The Empire wants and needs to have a 'Bob Dylan,' but it wants him as an *entertainer,* who cannot be allowed to arouse people with his anti-war songs like the furious *Masters of War* or *Blowing in the Wind.*

Here is one blogger's comment ('Sherlok Clone'): 'I was a big fan up through the "Blonde On Blonde" album which was recorded in early 1966. Then, in July of '66 was "the motorcycle accident." This was followed by a long absence and then the release of the twangy, cornball "John Wesley Harding" album in which the fake Dylan bozo couldn't even spell or pronounce the guy's name correctly (it's Hardin, not Harding) and everybody in the business at that time seemed to just pretend it was cool to misspell it like that.'

When Dylan finally emerged we all experienced the startling change in his voice and musical style, with stories being put about that his vocal chords had been affected by the accident.

Ask people about any Dylan songs they like, and you'll mainly get those from that early period, up until 1966. Why indeed did Scorsese choose to make his 2005 film-bio covering only those years 1961-6? The guy who reappeared afterwards was more surly and aggressive in interviews, no longer polite as earlier, and politically quite passive. Dylan's early music kept being shot through with rays of hope and themes of redemption, rather lacking in his later songs where instead "Its Doom alone that counts" (*Blood on the Tracks*, 1971).

His biographers face an unenviable task, with his various different marriages and families, rather hidden away. He has been the most mercurial and changeable of characters throughout his long career, whereby we have come to accept startling mutations in his appearance and music style. But could there be another explanation?

One would like to see a university physiology-department study of the colour of his eyes over the years, as too with Paul/Faul. These are maybe the most photographed people in the world so there should be enough colour pictures.

Here is another blogger: 'I went this summer (of 2009) to see Bob Dylan play in a concert with John Mellencamp and Willie Nelson. Having listened to all of his records day and night for months on end in the early days, I think I have an inkling as to whether he was there or not. I didn't notice Bob Dylan being at that event. It wasn't just that his voice was broken, which it (conveniently?) was. It was that nothing resembled his style and his articulation and phrasing had any of the artistry of the original.'

At the top of the food-chain, does identity-substitution become a bit of a risk? Kris Kristofferson worked with Dylan and as the son of a Pentagon major-general, he should know. Looking back in 1995 he sang:

> Well I was there the day they say that Bobby Dylan died
> You and I both know he got away
> He's out there stealin' horses
> Really learnin' how to ride
> And he's the reason I am free today
>
> Singin', You can be the new mister me, me, me
> Ain't it true that's what you wanna be, yes indeed
> And I'll be somewhere sunny where it's funny and its free
> And you can be the new mister me.

('New Mister Me' on the album, *A Moment of Forever*)

Endgame

Dylan's replacement had – or so it is averred - a shorter, more square face while the original Robert Zimmerman had a roundish, long, narrow face. Does not an utterly different chin structure appear, between the first Dylan album here shown, to *Blonde on Blonde* in 1966? As he has famously remarked, 'All I can do is be me. Whoever that is.'

Now in his seventies, Dylan keeps on touring, with a heavy schedule of at least a hundred concerts per year, which reminds us of Faul - neither of them can stop! In a rare interview of 2004 'Dylan' explained what kept him going. He first admitted that his early songs were 'almost magically written:' 'There's a magic to that, and it's not Siegfried & Roy kind of magic, it's a different kind of penetrating magic.' ('What happened to bob Dylan') And then, as to why he still tours:

> "Well it goes back to the destiny thing. I made a bargain with ... it, a long time ago, and I'm holding up my end.'
> 'What was your bargain?'
> "To get where I am now"
> 'Should I ask who you made the bargain with?'
> [Laughs] With the Chief Commander'
> 'What, on this Earth?' [Laughs]
> 'In this Earth and in the world we can't see.'

This appeared in an interview with Ed Bradley, over the release of his memoirs, *Chronicles* ('Dylan Looks Back', CBS, 5.12.04) Dylan spoke quite slowly and deliberately, one word at a time, a contrast with the ever-garrulous Faul. We may note that the 21st century Bob Dylan *did not ever criticise* President Bush, and then later on was effusive in praise of Obama.

In a remarkable September 2012 *Rolling Stone* interview[4], Dylan was insisting: 'You're asking questions to a person who's long dead. You're asking them to a person who doesn't exist. But people make that mistake about me all the time.' He then alluded to a book entitled, *No Man knows my History* and averred, 'The title could refer to me.' He had become who he was, out of the dead or vanished person, by *transfiguration*. 'You can learn about it in some old mystical books, but it's a real concept,' he said, This wasn't transmigration, he said: 'Its not anything to do with the past or the future.'

'I couldn't go back and find Bobby in a million years, neither could you or anybody else on the face of the earth. He's gone. If I could, I would go back. I'd like to go back. At this point in time, I would love to go back and find him, put out my hand. And tell him he's got a friend. But I can't. He's gone. He doesn't exist.' the baffled interviewer asked, '*I'm trying to determine whom you've been transfigured from?*'

As to what had been involved in that 'transfiguration' process, one could here be reminded of Dylan's cryptic words, 'I came in from the wilderness, a creature void of form.' ('Shelter from the Storm', 1975)

Later in the interview, the subject of the 1966 mutation in his life arose: 'With *John Wesley Harding* and *Nashville Skyline*', the interviewer asked, 'some were bewildered by your transformation. You came back from that hiatus looking different, sounding different, in voice, music and words.' Dylan then grew quite angry – for the only time in the interview – as if maybe his privacy were being invaded and he accused those who had sought to interpret that event, or to conjecture about it: '*They want to know what can't be known. They are searching – they are seekers…* Why are they doing this?' One feels here that Dylan himself may not be too sure what happened then.

For comparison, 'The Long & Winding Road', on the *Let it Be* album, has Faul trying to look back and wishing he could meet the old Paul - whose life he had to take over.

Dylan is the only artist with a comparable productivity to Faul, having composed over five hundred songs on forty-six albums. We get a possibly comparable - and rather weird - philosophy of magic from both characters. Both remind us of Wagner's 'Flying Dutchman': in their seventies, neither can stop, but have to keep going, ever roaming around the world, as if they had no home nor any wish to retire.

---

4 *Rolling Stone*, September 2012, 'Bob Dylan The Rolling Stone Interview' pp.42-51.

George sung about somebody needing the 'blood from a clone.' It was after John's brutal murder and he was feeling rather shattered, but what could he have meant?

> Beating my head on a brick wall
> Hard like a stone
> Don't have time for the music
> They want the blood from a clone

> George Harrison, 1981, 'Somewhere in England'

The word 'clone' has not been used throughout this book: trying to maintain what one might call a level-headed approach. But, both Faul and George have used it: in Chapter Three we quoted the former as commenting in a jocular manner upon his identity-problem: 'Oh no, I'm just a clone' - and now here is George with an eerie phrase about someone wanting the blood of a clone.

Ringo (Richard Starkey) does not ever say much. But, in 2011, at a 'Comic relief' event, he stated *twice* quite distinctly that he was the last remaining Beatle – 'I was in the biggest rock 'n' roll band in the history of music… I am the last remaining Beatle,' he affirmed.

Asked to explain, he added, 'I think it's people on the outside who perceive Paul as thinking he's the only one left. Actually, it's me. I am the last remaining Beatle.' Then he added, concerning Faul, 'We are good friends… We're the only two who've experienced all this who are still here.' (May, 2011) A distinction is made, that only he and Faul have 'experienced all this' and 'are still here,' *but* Ringo is the 'last remaining Beatle.'

His remarks were not made in any spirit of bitterness, but were thoughtfully stated, as a matter-of-fact truthful statement: *he was the only one left.*

A US survey in 2014 found PID to be the *least* popular of conspiracy theories –

	9/11 the US govt knew	Roswell Space aliens	Moon landing faked	Di killed by UK royals	AIDs virus from CIA	PID
Believers	25%	20%	14%	13%	8%	3%
Undecided	19%	33%	12%	20%	20%	15%

(by 'Rasmussen Reports', from asking a thousand people).

The figures seem about right for the Roswell space alien story, and the faking of the moon landing, but otherwise are rather low. I'd say a lot more believe in the PID story these days.

Faul should not be called or remembered as a fraud and impostor. He is so much more than that! But as we warned at the beginning, his original identity remains an enigma. Here in conclusion are a couple of Kenya images of the early Faul, which Mal Evans took in November of '66, but were only released years after his death, in the 1980s.[5] They are the very earliest images of Faul. As we have here argued in some detail, these have to be the same guy who composed *Sgt Pepper* and who was the star of MMT. A photo given on the *White Album* is shown for comparison, also rumoured to be Faul before surgery.

We saw how the Beatle message was or became 'psychedelic,' in that it *made manifest the psyche.* In vivid colours a language of the soul has been indelibly expressed in that music. The house of George Harrison at Kinfauns where the *White Album* was composed (check it online to see the radiant flower-power hues George painted it with) ought to have endured as a main tourist attraction of Surrey and a wonderful focus of Beatle-appreciation conferences. Instead it was demolished and replaced by a squat, ugly thing, as if people did not want to be reminded of those days of happiness which it expressed.

There was a darker side too - At the end of his fine Beatle-bio *Shout!*[6] Mr Phillip Norman commented on how '*The story left others dead: an uncanny number.*' He then counts sombrely through that 'uncanny number,' as if surveying the remains of some tragic battlefield. He can't explain it of course. But a secret had to be kept.

---

5 They are stills from an online video, featuring him and Mal Evans.
6 Philip Norman, *Shout! The True story of the Beatles* p.416

Appendix A: Chronology

1957 July McCartney meets Lennon after a Quarryman performance, at a garden fete

1961 February The Beatles perform in the Cavern at Liverpool

April They perform in Hamburg clubs, during which period Paul replaces Stuart as the bass player.

December Brian Epstein becomes their manager

1962 April Stuart Sutcliff dies of a brain tumour in Hamburg,

August Ringo Starr performs as the Beatles drummer

December Erika Hubers gives birth to Paul's daughter Bettina, conceived in Hamburg.

1963 February First album Please Please Me recorded in one day at the Abbey Road studio (EMI)

April Paul meets Jane Asher

November Paul moves into Wimpole Street Asher residence

1964 February The Band perform on the Ed Sullivan show in New York to audience of 74 million.

December Epstein moves into Belgravia flat in London.

1965 April Paul buys Cavendish Avenue house and renovates it.

May Paul composes Yesterday

August They perform at the Shea stadium before an audience of some 56,000 fans.

November Indica Gallery opens

December Final British tour

1966 March Paul moves into his own home at Cavendish Avenue

April-June recording sessions for *Revolver*

July A US magazine republishes Lennon's comment about how Beatles are 'more popular than Jesus'

August: Beatles final US tour on 5th, *Revolver* album released.

22 August Beatles give a press conference in New York City

28 August the last Beatles press interview, at Hollywood.

29 August The Last Concert, at San Francisco Candlestick Park

6th September Lennon has short haircut and starts acting for a war-film, in Germany

9 September, Revolver goes platinum, ie sells a million copies, their 20th album to do this.

10 September Last interview of Paul published in *Disc & Music Echo*

11th **Paul dies**

13 September *Melody Maker* Awards ceremony (cancelled)

14th September George Harrison and Patti go to India

17th September Lennon & Neil Aspinall come to Paris for first meeting with Faul, with Epstein.

14 October *International Times* launch party: McCartney arrives (?) disguised as an Arab.

9th November Lennon meets Yoko Ono at Indica Gallery (may have been a day or two earlier)

Chronology

19th November, Mal Evans and McCartney return from Kenya.

24 November Recording of *Strawberry Fields Forever* begins at Abbey Road

November – April 1967, recording for *Sgt Pepper*

December – Guinness heir Tara Browne dies, in supposed car crash

20 December Beatle Press interview outside EMI, Faul is present.

1967   January   *The Beatles Book* issue 43 denies rumours that Paul was killed in a car accident. IT interviews Paul McCartney.

30-31st January filming of *Strawberry Fields* in Knole Park,

February Release of *Strawberry Fields forever*

May McCartney meets Linda Eastman

1st June *Sgt Pepper* released, perform *All you Need is Love* on Our World International Telecast

July *All you need is love / Baby You're a Rich man* single released.

August They meet the Maharishi on 24th, and on 25th they go with him to Bangor, North Wales

August 27th Epstein is found dead in his home.

September-October *Magical Mystery Tour*

December *Magical Mystery Tour* shown on BBC (ie in black and white),

1968 January Apple Corps founded.

February-April visit Maharishi in Rishikesh, India

March *Lady Madonna* single released

July Yellow submarine cartoon film,

August *Hey Jude* release

1969 January Rooftop concert at Savile row, stopped by police after 45 minutes, later included in *Let it Be* film.

March 'McCartney' marries Linda Eastman, McCartney family not invited. John marries Yoko Ono

April Richard Asher Jane's father dead from 'suicide.' The single *Saint Paul* released by Terry Knight in Detroit.

April-August Recording sessions for *Abbey Road*

July Death of Brian Jones

17 September first PID article published, in Drake University's Times-Delphic newspaper.

12 October Paul-is-dead hysteria breaks out in Detroit, story becomes global.

22 October Newswire: Paul not dead. Faul travels up to Scottish home.

29-30 *Life* Magazine interviews Faul in Scottish highland farm.

7 November *Life* magazine 'Paul is still with us.'

1970 10 April: McCartney announces breakup of the Band, The Sixties come to an end.

May *Let it be* album released

1971 January Lennon records *Imagine*, his last great album

August John and Yoko move to New York, McCartney band *Wings* is formed.

1976 January Mal Evans shot by LA police

22 March Paul's father's funeral, Faul does not attend.

1980 December Lennon assassinated in New York

1997 November McCartney is knighted.

1999 December Crazed killer attacks George Harrison

2001 November George Harrison dies of cancer

2006 November first *Rotten Apple* video appears.

2007 June *Memory Almost Full* CD, with Faul on credits as 'King of Cosmania'

2008 March Death of Neil Aspinall

2009 15 July *Wired Italia* Magazine published Italian PID forensic research by Carlesi and Gavazzeni; Faul does a NY rooftop concert same day, then on 17th appears on David Letterman show, discussing (in Part 2 of video online) PID.

September *Memoirs of Billy Shears* 666 pages long is published on 9.9.09, the same day on which the entire *Beatles Original Studio Recordings* (16 CD pack) were released.

2010 11 September *The Winged Beetle* goes online, by 'Iamaphoney'

2011 May Richard Starkey declares, 'I am the last remaining Beatle'

Nicholas Kollerstrom

Appendix A
Tara Browne,
a Mystery death

'Those whom the gods love, die young'

Roman proverb

Kathy Etchingham, Jimi Hendrix's partner, recalled how:

On the night of the 17th December 1966 Jimi and I went to a party. Brian Jones had come round and insisted we should go to a party to see his friend Tara Browne before he went off to Ireland for Christmas. We arrived late and met Tara Browne and his girlfriend, the model Suki Potier who had both been spending that day with Brian, and they chatted with us around the dining room table. We exchanged phone numbers and said we would keep in touch and then they left.

Tara was driving his sports car and had a fatal crash in Redcliffe Gardens just minutes later. Suki survived and later became the girlfriend of Brian Jones. Jimi and I were shocked when we heard of the car crash. Tara was the first one of our circle who died.

All three of the young men here alluded to had died three years later. The Beautiful People in the 1960s did have a tendency to die off. But is this story relevant? Let'say, it hovers on the cusp of relevance.[1]

The words of Lennon's song *A Day in the Life*

> He blew his mind out in a car / He hadn't noticed that the lights had changed

---

[1] Blogger SunKing denounced it as 'way off base' for the PID story.

were about the tragic end of Tara Browne's life, because of that song's allusion to the House of Lords – as heir to the Guinness fortune he was due to become a Lord when his Father died.[2] In reality there *were no traffic lights*, neither in the newspaper reports nor at the road-junction in question. Yes, they are eternally there in the story, because Lennon's song put them there - but such mundane details hardly seem to matter.[3]

The young Tara Browne was, so to speak, too happy. He seemed to think he was here to enjoy life. At the mere age of twenty-one he had got married, had two kids, opened a couple of boutiques in London, got his fast car psychedelically painted, had raced in another of his cars, was mingling with the Indica gallery in-crowd, and knew the Beatles, Rolling Stones and Jimi Hendrix.

Figure: the rather Apollonian trendsetter Tara Browne in '66

With a private jet he flew over a crowd of the Beat generation glitterati to party at his parent's glorious Irish stately home. Here, surrounded by majestic mountains, culture blossomed: "On any given weekend Luggala was filled with the likes of Van Morrison or Marianne Faithful singing to us. Seamus Heaney reciting poetry while Edward Delaney sculpted in the gardens. There were long conversations over dinner with film director John Boorman and actor John Hurt. More often than not Ronan Browne (no relation) or Seamus Ennis would play the pipes while I was mesmerized by the footwork of the Irish folk dancers."[4]

From such a centre there emanated a cultural mood of optimism and well-being, nourishing the Swinging Sixties. On his 21st birthday party in the spring of '66, Tara had private jets fly his two hundred showbiz and glitterati guests to Ireland, including John Paul Getty, Mick Jagger, Brian Jones and his girlfriend Anita Pallenberg, and Paul McCartney. Surely, this sort of thing could not be allowed to continue.

---

2. As likewise the small white car on the Sgt Pepper cover, RHS on the lap of the child Shirley Temple.
3 There are some pedestrian traffic lights, for crossing the road.
4 Julie Anne Rhodes, 'Luggala, Escape to my Shamrock Paradise', 2010.

Appendix A

Tara co-opened the night club *Sybilla's* where George Harrison was a significant investor and these two names soon made it a hot spot with the in-crowd. Tara also ran a with-it store called *Dandie Fashions* and Faul wore a jacket made there in the flower-power days of '67; Apple took it over after its owner's demise.

Tare was due to inherit a million in a few years' time. The Establishment may well not have wanted so powerful a support and nurturing for a 'druggie' counter-culture. Why, with such millionaire backing it could soon develop to a degree that could no longer be controlled! That death would have sent a message loud and clear throughout the blossoming flower-power movement or whatever one calls it, not to get ideas above their station. In the US in the 1960s, the clandestine Operation Paperclip and Cointelpro were taking out so-called 'dangerous' activists.

The destiny of America was altered by the assassinations of John and Robert Kennedy and Martin Luther King. In this 21st century we're in a better position to appreciate the sorrowful truth, that the hippie flower-power movement did not just die - it was killed. In the wake of Paul's death there followed a series of strange demises, meant to look accidental. Tara would have been aware of the swapover, as a friend of the Beatles, and who knows that might have been a factor.

Certain members of the Irish home of the Guinness family could have been uneasy at this heir behaving in so hedonistic a manner: Tara had a livid ex-wife from whom he had taken their two children, and she was seeking to regain possession. A court case was going on that very day in London over ownership, and after the crash his wife gained access to his documents found in the car, telling her where her children were. I'm not suggesting she caused the event, but it would have been a convenient cover-story for anyone intending to do the act.

Cryptic Car Crash

The car-crash story makes no sense, however one examines it. Tara was driving at midnight away from Earl's Court, from Brian Jones' pad, going down a one-way street Redcliffe Gardens, when at a small junction with Redcliffe Square a vehicle suddenly emerged causing Tara to swerve over the right, where he hit a stationary van. The image of the car shows its middle part battered in as if with a hammer and its steering-wheel broken, but its front hardly crushed in. Its top has been removed (in the middle of winter) while its bonnet appears as unharmed. The front wheel was undamaged. There is no blood anywhere.

The various newspaper reports have Tara killed by 'brain haemorrhage' dying a couple of hours later while the model Suki Potier in the seat adjacent was unharmed. She would have experienced an identical deceleration to him, and if the impact was sudden enough to kill him how could she have escaped unharmed? If the car supposedly impacted on its right hand side that would not somehow exempt her from the laws of physics as the reports seemed to suggest. She had no seat-belt.

The first person to arrive on the scene of the crash was Mrs Maggie Postlewaite, a fashion model, who lived in Redcliffe Gardens. She testified how she with her children's nurse wrapped Mr Browne in 'travelling rugs.' (*Daily Express,* 19.12.66). – in other words the top of the car must by then have been lifted off, so she could get access.

A Mr James Murray was also present, and testified at the Inquest: 'When I reached the car I was surprised to find anyone in it, but I saw Tara Browne, lying in the driver's seat severely injured' Neither of these first accounts give any hint that Ms Potier was present, (*Irish Times,* 5.1.67) nor do any others at the scene. If his body could be wrapped in rugs it means that the steering-wheel had not gone into his chest, so why is it broken off in the picture? Our images of this glorious young life are replaced by these horror-images that don't add up – as was, maybe, the intention. If he was 'severely injured' he was not dead.

The post-mortem showed no more than half a pint of beer in his system. Proverbially he drove his turquoise Lotus Elan through a red light at high speed (Wiki account) although Ms Potier testified to how she had not felt unsafe in Mr Browne's car, how he had not been driving abnormally and drove 'not very fast.' (*Irish Times* 5.1.67)

The one published photo of the car is taken from the driver's side, and shows a car interior so badly damaged that one would expect the passenger to have had much worse injuries than a few bruises.

No van or any vehicle was visible in the picture of the crashed car, meaning it has been towed away or was never there in the first place. Wiki has a lorry being hit while early reports said it was a van, again suggesting that the event did not happen. At the Inquest, testimony was heard that 'shortly before the accident he [Mr Murray] had seen a white E-type Jaguar travelling very slowly towards Redcliffe Gardens'[5] – which could be a glimpse of the perpetrators.

---

[5] *Irish Times,* 5.1.67, 'Verdict on Tara Browne', testimony of James Chester Murray, a child care officer.

Appendix A

Through the swirling mist of conspiracy-theory, parallels are drawn between this mystery car-cash and that of Paul months earlier, where he and 'Rita' crashed together and were both killed.[6]

Kiss of the spider-woman

The nineteen-year old Suki Potier had starred in the first James Bond film, *Casino Royale*, where her character had made an amazing escape. The crash with Tara was the second time in less than ten days that one of Mr Potier's daughters had had a lucky escape: his elder daughter Sarah, 20, escaped without a scratch when her car landed on its back in a field in Northern France after hitting a lorry.

Brian Jones declined to comment on Tara's crash: 'I do not really want to talk about it – I am too cut up. Tara was a very close friend.' (*Daily Sketch* 19th December) Soon after Ms Potier moved into Brian Jones' home to grieve, becoming his girlfriend and moving into his 15th century farmhouse in Sussex a few months before his death. She was there on the night of his mystery death in his own pool a couple of years later. Later on, Ms Potier married a Hong Kong businessman named Ho, and one night in 1981 he allegedly told her he wanted a divorce, and her reaction caused the car to go over a cliff where they both died.

---

6 There is the story that Paul 'first took LSD' with Tara, and that a forthcoming book about him, inevitably entitled 'A lucky man who made the grade' will tell all.

Appendix B: The Endeavour of Forensic Analysis

Over the years 1960-62, Paul had an affair with 16-year old Erika Huber, in Hamburg. Erika had been faithful to him, and so when a daughter Bettina was born to her, she was sure that the child had to be Paul's daughter.

Upon asking for alimony, Erika soon had his lawyer (David Jacobs) trying to buy her silence. In 1966, she was paid 16,000 German marks [then about £7,000] to as she said "keep my mouth shut."[1] Through this act, she argued, Paul had acknowledged his paternity. Because of this gag order, her daughter did not discover who her father was until she was 12 years old.

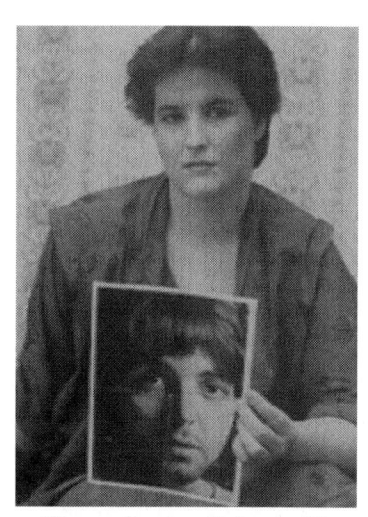

Figure: Bettina Huber holding a picture of Faul (!)

Bettina when she was seventeen, wrote an "Open Letter to Paul McCartney," published in the youth magazine *Bravo* in 1982. "Dear Daddy," she wrote, "here is someone who wants to meet you absolutely. Your daughter Bettina. I want to finally talk to my father and finally take him into my arms." This could alas never be. Once she turned 18, the Hubers went to a Berlin court asking for maintenance: they wanted £375 per month and a declaration from Sir Paul that he was the father.

---

1 But, Albert Goldman (Lies of John Lennon p.120) says it was 2,700

In response, Sir Paul allowed DNA to be sampled from his blood – the only time he has done such a thing. The match was negative, showing that he was *not* the father. His cautious comment was:

> It seems the girl's blood contains something that is not in mine or the mother's, so it must have come from the real father.

Surprisingly, the court rejected this scientific evidence and ordered him to pay full maintenance (Bettina then posed naked for High Society magazine for £600, saying she had to do it because of delays in maintenance payments.)

In spring 2007, mother and daughter went back to the court because her lawyers believed he had discovered inconsistencies in the DNA report of 1983. They made the claim: "Sir Paul sent a double to carry out a paternity test 20 years ago, which appeared to prove that he was not her father," and added, "The signature on the documents he signed at the time was false," she said. "We found the signature is from a right-handed person and he is not."

According to German law, if it could be shown that Bettina is Sir Paul's daughter, she would be entitled to ten per cent of his estate after his death, totalling tens of millions of pounds.

We could here note that DNA testing can work with relatives several steps removed: DNA from the daughters of Stella McCartney will give characteristics of Sir Paul's DNA, in the event that the latter is not obtainable, while that of Mike McGear should match up with Bettina Krischbin.

Forensic Science

A forensic-science analysis compared the heads of Paul and Faul, published in *Wired Italia* magazine on 15 July, 2009. It was called, *'Chiedi chi era quel «Beatle»'* translation: 'Ask who was that "Beatle."'[2] Its Italian authors were Francesco Gavazzeni and Gabriella Carlesi: the latter is forensic pathologist who specializes in identification of people through craniometry (which compares certain features of the skull) and forensic odontology (which analyses structure of teeth); she has worked as a consultant identifying people via digital image processing for various high-profile investigations.

Her colleague Gavazzeni is a computer analyst. The two of them used computer analysis to derive high-precision measurements of Paul McCartney's skull from various photos of his face. A thorough bio-metric comparison found discrepancies in the two faces that could not be accounted for by plastic surgery.

---

2 Text of this article with English translation is up on the plastic macca site.

The Endeavour of Forensic Analysis

Using photos dated from before and after 1966, with the subject directly facing the camera, they were scaled to all have the same distance between the pupils. Comparing skull shape they found that both of the photos taken prior to 1966 matched one another perfectly, while photos taken after 1967 matched one another perfectly, however the photos prior to 1966 did **not** match those taken after 1967.

The frontal curvature of the jaw was different, i.e. the curve going from one ear to the other and passing through the chin, which one sees when looking directly into a face, and then the jaw arc was also different: i.e. the curve of the jaw that you would see if looking downward at the head from above.

Gavazzeni noticed a common feature of Faul's early photos not evident in more recent photos: a dark area shadowing the external corner of the left eye. That area now shows something half-way between a scar and something that resembles skin that was stretched as a consequence of cosmetic surgery, or, as Gavazzeni suggests, of an imperfect cosmetic surgery.

Faul's head appeared as more oblong than Paul's head and Gavazzeni inferred that some of the early printed photos of Faul must have been compressed in height in order to make his head appear shorter and more rounded – after all, the shape of the skull of an adult cannot be altered. There was a simple trick for stretching or compressing photos during the printing process in those days before computer photo editing became available, he observed, which could easily have been done.

DETTAGLI DI BOCCA PALATO E DENTATURA
CONFRONTO TRA IMMAGINI DI PAUL McCARTNEY A BOCCA APERTA

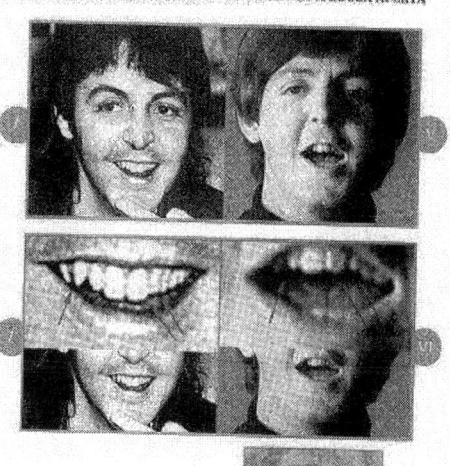

The position, relative to the skull, of the point where the nose detaches from the face cannot be modified by surgery. According to Carlesi, these points for Paul and Faul were considerably different.

In Germany, the identification of the shape of the right ear has the same legal value of that of a DNA test or fingerprints detection. Ear features are useful for ID purposes because they are not modifiable through surgery. Carlesi and Gavazzeni determined that the ears of Paul and Faul differed significantly.[3]

Carlesi noticed that the teeth configurations for Paul and Faul do not match. In Paul's mouth, his upper right canine tooth is pushed out of its normal position because there is not enough room in his jaw for all of his teeth to fit properly. In Faul's mouth, that same canine tooth is also crooked, but there is plenty of room in his jaw for all of his teeth. Since no other teeth are pushing against the crooked tooth, how did that tooth become crooked? Carlesi concluded that the crooked tooth in Faul's mouth was the result of a dental operation to simulate the crooked tooth in Paul's mouth.

Carlesi was startled by the difference in the shape of the palate. It was so narrow in Paul's mouth that some teeth were misaligned (such as the canine tooth mentioned above); when but Faul's palate was so wide that the front teeth did not rotate with respect to their axis, or tilt, as was happening for Paul, with the only exception of that upper right canine (mentioned above) which leans outward. Carlesi points out that altering the shape of a person's palate, although possible in the 1960s, would have required a traumatic surgical operation involving the breaking of a bone, and wearing of a brace for a year.

Their conclusion was: '*Multiple unique facial characteristics show significant differences between the 'old' and 'new' Paul,*' differences that could not be explained by natural aging. They added that a DNA test between Mike McGear and Sir Paul could readily resolve the matter.[4]

On the very same day as that *Wired Italia* article appeared, a stage had been constructed thousands of miles away above the famous Ed Sullivan Theatre in Broadway, Manhattan, the site of the Beatles' historic first American performance. On July 15, 2009, New Yorkers watched a fine performance by Sir Paul's band on that rooftop. The street below it was packed out with appreciative New Yorkers.

Two days after this concert, on 17th, came his interview in that very same studio on the David Letterman show - which some claim was then the world's most viewed TV program. Readers are urged not to deny themselves the fun of watching this.

---

3 'On the Internet, our ears are readily compared. Paul's round ears are both attached at the bottom. My earlobes hang down. Our images also show our head shapes. His is round, like his ears. Mine is longer-like my ears.' *Memoirs of Billy Shears*, p.609.
4 There is no English translation of the *Wired* article, but there's a good summary by Jim Fetzer, on *Veterans Today:* 'Ringo's Confession,' March 2105 (An imaginary story of Ringo making a PID confession, which generated some publicity).

Taking literally, Sir Paul's words clearly affirmed that he *was* the double:

DL: Towards the end of the sixties, is that when the rumours about you being dead surfaced, do you remember that?
Sir Paul: (Explains *Abbey Road* cover, then adds) People did start looking at me like, 'Is it him, or a very good double?'
DL: That was the idea, that was the other part of it, that there was a guy who looked like you taking your place:
Sir Paul: No well, *this is him.* (Points to himself)
Pause...
DL (smiling): Or is it?

Amidst the banter, the two never alluded to the article just published that day. That is in the second of a three-part video - and it makes a fine opening sequence of the *Winged Beetle.*

Thus the Empire responds: it cannot discuss, or give argument, but it did put on a rather brilliant, synchronous and pre-planned event that successfully knocked the appearance of this article off from any possible headlines.

Voice comparison

Paul McCartney's voice was of a lower register, deeper than Faul's, with more resonance and vibrato. The latter's singing voice is higher and thinner than Paul's was, and what Liverpool accent he had is noticeably less thick and consistent than JPM's.

Miami professor Dr Henry Truby was Director of the university's Language and Linguistic Research Department. He was renowned for his claim that, just like fingerprints and DNA, no two voices in the world are similar. Through the use of ultrasound techniques, he would measure the unique characteristics of a voice and create unique voice-profiles, his 'sonograms'. In his audio lab, Truby created three 'sound fingerprint tests' as he called them, and compared them to see if they would match, one of Paul singing *Yesterday* in 1965, then *Penny Lane* (recorded December '66, one of the very first sung by Faul) and *Hey Jude* in 1968.

He concluded: "somebody else was singing at a time when the fans and the label would indicate that it was Paul McCartney' (*Rotten Apple* 77, at 2 mins 44s). He produced three very different sonograms and did that mean that there were three McCartneys? "I'm not prepared to say that this is the final word," Truby told *Rolling Stone* Magazine, "but it's a beginning." (Reeve, 105)

Life magazine interviewed him for their November 7th issue. Compared these three songs he concluded: 'On the basis of singing voice plus musical background analysis, I have not been able to say that there were less than three voices, all of which are attributed to Paul McCartney. I *cannot* conclude that the same voice appears in these early and late passages.'[5]

Details of what he did have alas disappeared, and we only have these two interviews. The *Life* article publishing these sonograms and quoted Truby that they appeared "suspiciously different." "Could there have been more than one 'McCartney'?", the *Life* article asked" These statements caused Dr Truby some grief at his university, and he never pursued the matter: he published nothing.

We are conditioned to look for 'proof' that will demonstrate, like a fingerprint, whether two voices come from the same person or not. But, that proof never comes - as Batman explained to Robin (Chapter 7), it's not that easy. It's much better to listen to the two voices. What does your intuition tell you? Here is Paul at the last Beatles press conference, August '66: www.earthplanet.net/PaulReally2.mp3 , then one year later we have Faul answering questions about LSD in the summer of '67: www.earthplanet.net/FaulReally2.mp3 The difference is as plain as day - isn't it?

Let's hear a professional musician evaluating the two voices:

But, to me, the voice, starting with «Hello, Goodbye» [1967] diverges. He has gotten higher and more sustaining. Before ‹66 Paul had a high baritone ceiling. I make my living accompanying vocalists, playing shows, and doing recordings with singers. Some I have worked with since 1975.

Nobody I have ever worked with changes this much. I have worked with A LOT of male and female singers. I have worked with some of them off and on since 1975. I have recordings of their voices then, and now. They mature, they grow, but they don›t change that much...

If McCartney is the same man, then a RARE phenomenal change happened to his vocal cords, tone production, breathing, vibrato, vowel phonemes, support, placement........ If the same man that sang *Yesterday, Michelle, Paperback Writer* and *We Can Work it Ou*t [1965] also sang *Let it Be, Hey Jude, Jet, Say Say Say*, [1968-1983] then McCartney was changing in ways that would shock most voice teachers.

I am not saying the pre '66 Paul was bad. Not at all. I loved that voice. It is just, to me, a different instrument, a different technique, different

---

5 WKBW radio, in *Turn me on Dead Man* Reeve, p.105.

breathing and diction, different cranial resonators. Newer Paul "rings" his head resonators a lot (as opposed to falsetto, true head voice can be very powerful) ; older Paul seemed a bit trapped in his "chest voice." Paul in the sixties had to "reach" to hit E's and F's (just above middle C) and really had to push to tackle G's and Ab's. 70's and 80's Paul could soar effortlessly to G's and hover in that tessitura.

Plus, there is a total discard of the simple, unaffected, troubadour-balladeer approach that we hear in early work.

Turn the stereo balance all the way to the side that is predominately voice. Toggle between *Yesterday* and *Hey Jude*. Play the first "A" section of each song listening only to the left track. Go back and forth. *Yesterday* takes a lot of breath pressure to ascend to "all my troubles seem so FAR AWAY"... Compare this to "speaking words of wisdom" in *Let it Be*. Of course, there is a change of recording apparatus. But that's true for John on that album and he still sounds like John from the past.

Listen to the letter "K" or hard "C". Early Paul makes a very percussive, sharp unmistakeable sound on that consonant. Listen to *Eleanor Rigby*: check the words MacKenzie, church, socks, worKing, , or Ah, looKK at all the lonely people......etc. Listen to just the right side. *Paperback Writer*: listen to the right channel. paperbac (KKK) writer.... Whereas, "Hey Jude, don't make it bad..." the "K" in make is just not as forceful. Early Paul's "k's" are very loud and wet.

Also, low-range tones become more resonant before '67. In *Eleanor Rigby*, the verses range from E 3rd space bass clef to D just above the bass clef. Most of the notes are E-B, a very comfortable, rich range for a baritone. Paul is very at home here.

In *Hey Jude,* which begins on a tenory middle "C", dips only to that same "E" in Rigby briefly on the phrase..."make it BET-ter." On the syllable "BET" it sounds like he is scraping the bottom of the range.

He is either way, way hoarse, or he is a tenor. Tenors are funny, some can relax and croon down to low Bbs and lower, but it tends to be very thin. But this is middle E, for goodness sakes. The singer is a tenor.[6]

To reiterate: It's in the nature of a studio recording that we do not ultimately know who is singing, or what the great maestro producer George Martin did with the voices...

---

6 Comment by Perplexed, 'Paul's Bass Work' thread on invanddis.proboards.com.

Eye Colour

As regards the facial appearance, let's quote from the legendary '60if' document. This was alleged to be a statement by George Harrison which he had written in an Indian-language text, fearing for what might happen if it were in English, with instructions for it only to be released after his death. After he died in 2001 it somehow went to Italy and an Italian who called himself 'Sun King' got a hold of it, and it then appeared in broken English. The name '60if' alluded to the Abbey Road car number-plate, i.e. that Paul would be sixty years old in 2002 when this was published. In fact it was probably just a channelled message, because no other corroborating evidence ever surfaced, such as an original text.

> Faul had an appearance older in respect to Paul and for confuse this we left grow our beard and moustaches for seeming all "a bit older." Despite they must wear contact lenses for darken their natural green color, Faul's eyes were made discreet but someone noticed that something had changed: the surgeons had forgotten to duplicate the small ditching that Paul had on his chin. This was retouched in the photos.

> And Faul was endured to other sittings of plastic surgery until better results turned out possible but still not perfect. The surgeons altered his mouth again, the teeth and his chin fully rebuilt; the cheeks (and the chin) increased with time limited botuline injections when we must be in public or for the photos because his face was too thin respect to that of Paul. In spite of these operations today's traces of the old scar can be seen on Faul's chin and different oriented ears and overall a nose that is not the same one, Faul has a smaller with a different shape. and above all the distance among the eyes was wholly different: Paul had a very large one. This is the main reason why many photos were retouched.

For Paul's brown eyes, see *Paperback Writer* and *Rain* videos along with the movie *Help!* which are in colour. Paul's eyes are lighter than George's which were a dark brown, and John's were hazel. In MMT, the green eyes of Faul look hazel, as Faul is (presumably) wearing his brown contacts. We do see his green eyes in the *Strawberry Fields* video, probably because coloured contacts weren't advanced enough to hide the green totally.

Fingerprints: During the PID furore of 1969, Alex Bennett of a NY City radio station remarked that, 'The only way McCartney is going to quell the rumours is by coming up with a set if fingerprints from a 1965 passport which can be compared to his present prints.' Passports then carried fingerprints.[7]

---

7 Patterson, *The Walrus was Paul* p32.

In Japan[8] In January 1980 Faul was arrested in Japan for possession, and spent ten days in jail: they found his fingerprints did not match earlier Paul fingerprints from Paul's arrest in Germany in 1960, also the two signatures were quite different. They asked why he was impersonating Paul McCartney, and eventually Faul admitted that he was 'another James Paul McCartney.' That is the story told in *Memoirs of Billy Shears,* p.538.Various customs offices would have had fingerprints of the old Paul.

After Faul was arrested in Japan in January 1980, for trying to bring a huge stash of dope into that country, then in consequence a whole lot of sold-out *Wings* concerts had to be cancelled as Faul spent nine days in a Japanese jail. Denny Lane in particular in the *Wings* group became very fed up with the aborting of their whole Japanese tour and loss of income - why had Faul done that?

The *Wings* group broke up a year later, partly from the stress of this episode. The Japanese police interrogated him for two days, and according to the *Memoirs of Billy Shears* they asked him: 'The fingerprints that we received from you today were not the same as Mr McCartney's when he was arrested in Germany in 1960. You also have entirely different signatures... Who are you?'

They concluded that a celebrity impersonator had been sent to defraud the Japanese people. The British government had to intercede on his behalf, pointing out that he had been given an MBE by the Queen. The Japanese police persisted, wanting to know his identity. For them this was more important than the drug smuggling: 'They said that Paul may have an MBE, but who is this yahoo with all the marijuana? They also persisted in their suggestion that I was a government operative.' (p.539), which was sort of true. A Scotland Yard official eventually secured his release. This vivid, close-up detail is not present in the historical record and only exists in the *Billy Shears Memoirs*.

8

Nicholas Kollerstrom

Appendix C:
Two Alleged Disclosures

We have viewed two PID 'disclosures' as genuine: that of *The Rotten-Apple* and *Winged Beetle*, and then the book *Memoirs of Billy Shears*. A couple of others deserve mention, which are in contrast generally viewed as in some way bogus or unsound.

60if

In 2002 a text called '60if' appeared, by one 'Sun King' in Italy. Its title was alluding to the fact that Paul would then have been sixty years of age, echoing the '27if' car number-plate on Abbey Road. It was a whole story of the death and replacement as if narrated by George. It was said to have been a channelled message. SunKing posted:

> Sorry Friends,
> I had clear and strict directions.
> "60IF" couldn't be modified starting from 8th December 2002. It will remain "as is" until it will be on the Internet.
>
> Before receiving "60IF" I DID know NOTHING about Beatles story.
> I never mind it.
> What discrepancies?
> Possibly problems with my english? (I'm not of english language)
> Like you all I don't know if "60IF" is ALL true or not yet.

He averred that the message had been written during George's life in an Indian language, then somehow received by him in Italy. The early websites have vanished and it's hard to gather much of the story, but this message helped and inspired the growing PID movement. In its broken pidgin English it averred for example that, after Paul's death:

... the main problem was to find one with a most possible similar voice. We had to convoked a lot of imitators, there were many at that time, and find one with the face compatible with that of Paul. We found a boy with a beautiful voice that was able to imitate Paul in a cogent manner but his face presented problems not repairable with the cosmetic surgery. We decided however of hold him for complete the songs and went out the album that was in preparation in the short possible time or divert the suspects and the rumours that began to pursue.

When we hoped no more the right man was found. His name was William Sheppard and he was in force to the Commonwealth police in Canada. He liked sing and knew to strum a bit the piano. He had a beautiful voice but his Paul's voice imitation quality was worst than that of the boy already worked with us but his face presented wonderful compatible as concern the profile and the jaw, two determining elements for the choice by the cosmetic surgeons.

A 'Mocumentary Spoof'

In 2010 the heavily-reviled video 'Paul is Really Dead: The Last Testament of George Harrison' appeared, which can be viewed online, released within a week or so of the *Winged Beetle* video.

Highway 61 Entertainment in Hollywood, L.A. was known for pop music documentaries eg of Bob Dylan. But Joel Gilbert its manager has also made two 'mocumentaries' one 'Elvis Found Alive' and this one, covering the PID story. We are puzzled by his genuine, sincere-looking face staring into the camera and telling us about how his company received in July 2005 an unsolicited parcel postmarked from London, containing two audio tape-cassettes entitled 'the Last Testament of George Harrison' dated 30th December, 1999 – the date of the attack.

On these tapes, his team were shocked to hear 'a voice eerily similar to Harrison's' which told a story. For five years they wondered what to do with them, while they made several attempts to authenticate them in different laboratories, which were inconclusive. The company then decided to build up a film around the message of the tapes. It starts off with a short early interview with George, to remind us what his voice sounds like.

The advert for the film states: 'Highway 61 Entertainment has investigated this stunning new account of the conspiracy to hide McCartney's tragic death,' describing it as: 'What may prove to be the most important document in rock and roll history.' It that a lie, or just part of an American art-form whereby made-up news can be published? The video is freely available, so no great profit can accrue by its production. Tina Foster on her Plastic Macca site has covered a long list of impossible themes in this story, which have to be deliberate.

The video has George in hospital recovering from the brutal murder attempt (which was before dawn on Thursday, 30th December 1999) and asking his wife for the tape cassettes to talk into, to tell his story. On that day – when he would hardly have been in a condition to speak, if he was even conscious - he narrates the Memoir, and does so *'in the hope that the cassettes will protect me'* – in other words, by coming out with the story, with instructions for it to be released after his death, that may annul the motive of those who were seeking his death.

He says, 'I don't know why I was attacked, but ... I have my suspicions.' This video is riddled with fictional elements, eg the young Heather Mills being the girl who was (according to the urban myth) in the car with Paul when he crashed, in '66, whereas she had not yet been born then.

It does have some good sequences, eg of Paul and John acting in a Shakespeare play, Midsummer Night's Dream in 1965, where Paul exclaims 'Thus I die', 'Now am I dead', etc,; plus it has an extensive sequence of the Beatles with the Maharishi in India, and the Maharishi holding forth about his philosophy, filmed we may guess by George. But, it has Paul die on November 9th 1965, *after* which the remaining group decide to put clues into their next album, *Rubber Soul*, even though this came out at the beginning of December, 1965.

Let's give the last word here to 'Russ' on the pid.freeforums.net: '60IF was kind of compelling except that it was just toooo ridiculous in places. I think it worked as well as it did because he covered so many bases. It really lives on in that George Harrison "documentary" that came out a couple of years ago. All of these stories have a chance of being believed because of the vacuum ... any explanation feels better than the complete void that's really there.' (2014)

Appendix D: Copyright Issues

According to the copyright provisions of sections 17 U.S.C. § 106 and 17 U.S.C. § 106A, the fair use of a copyrighted work for purposes such as criticism, comment, news reporting, teaching, scholarship or research, is not an infringement of copyright. This book satisfies those criteria insofar as its purposes are those of criticism, comment and news reporting on a major deception of the public by offering a substitute musician as though he were Paul James McCartney, an original member of the Beatles.

Its contents are suitable for the further purposes of teaching critical thinking and research into issues of immense public interest, where the author is an accomplished scholar and adopts a scholarly approach to the evidence, including clues found in the lyrics from Beatles' songs. The copyrighted material has been readily available on the Internet for decades, where the failure to assert the copyright privilege has waived its applicability in this case, especially since they serve as evidence in solving a crime.

The author therefore asserts on these grounds and others unnamed that the use of the lyrics to Beatles' songs does not violate any proper copyright claim but, on the contrary, satisfies multiple criteria to qualify for exception. And the fact that the book constitutes an investigation into the apparent death and replacement of the man who may be the most popular musician of recent history reinforces the importance of permitting the use of those lyrics in resolving what appears to be an immense deception of the public.

Nicholas Kollerstrom

BIBLIOGRAPHY

Daily, Forrest, *The Fifth Magician, The great Beatles Impostor Story* 2003

Lev, Doctor, *Billy Shears The Secret History of the Beatles* 2002

MacDonald, Ian, *Revolution in the Head The Beatles Records and the Sixties* 2008

Martin, George, *The Making of Sgt Pepper* 1994

McCartney, Michael, *Remember the recollections and photographs of Mike McCartney* 1992

Miles, Bary, *Paul McCartney Many Years from Now* 1998

Reeve, Andru J., *Turn me on, Dead Man The Beatles and the Paul-Is-Dead Hoax* 2004

Patterson, Gary, *The Walrus Was Paul* 1998

Salewicz, Chris, *McCartney the Biography*

Schultz, Ernie, *Beatles the Untold Story the death and replacement of Paul McCartney*

The Beatles Anthology -set of 5 DVDs 2003

Uharriet, Thomas E., *The Memoirs of Billy Shears* 2009

Nicholas Kollerstrom

INDEX

#

28 IF, 144

60if, 218, 220

9/11, 195

A

A Day in the Life, 41, 207

A Whiter Shade of Pale, 113

Abbey Road, 68, 73, 143, 144

Abram, Michael, 166

Alistair Taylor, 112

Anthology project, 157

Apollo C. Vermouth', 158

Apple, 76

Apple Corps Ltd., 161

Apple Studios, 74

Asher, Dr Richard, 118

Asher, Jane, 17, 107, 109

Asher, Margaret, 130

Aspinall, Neil, 16, 58

Aston-Martin car, 140

Astrid, 129

Aunty Jin, 125

B

Back off, Boogaloo, 54

Bag of Nails nightclub, 113

Band on the Run, 33, 55

Barry Miles, 64

Barry, Dave, 145

Batman comic, 86

BBC Radio 4, 81

Beatlemania, *12*, 13, 73

Beatles Book, 94, 102

Beatles Book, The, 59

Beatles' Book, 144

Bee-Gees, 102

Best, Pete, 128

Bill Shepherd and the Ranch Hands', 98

Billy Martin, 161

Billy Pepper and the Pepperpots, 97

Billy Shears Memoirs, 174

Billy Shepherd, 195

Black carnations, 71

Blackbird, 32

Bob Dylan, 42, 196

Bonzo Dog Band, 42, 181

Bonzo Dog Band's, 70

Boogaloo, 55, 147

Book of Worst Songs, 145

Bramwell, Tony, 116

Brian Epstein, 100, 129

233

Brian Jones, 76, 207

Brigitte Bardot, 126

Browne, Tara, 133, 208

Butcher's album, 137

C

Caine, Michael, 108

Caldwell, Mrs, 127

Campbeltown, 81

Carl Jung, 142

Carlesi, 215

carry that weight, 52

Casino Royale,, 210

Cavendish Avenue, 60, 63, 109

Chaos and Creation, 21

Charles II, 167

Cliff Richard, 93

clone, 200

Come Together, 16, 51

cor anglaise, 141

Cowboy Favorites, 98

Cranberry sauce, 18

Crowley, 171

Crowley, Aleister, 172, 195

Crowleyite magic, 64

D

Daily Mail, 93

Dakota building, 154

Dark Horse, 187

Death Cab for Cutie, 42, 72

Denny Lane, 105

Derek Taylor, 83

Detroit, 73

Dick Cavett Show, 194

Disc and Music Echo, 91

DNA test, 214

DNA testing, 213

Don't Pass me by, 47

Donovan, 41, 46

doppelganger, 34, 192

Double Fantasy, 155

Dusty Springfield, 93

E

Eastman, Linda, 112

Ed Sullivan Theatre, 215

Eleanor Rigby, 119

Elvis accent, 72

EMI studio, 129

Emilo Lari's, 159

Epistle to Dippy, 41

Index

Epstein, 59

Eric Burdon, 116

Etchingham, Kathy, 207

F

Faul,, *13*

Fetzer, Jim, 17

Fields, W.C., 143

Forthlin Road, 126

Frankenstein, 54

Friends to Go, 56

Frost, David, 130, 169

Full Moon, 132

G

George Kelly, 60

George Martin, 63

Gilbert, Joel, 221

Gimme some truth, 148

Ginger Geezer, 69

Give my regards to Broad Street, 13

Glasgow Herald, 80

Glass Onion, 21, 137

Glastonbury Festival, 150

Glazier, Joel, 90

Golden Oldies, 59, 138

Golden Slumbers, 53

Goldman, Albert, 29, 148

Gotham News, 86

Grand Funk Railroad, 76

Guantanamo Bay, 150

Guardian journalist, 86

Guildhall School of Music, 130

Guinness family, 209

H

Hamburg, 128, 212

Happiness is a Warm Gun, 149

Harrison, George, 218

Heart of the Country, 31

Heather Mills, 158

Help!, 18

Hendrix, Jimi, 207

Hey Jude, 45

High Park, 81, 112

Highway 61 Entertainment, 221

Hines, Brian, 105

Hoffner bass, 140

Hofner bass guitar, 124

Hofsra University, 84

Huber, Erica, 212

Hyacinthus, 139

I

I'm the Greatest, 54

Iamaphoney, 157

Imagine, 147

In his own Write, 136

India, 94

Indica Gallery, 42, 64, 96

Indra Club, 128

Instant Karma, 152

International Times, 170

invanddis website, 191

Iris Caldwell, 128

J

Jagger, Mick, 165

Jane Asher, 114

Jane Asher's cakes, 122

Janis Joplin, 114

JFK assassination, 134

Jim Mac's Jazz Band, 123

Jim McCartney, 37

Jimi Hendrix, 114

Jimmy Frazer', 97

Joe Ephgrave,, 140

John Lennon's death, 164

John Wesley Harding, 197

Johnny and the Moondogs, 126

Julius Caesar, 15

K

Ken Kesey, 67

Kenya, 60, 202

Kinfauns, 46, 202

King of Cosmania, 176

Knight, Terry, 74

Kris Kristofferson, 198

Kuehn, Clare, 59, 172

L

Labour, Fred, 77, 144

Lady Madonna, 77, 182

Lady Madonna', 40

Lakshmi, 28

Last Testament of George Harrison, 221

Lennon, Julian, 155

Leso, 85

Lester, Richard, 130

Let It Be, 143

Life article, 216

Life Magazine, 80

Liverpool, 124

Living the Beatles Legend, 60, 65

Living the Beatles' Legend, 163

Los Angeles, 196

LSD, 19

Lucy in the Sky with Diamonds, 25

Luggala, 208

Lulu, 113

Index

M

M1 motorway, 144

'MacLen' publishing, 75

Madam Tussauds, 139

magic, 170

Magical Mystery Tour, 13, 14, 18, 71

Magick, 173

Mal Evans, 60, 63, 103, 163

Mal Evans', 117

Many Years From Now, 33

Maple Leaf Four, 98

Marianne Faithful, 114, 208

Marianne Faithfull, 39

Mark Lane, 133

Mark Twain, 74

Marks, Jay, 115

Marlon Brando, 141

Martin, George, 19, 26, 130

Matrix, The, 138

Maybe I'm Amazed, 119

McCartney, Jim, 123

McCartney, Linda, 158

McGear, Mike, 125, 134

McGillion, Frank, 179

Melody Maker, 57

Melody Maker awards, 92

Memoirs of Billy Shears, 70, 100, 180

Merseymania, 97

Merseyside Convention, 90

Mick Jagger, 208

Mike Douglas chat show, 134

Mike McGear, 88

Miles, Barry, 170

Mills, Heather, 37, 191

Mirror, The, 193

Moody Blues, 105

Mull of Kintyre, 32

My Sweet Lady Jane, 122

N

Narobi, 61

Neil Aspinall, 102, 157, 177

Neil Aspinall, Neil, 177

New Musical Express, 111, 130

New York Times, 80, 115

Newswire picture, 82

No Direction Home, 196

Norman, Phillip, 202

North End Music Store, 129

O

Official Secrets Act, 57

Officially Pronounced Dead, 42, 143

Orpheus, 12, 39

P

Pattie Boyd, 165

Paul McCartney lookalike, 94

Penny Valentine, 196

Pepperland, 85

Peppers Press, 179

Peter and Gordon, 108

Pickwick International, 97

PID, 74

Plastic Macca site, 136

plastic surgery, 67

PlasticMacca website, 196

Post Office Tower, 93

Primitives, The, 99

psychedelic, 26

Pyramus and Thisbe, 96

R

Ram, 99

Ram album, 120

Raymond's Revue, 69

Reeves, Andru, 194

Revolution 9, 73

Revolution No 9, 84

Revolver, 94, 138

Rhone, Dorothy, 119, 126, 195

Rishikesh, 46

Robey Younge, 115

Rock and Roll Hall of Fame, 164

Rolling Stone, 151, 199

Rolling Stones, 76

Rory Storm, 127

Rory Storm and the Hurricanes, 126

Rosemary's Baby, 154

Roskilde, 191

Rotten Apple, 157, 173

Ruby Tuesday, 16

Russ Gibb, 77

S

Saint Paul, 74

San Francisco, 196

Satan's Bed, 151

Saturday night Live, 87

Scaffold, The, 134

Schwartz, Francine, 117

September 11th, 20, 21

Sgt Pepper, 13, 25, 139

Sgt Pepper Code, The, 161

Shakespeare, 12, 181

Shea Stadium, 123

Shepherd, Billy, 102

Sherlock Holmes, 97

Shirley Temple, 141

Index

Sibelius, 29

Silly Love songs, 145

Sonic torture, 150

Sonny Liston, 141

sonogram, 216

Standby Films, 157

Stanshall, Viv, 31

Stanshall, Vivien, 180

Stephen Crane, novelist, 140

Strawberry Fields, 18, 147

Strawberry fields Forever, 68

Strawberry Fields Forever, 83, 90

Summer of Love and Peace, 67

Sun King, 218

SunKing, 70

Sutcliffe, Stu, 128

Sutcliffe, Stuart, 42

T

Tayler, Derek, 167

Temple, Shirley, 172

The Beatles' Bible, 131

The Drake-Times Delphic, 76

The Fool on the Hill, 44

The Memoirs of Billy Shears, 16, 98

The Mystery Tour, 85

The Quarrymen, 125

The Winged Beetle, 21

Tom Jones, 92

Trabant, Peter, 161

transfiguration, 199

Truby, Dr Henry, 216

Turn me on, Dead Man, 73

Two Virgins, 152

U

Uharriet, 15, 180

V

Valentine, Penny, 57

Vivian Stanshall, 69

W

Walls and Bridges, 153

Washington Post, 80

While My guitar Gently Weeps', 50

White Album, 46, 49, 202

William Campbell', 77

William Campell, 181

William Wallace Shepherd, 189

Wilson, Harold, 25

Wimpole Street, 108

Winged Beetle, 158, 172, 186, 220

Wired Italia magazine, 213

Within you, Without you,, 163

Wonderful Christmas time', 34

Y

Yellow Submarine film, 141

Yoko Ono, 73, 96